Brother Warriors

Martha Norris McLeod

2017

Brother Warriors

Copyright, 1940

By MARTHA NORRIS McLEOD

"The most noble sentiment a southern woman or American could express."

BROTHER WARRIORS
By Martha Norris McLeod

THIS BOOK contains the reminiscences of a number of the last survivors of the Blue and Gray, and a few of the black race who were slaves until the signing of the Emancipation Proclamation in 1863.

IT RELATES, in the colorful words of those "old folks," who are now 92 to 125 years old, how they "swapped" coffee for tobacco, fought the bushwhackers. How a sergeant halted Lincoln and Grant by mistake, and other experiences so typical of that period.

THE READER will be inclined to wander, in imagination, if not through his own memories, to a camp fire reunion of these ancient men. They are arrayed in uniforms of Union and Confederate soldiers and having a big time spinning yarns. Each is trying to "out do" the last one, or perhaps telling a true experience of ro-mance, humor, pathos, or courage, coloring the incidents as he goes along.

THIS BOOK deserves a place on every bookshelf as an historical edition, as well as for preservation for posterity.

DARLING PUBLISHING (COMPANY
818 Ninth Street, N. W.
Washington, D. C.

Brother Warriors

THE REMINISENCES OF UNION AND CONFEDERATE VETERANS

EDITED
With an Introduction, Notes, and Maps,
by
MARTHA NORRIS McLEOD

The Darling Printing Company

1940

Washington, D. C.

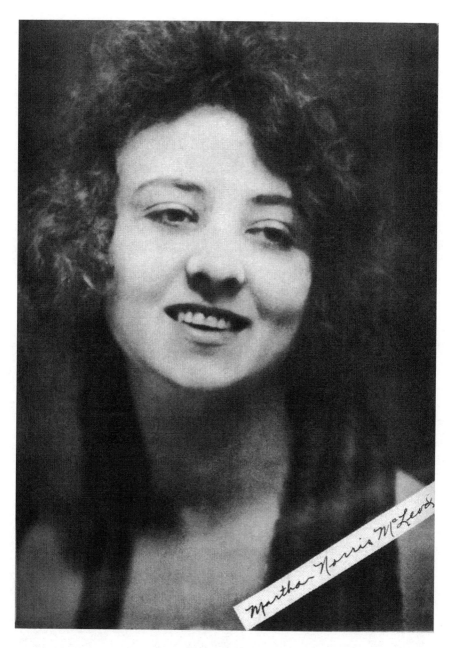

The Author

THIS BOOK IS AN EXPRESSION OF
LOVE AND RESPECT FOR THE VETERANS
OF THE NORTH AND THE
SOUTH, AND IT IS LOVINGLY
DEDICATED TO THE MEMORY OF
ONE OF THEM,—MY FATHER,
RODERICK DONALD McLEOD

Forward

Michelle McMillan Kirby
2014-2016 President, R. Don McLeod 2469
United Daughters of the Confederacy®

One sunny morning, in the little town of Sopchoppy, Florida, I first learned about Miss Martha McLeod's out-of-print book *Brother Warriors*. One of our UDC chapter officers had brought her recently and fortuitously acquired copy to share with the group and presented the question, "Could we possibly reprint it?" Carefully turning its discolored and fragile pages, my heart leapt with excitement and desire to return this valuable primary source work to the world. Not only does the book have vast historical significance but was the work of a woman who was so instrumental to our chapter. Miss Martha McLeod sponsored our chapter in many ways including providing $1,000 seed money for scholarships. Her father, Roderick Don McLeod, is our United Daughters of the Confederacy® chapter's namesake. It was meant to be. We knew little about how to do this but with desire and effort, and surely some divine intervention, we return this work back to the world.

Miss Martha once wrote, "A seed is planted, but it takes a lot of sunshine, water, and tender care to bring it to fruition." There are many who provided tender care. First, thanks to the ladies of Anna Jackson 224, United Daughters of the Confederacy®, for transferring the republication rights in which Miss McLeod had originally entrusted. A special thanks is due to Mrs. Sue Cowger, Florida Division President (1998-2000) and former president and agent in behalf of the Anna Jackson 224 Chapter, Tallahassee, Florida. Watering this seed project with vast hours of effort was Mrs. Charlotte Thompson, Honorary Florida Division President, United Daughters of the Confederacy® and 2015-2016 president of the Anna Jackson 224 UDC Chapter. Charlotte spent a plethora of hours scanning and converting the original book to an electronic version and repairing the faded photos and maps. Charlotte was also a wellspring of ideas for how to organize proofreading and final assembly of the book.

IX

She and I spent many hours on the phone and in person working through the challenging nuances of file conversion and formatting to further the work. My computer became my electronic pet for many weeks as I performed the second stage of conversion. Not all scans were ideal with some in awkward text boxes which had to be removed and realigned. This involved toggling between two screens to compare the scanned pdf version with the Word conversion as well as several all-nighters. Once the manuscript was in rough draft format, the following volunteers from the Wakulla County Historical Society and our UDC chapter, R. Don McLeod 2469, rendered their time and hearts to proofread: Carolyn Harvey, Evelyn Stills, Mary Ann Laird, Judy Seaman, Betty Green, Tanya Lynn, Sherry Colvin, Linda Thompson, Mary Nichols, and Jane Raker. Also, a special thanks to Arlene Vause for coordinating the proofreading efforts. We are grateful to Dale Cox who is an honorary member of our Chapter and who carried this project to its end result in publication through Old Kitchen Books. We also give thanks to God for shining upon us in the effort.

We made every attempt to keep the wording, capitalization and punctuation as originally published. There are obvious misspellings such as "Spottsylvania" with two "t"s, left intact as it was spelled that way by a majority of soldiers contributing to the work. We did, however, adjust a few out-of-place lines which were surely original publication errors. It is otherwise their words, their history. Once into a few stories, it should become obvious to the reader why Miss Martha McLeod named the book *"Brother Warriors"* as there is a common spirit of forgiveness and brotherhood throughout. In our modern world of continued challenge for political correctness, *Brother Warriors* presents a reminder of the value of civility and respect, regardless of one's political views. Also, if they could forgive, why can't we? Further exemplifying the spirit of brotherhood was the book's first copy off the press being co-presented, on June 30, 1941, to President Franklin Delano Roosevelt by Commander William W. Nixon, Commander in Chief, Grand Army of the Republic and Julius Franklin Howell, Commander in Chief, United Confederate Veterans. This was arranged by General Watson of the White House, who believed it was significant and timely, as All-American Day had just been inaugurated. The National League of Pen Women was represented at the presentation of *Brother Warriors*. Martha was invited by the group to become a member and present her book to them in a similar ceremony. Following this, she was considered an authority on the War Between the States and gave numerous lectures in person and on the radio in Washington, DC, Maryland, and New York. "The Women of Achievement" program had her dramatize *Brother Warriors* for its series and become one of its members. This work was respected and acknowledged for its historical significance. It deserves to be remembered and still be respected today.

The memorabilia of the co-presentation following this forward were found in the folds of Miss Martha's book which was loaned to me by her nephew, Don McLeod. These mementos offer added richness to the work as it provides a grand history of this book's impact on a national level. We also added a newspaper clipping inserted in Martha's book which provided an update on Julius Franklin Howell, Commander in Chief, United Confederate Veterans, upon his 100th birthday.

You may learn more about Miss McLeod, her father, R. Don McLeod, and the United Daughters of the Confederacy® on our chapter's website at www.rdonmcleod.org. May God richly bless those who read this book. May you deepen your understanding of the spirit of brotherhood and sisterhood, and the power of forgiveness.

BROTHER WARRIORS

First Copy off the Press Presented to:

PRESIDENT FRANKLIN DELANO ROOSEVELT

Ceremony held at Confederate Memorial
Hall, 1332 Vermont Avenue, Washington,
D. C., Monday Evening, June 30, 1941.
at 8 o'clock, by the last Commanders-
in- Chief of The War Between the States

Gen. William Nixon, Commander-in-Chief
        Grand Army of the Republic

Gen. Julius Franklin Howell, Commander-in
        Chief, United Confederate Veterans

Mrs. Lena Epperly MacDonald
cordially invites you to a Reception
in honor of
Miss Martha Norris McLeod
presenting her book
"Brother Warriors"
to
President Franklin Delano Roosevelt's Aide
Monday evening, June 30, 1941, eight o'clock

Confederate Memorial Hall
1332 Vermont Avenue, Northwest
Washington, D. C.

THE AMERICAN ODE
By Marx E. Kahn

BEHOLD the Emblem of our Country-the Greatest Flag of the Greatest Nation in the World: May it ever wave over a free and liberty-loving people. May it ever represent the highest ideals of American manhood, the loftiest standards of exalted womanhood, the purest principles of social democracy. May its generous folds, blessed by Almighty God and glorified by the blood of our forefathers ever succor and support, at home *and* abroad, on land and on sea, suffering mankind, struggling for human rights, human freedom and human advancement.

OATH OF THE UNITED STATES ARMY

And I do SOLEMNLY SWEAR that I will bear true faith and allegiance to the United States of America: that I will serve them honestly and faithfully against all their enemies whomsoever: and that I will obey the orders of the President of the United States, and the orders of the officers appointed over me, according to the Rules and Articles of War.

OATH OF ALLEGIANCE

I pledge allegiance to the Flag of the United States of America and to the Republic for which it stands. One nation indivisible, with liberty and justice to all.

SALUTE TO THE CONFEDERATE FLAG

I Salute the Confederate Flag with Affection, Reverence, and Undying Remembrance.

CONTENTS

REMINISCENCES OF SLAVES

ILLUSTRATIONS

John E. Andrews, Commander-in-Chief, Grand Army of the
Republic, and Julius Franklin Howell, Commander-in-Chief,
United Confederate Veterans, are shown on the front flap of the jacket.

Martha Norris McLeod, the Author, is shown on the fly-leaf.

M. A. Moore
Joseph Morgan
Elbert Nunn
Erastus Page
William Pierce
Louis F. Rieb
C. J. Rose
George Rummelhart
C. E. Scarlett
Robert P. Scott
D. W. Seigler
Peter Pierre Smith
Cyrus Stamet
Devalois W. Stevens and the Monument Erected
    to His Regiment
A. F. Tolman
John Wesley Turnbough
R. H. Wall
W. H. Wall
Emmett N. Waller
J. M. Wickersham
John M. Wildman
Robert Wilson
Jerry Withelm
Homer S. Woodworth
M. D. Vance

SLAVES

Jackson F. Fischer
R. A. Gwynn
S. J. Miles
Simon Phillips

PREFACE

This volume is a prized collection of reminiscences and anecdotes told to the author by Confederate and Union veterans who formed the rank and file in that unhappy conflict between the North and South during the years 1861 to 1865. Much has been written about the big battles and the brave officers who led the armies, but this is the only book which expresses the true feelings and recollections of the men who formed the very backbone of the man-power upon which the outcome of every battle was dependent. These stories depict typical experiences of those thousands of humble but noble men who gave in full measure of their loyalty and devotion to the Cause in which they believed and for which they fought.

We are no longer North or South, but a united nation whose high principles are the noble qualities molded out of that unhappy past. The influences that have been at work for seventy-five years in closing the chasm that temporarily divided our beloved country can better be judged and appreciated after an insight into the minds of the men who once were steeped in the bitterness and strife of that tragic epoch, but who survived it with victorious spirit, and who now tell us of their experiences of that day without rancor or prejudice.

The philosophy of this thinning remnant of heroes, whose ages range from ninety to one hundred and twenty-five years, reflects a full life, tempered by the wisdom of a century. Time has been liberal in sustaining their strength, their courage, and their spirit. As they tell their stories of daring, chivalry, intrigue, and romance, we forget whether they wore the Blue or the Gray and appreciate each narrative as that of a loyal soldier and patriot. It does not matter for which side they fought in those seemingly far-off days; today they are simply Americans. They will soon be gone; and preservation for oncoming generations of their thoughts and experiences as expressed in their own language is well worth while.

Present at the "Last Meeting of the Blue and the Gray," held from June 29 to July 6, 1938, on the seventy-fifth anniversary of the Battle of Gettysburg, were 486 Confederate and 1,397 Union veterans. These 1,883 old warriors came from every state in the Union. A great many of the stories herein recorded were told to the author during her visits with the veterans at that eventful reunion. Others were gathered by her while visiting the veterans in their homes. Many others were obtained through direct correspondence with the veterans, a considerable number of such stories having been written by the veterans in their own hands.

In many instances it has been necessary to revise the stories as told by the veterans for the sake of clarity, conciseness, and brevity. The substance, however, has not been changed, except, in some cases, in the interest of accuracy. Care has been taken to retain the individual flavor and style of the narratives, which constitute much of their charm.

The author is deeply indebted to Wilden F. Van Swearingen, Commander-in-Chief, District of Columbia and Maryland Division, Sons of Confederacy, Washington, D. C., as well as Margaret Gordon, Washington, D. C., E. Richard Colvin, Deland, Florida, W.O. Burtner, Washington, D. C., Louise Griffith, Dallas, Texas, Margaret Nero, Rome, New York, and to many others who lent their time, aid, and sympathy in making this work possible.

Martha Norris McLeod.

FROM GETTYSBURG ON TO MEET THE LORD

July 2, 1938.

Dear Comrades:

As we don our respective colors in recognition of what was once adjudged to be a just Cause, let us do it conscious of the fact that the reasons that gave rise to a most noble, yet sorrowful, struggle have long since been removed.

As we stand for the last time on ground made sacred by the blood of our slain brothers, may we stand as nobly now united for the peace, protection, and prosperity of those who shall carry on in the future, as we once stood divided.

Soon we all must answer the call of death. Time and the wisdom of God have helped us make peace between our now fast-fading ranks. Let us now, as individuals, make peace with God.

Our cannons are eaten by the rust of idleness; the graves of our departed buddies are covered deep with the foliage of passing years; our hearts have healed under the balm of friendship, and neighborly deeds; the lives and lot of our loved ones have been made happy by both a political and economic tranquility. Let us now, therefore, as true patriots of a common cause, surrender our hearts to Jesus Christ, who is "The Prince of Peace."

Robert P. Scott
Color Bearer, Dallas Confederate Camp No. 1853
Commander 3rd Bgd., Texas Division, U. C. V.

See "Gets All His Wounds Facing The Fight," by Robert P. Scott.

XXIX

OPERATIONS · IN · THE · EAST

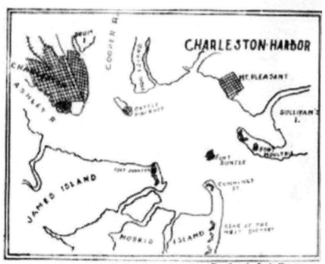

CHARLESTON · HARBOR

—Drawings by Leola Hayoux.

XXX

OPERATIONS IN THE WEST

OPERATIONS IN THE
SOUTHEAST

—Drawings by Leola Heuscom.

Brother Warriors

OPPOSES YANKS AT PORT GIBSON

JAMES GALVESTON AINSWORTH, Brig. Gen. Com.
2nd Bgd. Miss. Div. U.C.V. (1938), Wesson, Miss.
B. May 26, 1846, Copiah Co., Miss.

In 1863, I joined a scout troup at Hazelhurst, Miss. I was only seventeen years of age, but I was old enough to be keenly aware of the dark clouds of disaster hovering over my state and people and the immediate necessity of utilizing all our strength to combat the destructive forces. Lincoln, as Commander-in-Chief, had just issued his Emancipation Proclamation as a military order. The Yankees were making frequent raids and carrying away our slaves. It was about this time that negroes were first employed as soldiers, their first participation being in the siege of Vicksburg. My first assignment was along the river from Baton Rouge to Vicksburg, and my duty was to keep the slaves from going to the Yankees.

The Yankees used a lot of our negroes as spies to report our whereabouts. Our Lieutenant was cognizant of this and was watching for an opportunity to put an end to it. He was a native of Natchez, so knew nearly everybody, white or black, along the country roads. He knew pretty well who could or could not be trusted. He employed a reliable negro to help ferret out the guilty ones. This negro was not slow in exposing a few of them. He learned that the colored folks were going to have a frolic at one of the shanties and that a number of the offenders would be present. This was the golden opportunity our Lieutenant had been waiting for. He selected seven scouts to accompany him and take the party by surprise. The shanty was located a bout half way between Natchez and the Yank picket post. Our first problem was to get safely around the pickets. The night was cold, rainy and dark, which was disagreeable to the feelings but favorable to the safety. We rode near enough the post to see that there were three or four pickets hovering over a fire. This gave us a pretty good idea of their layout. We quit the road and circled around the pickets, making our way in the shadows of the forest. There were about twenty-five or thirty darkies at the party. We charged, then commenced firing, which

1

caused a bedlam of excitement. They started dodging and running, but didn't stop long enough to fire a shot back. We rounded up eight prisoners and hastened our return to safe ground. We inspected each prisoner closely and found that we had three spies. These three happened to fall into one of those deep ravines and we never heard anything more of them. We turned the other five over to our Colonel.

On April 30, 1863, I formed a small link of the South's opposition at Port Gibson. We tried hard to hold back Grant's forces, but they didn't seem to bother much about us; they came right on, pushing us out of the way, and shooting those who tarried too long. We were powerless to do anything but keep receding. It was here that one of my pals, riding right alongside of me, caught a bullet in his leg. He was helpless, so I took him away for treatment. His condition was considered serious, so I was detailed to care for him and take him home.

As a Confederate veteran and as Commander of the 2nd Brigade, Mississippi Division of the United Confederate Veterans, I want to thank the United States Government and the kind people who have made it possible for the North and the South to have this Last Meeting of the Blue and Gray. I arrived in time to enjoy the entire stay from June 29th to July 6, 1938. Though I am ninety-three years old, it has been lots of fun camping in tents, dining in mess halls, and taking part in various activities planned for our pleasure.

A PRISONER'S LETTER

(Excerpts from the Confederate papers of Tiphen Walsingham Allen, Allendale, Virginia, furnished by his daughter, Mrs. Allen Pierce.)

August 1, 1864
"Camp Chase Prison 3, Ohio
Mr. Wm. Ott,
Wheeling, Virginia.
Dear Sir:

You will please pardon me for presuming to address you, as I rather expect my name will sound unfamiliar, as many years have elapsed since I had the pleasure of your acquaintance. Was desirous of seeing you when in Wheeling, thinking it would afford you pleasure to hear from your relatives in. Woodstock. * * * I try to content myself as a prisoner here knowing that "God doeth all things well." In him I've long trusted-it would be sinful to murmur against the decree of God. We should bear our trials with fortitude and cheerfulness, placing confidence in our Savior, never doubting but that our trials were sent upon us for ultimate good. His motives are inscrutable.

I am glad to inform you that the officers of the prison are accommodating and that very kind physicians are in attendance upon the sick. My health has been rather indifferent, but I hope I am improving now. I need a Bible and some good books to read-would like to have "Park's Arithmetic," slate and pencil, also Kusham's English Grammar. If not asking too much or putting you to an inconvenience would be pleased if you know of any of my friends in Wheeling to request them to forward me a box of edibles and said books, as I will be very grateful indeed for the least manifestation of kinship. Your attention to the above will be considered a worthy favor conferred upon your friend for which I shall ever hold you in kind remembrance. Will be pleased at your earliest convenience to hear from you.

With kindest regards and best wishes for yourself and family, I am
Most respectfully your friend,
T. W. Allen"

VOTES FOR LINCOLN TWICE IN ONE DAY

JOSEPH H. ALVERSON, Batavia, Io. Union.
B. Sept. 16, 1844, Garret Co. Ky. Co. F.
3rd Reg. Io. Cav., Fairfield, Io., Feb. 26, 1864.
Dis. Aug. 9, 1865, Atlanta, Ga.

I was anxious to get into the army, but didn't know just how I would get by the physical examination as three fingers on one hand were missing. Fellows who didn't want to go would say to me, "Joe, that's a good sign that you shouldn't go; you'll be killed in the first battle." When I took the oath, I held up only one hand and the examining officer let me pass. Seventy-five years have passed since that time and I am still hale and hearty.

The story of my experiences is one of misfortune as I was anxious to fight and didn't get into many battles. There was an epidemic of fever and I had to spend many months in the Washington General Hospital at Memphis. After that I was furloughed.

When I left Memphis to return to my regiment, I voted for Lincoln twice; once before crossing the bridge and then again on the other side.

Roy T. Alverson was my attendant at the Gettysburg Reunion. We stood the trip fine.

5

TRADES TOBACCO FOR COFFEE

H. V. ANDERSON, Troy, Tenn. Confederate.
B. Nov. 12, 1846, Wayne, N. C. Co. D, 40th
N. C. Regt., Goldsboro, N. C.

Seventy-four years have passed since I took the Oath of Allegiance, July 19, 1865, and secured my release from prison. I was captured at Fort Fisher on January 15, 1865. So far as bitterness is concerned, there have been too many other things to remember that are healthful to the mind and well-being of a person.

As to the battles I took part in, we Johnnies always know'd the Yankees had seven men to our one, but we had a principle and were willing to fight it through, win or lose. I served under the command of General Hoke and General Whidon. I came through battles, starvation, imprisonment, and deprivation of every kind, so the good Lord must have been with me.

All relationships between the opposing armies were not stinging and resentful. We frequently met the Yanks between battles and played cards together. Of course, we had to hide from our officers for if they had ever ketched us, we would have been court martialed. There was a creek dividing the Union and Confederate armies, and we would take turns with the Yanks as to who should run the risk of swimming the creek. Then we had to crawl through the weeds until we could find a secure spot. If an officer came too near, we stayed quiet as a mouse until we got a good chance to make a getaway, then we'd run like rabbits.

I shall never forget the dejected feeling I had once when I returned to camp, after being off picket duty, and found that our command had done left the country. That was at Franklin, Virginia. Two of my buddies were left behind with me. We were as hungry as wolves and there was nothing left for us. During our encampment there, some shoats had been pestering the life out of us, so we decided that this would be a good time to get even. I said, "Mose, let's kill one of those shoats." He said, "All right, but you shoot him." I put my gun to my shoulder and was getting a good aim when a fellow up the hill intercepted. He called us to come up there. My knees

7

grew weak and my courage faint, for I know'd we were into it plenty deep, since the swine belonged to him. But, do you know, instead of bawling us out, that fellow gave us a feed that I won't fergit if I live to be a hundred years old.

These Yankee soldiers are still out-numbering us at the Last Meeting of the Blue and Gray, but there is not much fight left in any of us now. My attendant is Robert Bright.

ACCEPTS BOUNTY AND SUBSTITUTES

FRANCIS GOODSPEED BABCOCK, Washington, D. C. Union.
B. Apr. 5, 1846, Westfield, Pa. Co. D. 4th U. S.
Art., Elmira, N.Y. Dis. July 6, 1870, Fort McHenry, Md.

The main issue of the war was a national problem and one a little too deep for my tender years, but I was eager to go to war and avenge the death of my eldest brother, Richard Philip Babcock. Richard was the pride of our family; the first boy to enlist from Westfield, Pennsylvania, and the first from that town to be killed in battle. They buried him in Arlington Cemetery with great ceremony; and the Westfield G.A.R. Post is named in honor of him.

I did not know just what procedure to take to get into the army. My family thought that I was too young to be accepted, and that I should stay at home with my widowed mother. I ran away from home three times to enlist, but every time my uncle, who was a Supreme Court Judge in Philadelphia, was instrumental in having me sent back. One time, I had got clear down to-gosh, almost to Florida.

The war went on. News came that the enemy had killed my other brother. That made me fighting mad. The blood of revenge ran hot in my veins. I was determined to fight, law or no law. By that time I had managed to get work away from home, so it was easier for me to get away from the influence of my uncle. During the past two years volunteers had fallen off. Early in 1863 Congress passed the first national conscription act. It made all able-bodied citizens subject to draft, regardless of age. The act provided a commutation feature that a substitute might be obtained on the payment of three hundred dollars. A man named Sam Murdock knew of my desire to serve so he paid me a five-hundred-dollar bounty to act as his substitute. I was so tickled to be a soldier that I offered to return the money to him, but he wouldn't accept it.

The war ended ninety-three days after my enlistment, so I did not get to do any fighting after all. I guarded prisoners at York, Pa. By this time I was old enough to enlist in the regular army, which I did, and was sent to Fort McHenry, Md.

One of my proudest possessions is an honorable discharge from the United States army. It is framed and you will always find it hanging in my bed room.

"I have never known a truer patriot than Mr. Babcock has always been.'Loyal to death' has ever been his motto."
-Mrs. W. L. Munger

Samuel A. Ballard, G. A. R.

YOUNGEST MAN IN INDIANA CAVALRY

SAMUEL A. BALLARD, Eaton, Col. Union
B. May 12, 1848, New Castle, Co., Del.
Co. L, 10th Ind. Cav., Clifford, Ind. Dec. 5, 1863.
Dis. as corporal Aug. 31, 1865, Vicksburg, Miss.

I enlisted in the Union army at the age of fifteen, giving my age as seventeen. Twice previously I had run away to join the Union forces, feeling that if my older brothers could fight, I could too. The third time I ran away my father declared that if I could pass the examination he would not endeavor to keep me out of the war.

Even though I did not measure up to the standard height, nor top the scales at the standard weight required for soldiers, through the good graces of one of the doctors, who was a friend of the family, I passed the examination. When it came to the problem of height, the man who was making the examination said, "I think he can make himself taller. I won't look at his feet." So standing on tiptoes, I banished the problem of height, which had stood as a barrier to my acceptance in the army.

I was the youngest man of Company L, Indiana Cavalry, and during the war I became a non-commissioned officer. I was in actual service for two years and was not off duty a single day during that time, nor was I ever sick a day.

Though I was in the same company as my brother during the first part of my service, the company was later divided and my brother went with one division while I went with another. At the close of the war my brother reached home several days before I did and they thought that I had been killed. When I appeared on horseback one evening at the trough, my father, a farmer, was watering the horse, and his joy at seeing me alive was boundless. Going up to the house to see mother, I stopped at the gate and called "Hello! Do you suppose a fellow could get lodging here for the night?" Mother came out on the porch to look the wayfaring stranger over, and when I dismounted and repeated my question, she rushed to me, crying: "Sammy, Sammy!"

It was a joyful homecoming for me after I had run away and was thought to have been killed, and to return home without a single bullet wound, a testimonial to my ability as a good dodger.

After the war, I studied law and was admitted to the bar in Albany, Missouri, where I practiced before going west to Chadron, Nebraska, a town of about twelve thousand inhabitants. I specialized in Department of Interior land cases of the pioneer days, which were often taken to Washington for hearing, and I was never defeated in a single case. While residing in Chadron, I held the office of County Judge for six years, having started my first term about 1893. When the town was moved to a new location our family moved to New Chadron.

I moved to Douglas, Wyoming, for the benefit of an invalid daughter, but people still came from Nebraska seeking advice from me. Since my retirement, after leaving Nebraska, I have also lived in Casper, Wyoming. At the present time I live with my daughter, Mrs. Gillis.

Though my eyesight and hearing are somewhat impaired, I am keenly interested in current events and see more clearly through the eyes of my daughter, Grace Gertrude Gillis.

I attended the Gettysburg reunion of civil war veterans on the seventy-fifth anniversary of the battle, for which trip all expenses were paid by the government for me and my attendant. Here the Blue and the Gray gathered on the historic battle ground for the last world-wide reunion of civil war veterans, whose numbers are gradually diminishing as, one by one, the old soldiers slip into the Great Beyond.

When I left home, at the depot that Monday evening, there were several legionnaires of the Norman Hutchison Post to give us a big send-off and assist us in boarding the train. Mayor Deffke and a large number of townspeople were there; and the school band, under the direction of W.J. Evans, played several selections before the train pulled into the station. As we veterans boarded the train they broke into the strains of the national anthem. I made a brief talk and then we were off for a glorious journey to Gettysburg and a trip through the East.

Outstanding among my memories of this reunion will be the President's reference to us when he said: "Men who wore the Blue and men who wore the Gray are here together, a fragment spared by time. They are brought here by the memories of old divided loyalties, but they meet here in united loyalty to a united cause which the unfolding years have made it easier to see."

Louis F. Rieb

James R. Barker

John B. Burket

UNION HEROES

MEETS SAD-FACED MAN HE FAILED TO SHOOT SEVENTY-FIVE YEARS AGO

JAMES R. BARKER, Green Valley, Ill. Union
B. Dec. 24, 1846, Canada. 11th Ill. Cav.
Co. C, Sept. 27, 1864, Springfield, Ohio.

My early life was filled with many adventures as I was born in the days when the blood of the pioneer ran strong in the veins of the ambitious and the word "fear" was not known. We knew but to "do and dare" and bear the resulting hardships like a man. We did not have government relief then. When a boy was big enough to "go on his own" he ventured out into the world to carve a career for himself, and he usually succeeded.

My father, William Barker, was a carpenter and wheelwright, specializing in the building of hauling carts. His trade took him to various localities, but he always regarded Cleveland as his home. When the railroad was being built in Canada, it seemed a likely prospect for a man, so father went there. I was born there. After my mother passed away, father returned to our old home in Ohio.

I often compare the meager opportunities of my childhood days with those of the average boy of today. When I was fourteen, father agreed to let me go to Illinois in a covered wagon with Julius Murray, a wealthy citizen of Kingsville, Ohio. Mr. Murray allowed me to sell matches along the way to pay my expenses. I later returned to Ohio and worked as an apprentice in a cobbler shop. The call of the Illinois prairie began to surge in my veins again. The people passing my window seemed a part of the scheme to beckon me to join in the march. So with father's blessings and $1 in cash, I started to Peoria, Illinois, by train. From there I went to Pekin by boat. I stayed at the Birkenbusch Hotel and paid the whole sum of fifteen cents for a night's lodging and breakfast.

Brother Warriors

On September 27, 1864, I walked eight miles to Coon's Grove, where I met my best friend, Jim McClung. We went to Mr. Gregory's and he hitched up the team to a lumber wagon and took us, with his son, Ben, to within a few miles of Springfield. Here, we stood our examinations and were mustered in on September 28, 1864, at Camp Butler. My officer was Colonel Robert Ingersoll of Peoria, who later resigned saying he was a "better speaker than fighter," and who was succeeded by Colonel Funk.

The winter of 1864 was very bitter. One day during a blizzard we were commanded to march. We had no idea where we were going, but when ordered to dismount and encamp we were in a wooded section near Memphis, Tennessee. We set about cutting the fine timber and converting it into shingles and materials for barracks. We were told to keep our pistols at hand for instant use if the enemy should approach.

Frequent skirmishes were to be expected. I was in a number of them, but survived without getting seriously wounded, nor was I sick more than two or three days.

We were always hungry and glad to eat whatever we could get. Rations usually consisted of bacon and foraged foods. Raw meat was eaten with apparent relish when there was nothing else to be had for several days. On one occasion we went without rations for more than two days. We camped along the banks of the Mississippi then and the "John Rain," longest boat on the river, came along. Our captain hailed it and asked for food "in the name of the United States Army." We were given a supply of crackers. It was late at night, and, being very hungry, we feasted on them and thought they were delicious. The next morning we made another dash for the crackers. You can imagine our surprise to find that their unusually good flavor was derived from their fertility with meal worms.

How I recall, one evening, when I returned to camp from scout duty. I was wet and chilled to the bone. I had visions of staying in the next day and getting nice and warm. I made appropriate excuses why I should not be required to report. The next morning, I found out that if I remained in camp it would mean doing camp duty, so I hastily dressed and rode off with my comrades.

Once, in Memphis, some of the boys brought some whiskey to warm us up. When we returned to White Station and dismounted most of the fellows "doubled up." The captain remarked: "My pets are in a bad fix." I leaned against a tree for support. Some of the men had to be dragged to camp.

One wet, cold night, we were lucky to find a Negro shanty to sleep in. The front door provided the only opening and, as we were afraid the rebels might slip in and attack us, we loosened a chunk of dirt in the chimney just in case a hurried departure became necessary. This little shanty was luxurious compared to the fare we had been used to. We built a cheerful fire and made some coffee, then while our dripping clothes adorned the ceiling beam, we gathered around the hearth for refreshments.

One day, while out scouting on my horse, I suddenly met five mounted Johnnies. I did not know just what they might do to me, but I made up my mind if they dared molest me that I would shoot at least two of them, and that I might be able to get the other three. One of these men had a peculiar and particularly long, sad face. The orderly was wearing boots that looked like Jim McClung's. I distinctly remembered Jim's boots for when we started to war we had a pair exactly alike, made by the same cobbler. On my return to camp I learned that the men were General Forrest and his staff, who were on their way to Memphis to surrender. At the close of the war, I ran into Jim McClung, in Springfield, when we were waiting for our discharges. He told me that he had been wounded in a skirmish against Forrest and that a rebel had taken his boots and left him a pair of worn-out shoes.

In the war it was always a question of who could shoot first and those things are best untold. Many times we risked our lives or faced death at close range. One time when we thought we saw the enemy approaching, I volunteered to investigate. It was a great relief to find that they were Union soldiers who were lost.

We often played pranks to relieve the tension of the tragedies occurring around us. I remember particularly that our adjutant wrote his letters on a fire-arms box, upon which I often lounged when at headquarters on errands. This was disagreeable to him, so on one of my visits there appeared a small hole in the box. My hand fell over the hole, but I withdrew it quickly-just in time to miss a long needle that sprung through it. Well, I didn't let him know that I saw it, but he looked mighty disappointed.

I told my tent mates about the joke and we decided to try it on Pete Wolf, who was a cautious young German. I fixed up a similar box with a needle and spring under the lid. We invited Pete for a game of "seven-up," but he refused to accept until we promised not to play for money. Anticipation of the joke excited all of us but poor, unsuspecting Pete. When they were absorbed in the game, I sprung the needle, but it failed to work. So I had to hatch up an excuse to turn out the lights and re-set the trap. All set, the boys started arguing about who was the rightful holder of the card trick. Pete replied, indignantly. "Meine Guteness! Das ist mein trick." He reached for the cards and I sprung the needle. Well, poor ole Pete let out a howl and sprung about three feet into the air. Today I still chuckle when I think of Pete's affright.

While at the Gettysburg reunion, I needed a haircut, and, as the Union barber shop had not been set up, I went to the Confederate shop. I waited my turn and it was noon before I was served. The Union mess tent to which my attendant, Mary Olive Latham, and I were assigned was quite a distance. I was wearing civilian clothes, so we thought it would be quite a lark to slip in the Confederate mess hall, which we did. We seated ourselves near two men who were wearing Confederate uniforms. The one at my right leaned across the table and asked the one across from me, "Where were you when you surrendered?" The man answered, "I was one of General Forrest's staff, I was with him when he surrendered at Memphis." Immediately, I looked at the man facing me, and, behold, there sitting before me was the man with the long, sad face—the one whom I had picked out to kill some seventy-four years ago, had they attempted to molest me on that wooded road.

FIGHTS BUSHWHACKERS

CHARLES BAROTHY, Omaha, Nebr. Union.
B. Sept. 15, 1846, Hamberg, Germany.
Co. B, 1st Reg. Neb. Vet. Cav. Vol., Omaha, Neb.

I am the only surviving Civil War veteran in Omaha who enlisted here. I recall as if it were yesterday the time I enlisted with two other boys—all from Fontenelle, Nebraska. We walked into the recruiting office late at night. I was only sixteen, but I had high hopes. I didn't want to lie to get in, so I prepared a piece of cardboard with the figure "18" on it. When I stood before the officer and he asked my age, I said, "Sir, I am standing on 18."

I returned home for ten days and then came back to Omaha to get my army clothes. No doubt, they ordered my suit for an eighteen year old boy for it was much too large for me.

I did guard duty for several months and helped fight the bushwhackers. They would not fight for their country, and fitted in as pests for all concerned.

The only injury I received was a gunshot wound in my left leg. After the Civil War, I fought the Indians until 1866, when I was mustered out of the army.

My present home is not over twenty feet from where my father came into Omaha in 1855. I took a homestead in Washington County in 1866. In 1874, I opened an implement business and later went on the road as a salesman.

In 1865, I whipped the Rebels, but times has changed and now in 1938 we are all good fellows together. We've had a good time singing old-time songs together. Our chorus is composed of Joshua Henry, 95, of Kansas, H. S. Woodworth, 95, Jerry Withelm, 94, and myself of Nebraska; J. R.

Huddleston, 95 of Illinois, and C. E. Scarlett of Missouri. So, I will say the Gettysburg meeting is a grand reunion.

COMMANDER OF "LOUISIANA TIGERS"
AT LITTLE ROUND TOP

COLONEL WILLIAM BEATTY, Cromwell, Ky. Confederate.
B. July 9, 1842, New Orleans, La., 2nd Bgd., 2nd
Div., New Orleans, La.

On April 6-7, 1862, I was in the Battle of Shiloh, General Albert Sidney Johnston being my commanding officer. We took the enemy by surprise and drove them behind their guns the first day. About two o'clock in the afternoon of the second day's fight General Johnston was riding along his advancing lines and was struck in the thigh by a bullet. We took him off his horse and tried to stanch the flow of blood from a severed artery. His staff surgeon had left him just a few minutes before to look after wounded federal prisoners. Our beloved leader died about four o'clock that same afternoon. This was a great loss to the South as Johnston was fearless in leading his men into the fray. Once when he was advised to delay action, he said: "I would fight them if they were a million."

General G. T. Beauregard, highest ranking officer, took command. He issued orders for us to fall back and hold our position. We told him that would never do as General Grant and General Buell were coming up the Tennessee River with reinforcements. That day we were forced to retreat back to Corinth.

We were without reinforcements and the strenuous fighting of the past few days had been too much for us.

It was said that once during a battle, when the first shots rang out, a man standing in the federal forces threw down his gun and started running. The command was sounded to halt, but he kept running. Someone called out, "John why are you running?" He replied, "Cause I haven't got wings to fly."

On September 17, 1862, I entered my second battle at Antietam. Our forces consisted of 40,000 men, and we stood our ground very well against McClellan's 75,000. I went from there to Richmond.

During the Battle of Gettysburg, I was helping defend Little Round Top. General Lee said to Pickett, "I want those guns." Pickett said, "I can but try." Pickett came to me and asked if I would support him in the charge, the Louisiana Tigers being my brigade. I told him "Yes." We took the guns, spiking them. During this time General Longstreet hadn't moved his corps stationed near Little Round Top. Lee had given Longstreet orders to charge in the morning when he heard the roar of guns, but Longstreet failed to do so.

In the battle of Gettysburg, when the bugle was sounded for retreat, a wounded Union soldier lay pleading for water. He asked me for water; I had none, but I had a pint of brandy which I carried in case of emergency. I dismounted my horse, preparing to give him the brandy, when he whirled over on his elbow and shot me through the upper lobe of the right lung. After this deed he fell over dead. I got on my horse with great difficulty and went to headquarters where I was taken care of by a doctor. The bullet lodged in my back and remains there to this day.

Three of my brothers were killed in the War Between the States: Leonardus was shot while accompanying Stonewall Jackson, the night Jackson was mistaken for the enemy and felled by a volley from his own men; Greenbury was killed in the Atlanta Campaign; James was in the Navy and was killed at Mobile Bay opposing Farragut.

I believe I am the only surviving officer of General Robert E. Lee's staff. As I have lived to see this day, I thank God that He gave to the world such a commander as our wonderful, brave, gallant Lee.

The Gettysburg Reunion, founded on brotherly love, has been a success. President Roosevelt's words spoken on that famous battleground will become memorable as did Lincoln's.

STANDS INSPECTION BAREFOOTED AND REFERRED TO AS "GOOD SOLDIER"

EZRA BERKSHIRE, W. Los Angeles, Calif. Union.
B. Mar. 1, 1847, Jacobsport, Ohio. Co. K. 61st
Ill. Vol., Inf. Springfield, Ill.

When the war came on in '61, my brothers John and Robert joined immediately, but Israel and I had to remain at home and help father on the farm. I joined two years later.

With very little military training, I was sent to winter quarters of the 61st Illinois Volunteers, at Little Rock. My regiment was commanded by Colonel Nulton and Major Grass; Company K was commanded by Captain Judy.

When spring came, the bushwhackers and guerillas started raiding our lines. When we were not engaged with them we were often sent out on skirmishing parties. So our activities were of a lesser nature.

Later on in the year we went to Tennessee. We were on the move continually, travelling by foot, by boat, and sometimes by train, and occasionally engaging the Confederates in a small battle.

Our rations was the usual hardtack and sowbelly. Sometimes we were able by various means to obtain a little fresh food.

In the summer of '64, General Shelby, a daring and fearless Confederate soldier, was making life miserable for the Union forces. We determined to rid Arkansas of him. We were sent to support a battery of light field artillery which was engaged in a spirited dual with Shelby's artillery. The infantry was to stand in the rear of the field pieces and not take any part in the action unless the enemy infantry attempted to capture the guns. It was anything but pleasant when the other fellow was shooting at us not to be permitted to shoot back. One time, a shell came along, clipped off the limb of a nearby cottonwood tree and then went screaming over my head—a very discomforting experience.

Once we were issued "one ration" and sent out scouting. We expected to be back in camp in time for supper. For three days we continued a hot pursuit of a raiding party who led us a merry chase through swamps. They managed to keep just out of our reach, which incited us on. Exposure, exhaustion and deprivation of food took a heavy toll. None of us escaped being ill, and our officers said that we could not have lost more men if we had been in a continuous engagement during this time. When we returned to camp, we were muddy from head to foot and too tired to clean up. Without even attempting to cook, we ate our fill—salt, fat and all of sowbelly and wormy hardtack. Thus, wet, tired, and filled with the most unappetizing and indigestible food imaginable, we rolled up in blankets and had a long sleep.

Early the next morning, our sergeant aroused us from a sound sleep with a loud, "Prepare for inspection!" Inspection at any time was a bane to a soldier's life, but at this time it was worse than a horrible nightmare, as if fortune and luck had completely deserted us. The inspection officer was none other than the distinguished Colonel R. B. Marcy, a regular army officer, a West Pointer, and at this time Inspector-General. Well, we immediately attacked the mud covering our uniforms and guns, but with little enthusiasm. We gave vent to our feelings, too, for inspectors, inspecting-officers and one regular colonel, in particular. Volunteers and regulars differ in that regulars are known to be sticklers to regulations, regardless of conditions and circumstances. Here we were the dirtiest, most bedraggled company of soldiers in the army, about to be inspected by a regular. In my haste, the ramrod got stuck in the barrel of my musket. The harder I tried to remove it the firmer it stuck. It was still jammed there when the sergeant yelled, "Fall in for inspection." You can imagine the appearance we made, without shoes, breeches rolled up, some of the men minus blouses, and all looking as if we had wallowed in a pig-sty. The colonel took the musket out of my hands, gave it a shake, and, without a glance toward me, tossed it back. Completing his inspection, he started to walk away, then suddenly turned around and, in a voice loud enough for all of us to hear, said, "Good soldiers." We gave him a long and lusty cheer and changed our opinions of regulars—of one colonel in particular.

While in Tennessee, we were engaged in building block houses and guarding railroads. Near us there lived a farmer's family. There were two young ladies who were quite talented musically. We used to go up there to buy buttermilk. When we called for "Buttermilk," they would dash to their old-fashioned, square piano and accompany us, singing out, "Big Yank, Little Yank, run Yank or you die." Our reply was, "We did run, but the Rebs were running in front of us."

From Tennessee we went to Springfield, where we were discharged in September of '65. Arriving home, I learned that my dear mother had been buried just a few days before.

Returning home from the Gettysburg Reunion, July 1938, my son-attendant, Harry, and I stopped by our old home in Chauncy, Illinois. We visited the scenes of my boyhood and paid homage to departed loved ones who rest in the family cemetery there.

*

SHAKES HANDS WITH ABRAHAM LINCOLN

PETER BINKLEY, Omaha, Neb. Union.
B. Sept. 19, 1847, Chambersburg, Pa.
Co. B, 11th Reg. Pa. Cav. Vol.,
Chambersburg, Pa., Feb. 29, 1864.
Dis. Aug. 13, 1865. Died Mar. 24, 1938.

A succession of interesting things happened during my war service. Standing out most vividly in my memory is the time that Abraham Lincoln shook hands with me when I was hospitalized. Then there was the time I held General Spear's horse when General Lee surrendered at Appomattox.

Twice I had narrow escapes from death. One of these occasions resulted in wounds when I was fighting down at Apple River, Va. Another time, I was almost drowned when my horse, fell off a pontoon bridge, but saved myself by hanging onto the horse's tail and he swam out with me.

I was pretty badly injured near Portsmouth, Va., when my horse threw me on the stump of a tree. I was taken to the camp hospital and later to Yorktown Hospital. I was also in several other hospitals, and they finally sent me to Fortress Monroe, where I remained until I could go back to my regiment. I served altogether about eighteen months.

Though I am nearly ninety-two years old, until recently I walked three miles downtown and back to my home several times a week. If you want to keep your health you have to be active and kind to yourself.

SERVES THE ARMY AND THE NAVY

FREDERICK A. BOLAND, Syracuse, N. Y. Union.
B. Nov. 4, 1844, Chenango, Co., N. Y. Co. F,
127th N. Y. July 30, 1862, Staten Island, N. Y.
Re-enlisted in the U. S. Navy.

Standing on the dock at Poughkeepsie, I saw a big steamer coming down the river. My, but it looked pretty. The fare to New York was only $1, so without waiting to make up my mind I just got on. There was nothing for me to do after I got there, so I just hung around awhile until I went to Staten Island and enlisted.

My regiment was up near Yorktown for awhile and from there we went by train to Fredericksburg. We were sent into that battle with great force, but were not amply protected. We were out in the open just like a target set up for the Confederates to shoot at. We suffered a loss of 12,300 men to their loss of 4,500. I was with the Union forces through Dismal Swamp. Oh, I don't know, I was in fights, but I can't tell now what they were—down in Virginia.

I helped build breastworks around Washington, on the Virginia side. We were around there close to a year. I was a favorite of a general, so he gave me easy jobs, such as building. There was a strict order not to drink water from a certain spring. I didn't think about the reason for not wanting us to drink it, so I disobeyed orders and drank all I wanted. That put me out, I was sick for three or four months with ague. For a long time I stayed in a sick tent. Then I quit the army. On my way home, I felt so bad that I stopped in Harrisburg. A family who had lost a brother—a general—at Missionary Ridge, had a lot of sympathy for soldiers and took me in. They gave me a fine feather bed to sleep on and called their family physician to see me. Times has changed since then. Nowadays, people sleep with their feather beds (comforters) on top of 'em.

It didn't take me long to get well and back into the service, but this time I joined the Navy. I was on the flagship Hartford. We cleaned up the country then. I was given a gun on deck to man. I missed getting killed by a split-second once. I was temporarily relieved from duty just about the time a shell exploded on deck and killed everyone around it.

Hardtack was a staple food used by the government in feeding soldiers. We were mighty glad to get it and it tasted mighty good then. I can't remember having a meal without it. We used tin cups and had to drink coffee to get the hardtack.

I recall seeing Lincoln in Washington right after the war. They had parades there—big parades—up Pennsylvania Avenue. There were lots of people and flags on every building.

BELLE BOYD—NOTED CONFEDERATE SPY

Belle Boyd was born in 1843. She grew up to be one of the best horsewomen of her day. During the War Between the States, Belle killed a Yankee sergeant who entered her family home at Martinsburg, West Virginia, and made an attempt to pull down the Confederate flag. She was court martialed, but won her freedom when she vamped the federal officers.

She was quite friendly with the Northern officers, who used her home as a barrack, but retaliated for their invasion by appropriating their weapons for the use of the Confederacy.

J. E. B. Stuart found her invaluable as a spy. She used to eavesdrop on the officers and convey their conferences to the Confederacy in messages secreted in the rolls of her long, luxuriant hair.

She saved the life of General Jackson by warning him of General Shields' plan to trap him. He wrote her a note which read: "I thank you for myself and for the army for the immense service you have rendered your country today. Hastily, I am your friend—T. J. Jackson."

In 1862, Belle was captured at Front Royal, Virginia, and imprisoned for one month in old Capitol Prison, Washington, D. C. During an exchange of prisoners she was returned to the South. She was again captured in August 1863, and lodged in Carrol Prison for four months. She was released for lack of evidence.

In August 1864, Belle was married to Lieutenant Sam Wylde Haringe, a Union officer. She died in Kilbourne, Wisconsin, in 1900.

For personal accounts of the activities of Belle Boyd see the stories of Henry Evans and of Peter Pierre Smith.

LINCOLN SHEDS TEARS

JOHN B. BURKET, Warriors Mark, Pa. Union.
B. Mar. 31, 1849, Warriors Mark, Pa.
Co. A, 205th Reg. Pa. Inf., Altoona, Pa.,
Aug. 16, 1865. Dis. June 2, 1865.

I want to tell you that I am the only surviving soldier in this community who fought in the Civil War. The rest have all departed. It doesn't seem so very long ago since the day I stood on the mount at Warriors Mark Cemetery to listen to memorial address and it was crowded with soldiers. There was hardly enough room for us all to get on. On May 30, 1938, they had all answered the roll call. When I stood there before, little did I realize that I would be the last one. It won't be long though until I will have to follow them.

I want to tell you a little about the Civil War; what I have seen and gone through. I want to tell you from the start. There were four of us here in this community who decided we'd like to enter the army. Two of the fellows were eighteen years or over, one not quite eighteen, and I was fifteen years and four months old. I was as big as they were though. We all went to Harrisburg and took the physical examination and we all passed. When they asked my age I told them eighteen. The doctors all looked at each other and kind of smiled. Then one of them slapped me on the back and told me to go on my spunk. We then went to Altoona and were enlisted in the army.

From here we moved on to Harrisburg where we drilled for quite a great length of time. We were reviewed by the officers and given a good talking to. They told us boys they hoped we had the spunk to stand the test. The training finally came to an end and we were given our uniforms. Then we got the balance of our equipment and our guns,

After we were fully equipped we started for Washington in old box cars. We were packed in there like sardines, so we were. From Washington we moved to Arlington Heights. We were here for a couple of days. Then we went down to the wharf and were loaded onto vessels and went to Virginia to the headquarters of the army. Here we saw two corrals which had seven hundred head in each of them. A few days before we landed, the rebels took one of the corrals and drove them off.

After we had landed, it was found out that we did not have enough soldiers. We went into camp and threw out a picket line. The roads ran out of town straight through as far as you could see, but the country was covered with underbrush so thick that a dog could not get through. It started raining and then sleeting. Four of us and a non-commissioned officer went out about a mile to a little place and pitched camp. The officer said to us: "Two of you pick out a place and camp and the others will stand guard." One of the fellows and myself went to the side of the road. With my foot I scraped the hail from the ground. It was about five inches thick. I threw a blanket down on the ground. We lay on it and pulled another woolen blanket over our bodies and covered our faces, because the hail was still striking us.

We lay thus for almost an hour, when the officer came up to us and exclaimed: "The rebels are coming!" We sprang up and got our guns in readiness. Now we could hear the patter of hoofs. We hollered: "Hold on, who comes there?" No one answered. We hollered again and still no answer. We called a third time and then pulled the hammers of our guns and advanced. It turned out to be one of our own men, who was scared and shaking so that he was speechless. He told us that the colonel was out viewing the pickets and he had to ride alongside on his horse. No rebels came that night.

We camped at this site for quite awhile and then we marched to the front line. Up to this time I had never seen a rebel. I was out on picket duty near rebel lines one day. I was looking across a ravine and saw a man standing on the other side. He was staring at me and I looked at him. He hollered "Hello, Yank!" and I answered, "Hello Johnnie!" Then he said: "Where yo' all from?" I answered: "From Pennsylvania." He said: "Are all yo' men from Pennsylvania?" I said: "No, we come from different states in the North." That was all we said to each other.

On one end of the picket line there was a large field. Across the field there was a big house and not far away from the house a large horse-chestnut tree. In this tree was stationed a sharpshooter. The next night they put two sharpshooters in this tree. The rebels fired and one of the men fell down on the lower limb of the tree and hung there, limp-like. He never moved. They must have shot him down. The rebels then shot two more bullets into him. All we could do was watch him, but we did not dare go near him or take him down. He had to hang there until after dark.

We stayed here for quite awhile. The rebels waited until a real dark night to make an attack. They attacked the fort or house in which we were staying and took a few of our boys as prisoners. Of course, we heard the racket they were making and went into the line of battle right away. They hardly gave us time to get into our clothes. The rebels certainly did whoop and holler. The officer in command shouted: "Not a man shoot until he gets orders!" Then we got orders to fire. We killed them right and left, and they fell deader-than-a-door-nail. We thought we had killed them all, but there were a few left. We charged and got up pretty close to them, but they ran back. Then we saw another bunch of rebels coming toward us. There was a good number of them. I would say twice as many men as we had. We were ordered to move back a little and reload our guns. The rebels were advancing slowly. When they were close to our line, we were given orders to fire. They fell fast. Mr. Weston, who was one of my buddies, found two guns. He had one gun loaded. A rebel came along and bent his gun. The captain honored for me to get back. He said: "I believe this gun is loaded." I said "Let 'er go, maybe it will kill two." At this point we were given orders to stop firing.

We walked over the field. I noticed a man coming along, and, when I got up close to him, I saw it was Abe Lincoln. He had his black silk hat in his left hand. When he came upon a dead soldier he would just stand there and gaze at him. The tears would stream down his face and he would wipe them away with his hand. He treated the soldiers all alike, our boys and the rebels, wounded or dead.

Just about this time Lincoln was up for re-election. Congress had passed a law that all soldiers eighteen years and over could vote. I wasn't eighteen, but my records said I was. As I was walking along I had no intention of voting. The captain said to me: "Here, Burket, take this ticket and vote." I took it and, of course, I voted for Abe Lincoln.

In the meantime, the railways were bringing in many cannons daily. One night the officer told us he wanted us to fall in line. We went out and lay on the ground and had our cannons ready to fire. The rebels fired and shot right over the top of us. Some of the balls were cap shells that had to strike something before they went off. Others were fuse shots. The rebels had some of these and as they exploded many of our men were killed. I don't know how long this kept up but firing finally ceased.

Now, I will tell you something about the fort. It was about one hundred and seventy-five or two hundred feet straight across. Outside the fort was a ditch six feet deep and eight feet across. Outside the ditch was a row of prongs about four feet high. These were rammed against each other and wrapped with wire. When we got up close to make our charge, we thought we could go in there and throw them apart. We could not get the prongs apart, and our fancy uniforms were all spotted and torn.

We waited there until dinner-time and thought we would get a bite to eat. I had coffee on. Then a train came in loaded with soldiers and I could not get to drink my coffee because we had to start firing. We jumped into the ditch and rammed the bayonets into the ground until they formed four steps. When we climbed and got our heads above the top the rebels fired at us and aimed for our heads. Finally, we saw that we had to do something. At one side of the fort was a draw-bridge. Only a few of the rebels escaped by way of this bridge. Our fellows headed them off. Some of the boys rammed their bayonets right through the rebels. I saw two or three with bayonets plunged right through their hearts. A few of the rebels escaped us.

By this time it was getting dark and firing ceased. We now had to go to work and find our dead men and give aid to those who were wounded. We then had a bite of supper, which consisted of hardtack. I had coffee with mine. We all had enough to satisfy us and then lay down to sleep.

About midnight, or a little after, the whole earth shook around us. The rebels were retreating and we knew immediately that they were leaving. The officer did not call us, but let us rest until morning. In the morning when we got up we started to follow them. We trailed them for one and a half days before we finally caught up with them. We approached the rebels from the rear and completely surrounded them.

General Grant presented a prepared note to General Lee asking him to surrender. I can still picture General Grant on his horse, his long, black, beard flowing in the breeze. General Lee answered General Grant by asking what the terms were. General Lee said that he would let Mr. Grant know by four o'clock. Lee wasn't long in giving his answer. After a bit he came along. He was a fine man with gray whiskers. He went into the building and Mr. Grant was seated at a table. He had the terms all written out. General Grant arose from his chair and shook hands with General Lee. They talked over the terms for awhile, after which Lee read them. He must have been satisfied because he accepted the terms. General Lee had all his guns stacked on the field and he said to General Grant: "My men really own their own horses." General Grant answered him by saying: "Tell your men to take them back home and use them for farming." The rebels then fled like wild-fire, whooping and hollering.

Shortly after the surrender I talked, with one of the rebels. He said that he had not eaten anything for two days and two nights and that he was weak from hunger and exhaustion. General Grant opened up the provision train and said: "Give them all the hardtack they want and can eat." One fellow took one end of the hardtack, put it in his mouth, and pulled and pulled, but he could not break it. He commenced to swear, saying: "How do you fellows do it?" I said "Get a stone, break it, and put the pieces of the hardtack in the coffee, so the hardtack will absorb the coffee. We have to eat the cakes to get the coffee." That tickled him and he laughed and laughed. I didn't see anything of the fellow after he left.

After the war was over, we stayed in this place for a few days and then took trains for Washington. Half way back we met wagons loaded with bread and provisions. We sure were glad to get the bread. All of the bread was distributed among the soldiers. I ate half my loaf and had some coffee to go with it.

We arrived at Arlington Heights where we rested for awhile. We started making preparations for the big parade in Washington. Every man was given one-half of a candle which he put in the muzzle of his gun. These candles were lit at night. During the march from Arlington Heights to Washington and as far as I could see both ways these candles were burning and glowing. It was a beautiful sight to behold. As we were marching along we were proud to be in the parade. We could feel the tallow running down our backs, but the lighted candles did look pretty. Later on, we had to take knives to peel off the tallow that had run down our backs. When we finally got into the city there wasn't a square foot of space where somebody wasn't standing. It was a grand home-coming day, and one which we will all remember for a long time.

After the parade we got into trains and returned to Harrisburg, where we stayed for several days. We were given our discharge papers by the paymaster and soon were on our ways home.

I attended the Gettysburg reunion and was happy to be there with the hundreds of other veterans. In memory I thought of my three brothers who were in the Union army; James, Mahlon and William Burket. What a happy reunion it would have been for me if they had been there too!

SERVES THREE YEARS BEFORE HE IS EIGHTEEN AND REFERRED TO AS "BRAVEST MAN IN THE COMPANY"

JOSEPH T. BUSHONG, Hicksville, Ohio. Union.
B. Aug. 27, 1847, Logan Co. Ohio. Co. G, 81st
Inf. Vol., Aug. 26, 1862, Lima, Ohio. Dis.
July 13, 1865, Louisville, Ky.

When I was enlisted in the army they asked me if I was eighteen years old. I told them I was. That's the only lie I ever told in my life, but it was the proudest day of my life. I served three years lacking thirty-five days, and was home thirty-five days before I was eighteen.

The 81st Ohio was organized at Lima, Ohio, in September 1861. It was reorganized in August 1862. We, with five new companies of a hundred men each, joined a lot of recruits from old companies that had been in the battles of Shiloh, Corinth, and Iuka.

During the winter we camped at Corinth and made several raids. One raid, of eighteen days, was in the Tuscumbia Valley of Alabama. Old Joe Wheeler, a Confederate cavalry general, was giving us trouble and we went down after him.

In the spring we guarded a railroad bridge at Pocahontas, Tennessee. Then toward fall we did various kinds of guard duty at Pulaski, Tennessee. Toward spring, of 1864, we started south past Chattanooga and on to Resaca, Georgia, where our first hard battle was fought on May 14 and 15. My command was then sent up the river to effect a crossing and interfere with the rebel's retreat on the Rome Road. We charged across an open field and dropped by a low, cedar, rail fence, protected by a border of high, thick brush. We were within twenty feet of the river, which was narrow, with bottomland on both sides. Right .across from us, perched on a bluff about eighteen to twenty feet high, was a line of Johnnies. They fired down through that brush. Every now and then they would hit one of our boys. A neighbor boy, right beside me, was hit on the right shoulder. The shot penetrated the shoulder blade. Now in a place like that there was one of three thoughts in a soldier's mind, or all three, if possible. First was home and loved ones; second, eternity; third, victory to our flag. The instant the ball hit him, he cried; "Bless the Lord, bless the Lord, bless the Lord!" three times. Now, I never was easy to scare and I wasn't scared then, but it made a queer feeling run down my spine. We had been close boyhood friends and our families all belonged to the same church. They carried him away and I never saw him again. He died of that wound.

At the same time, right by his side, was another boy who got shot in the forehead. He died within a few minutes.

The next morning we crossed the river and drove the enemy back to the Rome Road and had quite a battle there. The battles of Resaca, Lays Ferry, and Rome Road were pretty close together. It was not long until the battle of Dallas, where the rebels charged us seven times in one night. We had a good line of field works, so they failed to break our line and did not hurt us much.

There were battles, like Big Shanty, Kennesaw Mountain, and others, I don't just recall, but it was not long before the Atlanta campaign. Joseph E. Johnston commanded the southern army until near Atlanta. The Confederate authorities thought he was falling back too much. They removed him and put in General John B. Hood. Johnston ought never to have allowed Sherman to cross the Chattahoochee River. Hood bolted right into Sherman and thought he would drive him right back across the river. His first effort to the right of Sherman, on July 20, 1864, failed. His second attempt was on July 22. Johnston massed his forces against the left and extended out beyond the end of Sherman's line. Our scouts got wise to this formation, so my command extended Sherman's line. If Hood could have preceded us there it would have been disastrous for us, since their position behind our line would have resulted in what is called an enfilade fire.

Our army formed what is called a column or line of battle, a front rank and a rear rank, placed twenty-eight inches apart. The men of the ranks stood just far enough apart for their elbows to touch. Hood mustered his forces so that he had three lines to our one. The 14th Regiment of Ohio Battery came with their horses on a dead run to strengthen us. My regiment was the last in formation. We had to run about two miles to get down to the end of the line. We made way and let the six gun battery pull right into our line. When Hood's men began to come on, the battery used shells on them until they got close enough for us to use grape-shot and canister, but that only carried about forty rods. We were ordered to lay down until they were close enough for us to use our muskets, this position caused them to shoot over us. They came right on up, but could not face the battery any closer than ten rods, so lay down on the ground. The ground sloped so the battery wasn't of much use and we were ordered to charge with our muskets. When we were lining up for the charge, the best officer we ever had pointed to me as he spoke to one of the sergeants. He said: "There is one of the bravest men in this company." "Why?" asked the sergeant. "What makes me think so! Look at him," the officer said, "boy as he is, he takes in, the whole situation, realizes the dangers, yet he has the courage to stand there like a statue-that's what I call a hero."

When we drove the rebels out of there, they went farther to the left and forced a division out of the breastworks. We were called to go and help that division out, so we took a pretty active part in that day's fighting. Four thousand of our men were killed or wounded and six thousand Confederates.

Hood's next onslaught was on the right of Sherman's line, the 28th of July, but I don't know so much about that. I was detailed to help cut a road through the timber so a battery could pass into a new fort.

Not long after this, my command was sent about twenty-two miles to cut off the rebel's communication and base of supplies from the south and to force them to evacuate Atlanta. That was called the battle of Jonesboro. It was the last hard fight of the Atlanta campaign. We were behind a good line of field works, built about breast high. We used what was called a "head log" for protection. For this we used a log eight to twelve inches thick-as large as the boys could very well handle. There was a chunk under the log the size of the wrist so the muzzle of the gun could fit through it. When the Johnnies charged us they were within about twenty feet of our works and knew that they could never get over that line of works alive. They stopped there. The orderly sergeant said to me: "Bushong, you are the next man on the roll. We are out of ammunition." The firing was too heavy for the ordinance wagons to come anywhere near us. They stopped fifty or sixty rods back in a hollow. I took off my cartridge belt, laid it on the bank of the ditch, and started to the rear. The cartridges were packed in pine boxes, a thousand rounds in a box, and weighed somewhere from eighty-six to a hundred pounds. When I got to the teams, the ammunition boxes had been unloaded and piled on the ground. I scanned the boxes until I caught sight of the calibre for our guns, "58". I jumped, setting my feet far enough apart to stoop, grabbed a box, and started back to the front. As I ran, the bullets flew thick and fast past my ears. The balls were pop, popping all around the ammunition and a hail storm of bullets were striking the ground in front of me until I felt that I was running to catch up with them, but not one touched me.

The enemy left Atlanta and their next move was to the Sea. We left Atlanta on the 14th day of November and landed in Savannah on the 21st of December. Our next move was through the Carolinas. We left Savannah on January 11th and crossed over to South Carolina, then into North Carolina, and were near Goldsboro at the time of Lee's surrender.

I never allowed the best of them, the worst of them, or all of them to induce me to smoke, chew, drink or gamble, and I sent home more money than a lot of men.

In my day there were not many schools. The terms were three months in the winter and two in the summer. Boys usually went to work as soon as they were large enough. I was a good speller and had a little idea of addition, subtraction, multiplication, and division, and could just write my name when I went to the war. I learned to write on the back of a knapsack or a cracker box lid. I never studied geography, grammar, or history, but I had a good memory most of my life.

The trip to the Gettysburg Reunion was one of the finest of my whole life. We met the last survivors of the Blue and the Gray-a group of century-old warriors, who were surprisingly young and chipper.

There follows short poetry that I blocked out in 1925. Maybe it will give one some idea of how an old soldier faces the reclining years:

THE BIRTH OF CHRIST

Christ our Lord in Bethlehem,
A child of lowly birth,
Was born to save the sons of men,
From all their sins on earth.

His blood was shed upon the cross,
To save the world from sin,
All else to him is only dross,
When there are souls to win.

What greater love hath man than this,
To lay down life for friends,
Descending like a holy kiss,
Is love that Jesus sends.

Oh, could the world but hear his voice,
The nation would be blest,
Accept the right because of choice,
'Tis Jesus' sweet request.

And were the world with great delight,
To hail "good will to men,"
And Christians keep their armour bright,
The world would prosper then.

Brother Warriors

FOUR BROTHER NONAGENARIANS SERVE CONFEDERACY

SEABORN LEWIS CAMP, Sulphur Springs, Tex.
Confederate. B. Sept. 5, 1848, Jonesboro,
Ga. 25th Ga. Inf., Co. C., Dalton, Ga.

Though I came of a family of brave soldiers, I did not get into the army until it was nearly over. I am glad that it was my privilege to give thirteen months service. Brigadier General Stephens was my commander.

When Sherman made his march toward Atlanta, I was serving General Joseph E. Johnston. He was a man of keen, sound judgment, but was replaced by General John B. Hood who was more of a dare-devil fighter. I recall when General Johnston was observing army maneuvers. I saw a shell from the enemy's gun fall directly under his horse. It grazed the earth and slid on some distance before exploding, so did not hurt him. General Johnston remained calm and collected as was ever his nature when facing danger.

My older brothers served the full four years of the war and all returned home. John, who later became a Baptist preacher, lived to be over ninety, and J. J., who became a doctor, lived to be ninety-two. Both of them were in the battle of Gettysburg, under the command of General Longstreet. B. M. joined the Confederates at Jonesboro, Georgia, in October 1861. He held the rank of Lieutenant in Company F, Second Georgia Cavalry and served in Wharton and Martin's Division, Army of Tennessee, under General Nathan Bedford Forrest. He was a special scout for General Joseph W. Wheeler, which brought him in close contact with dangers. B. M. lived to be more than ninety-seven years old.

Though the modern warfare equipment being shown at the Gettysburg Reunion is complete, I hope this country may never have to use it. Give me peace and love every time.

SNUBS PRESIDENTIAL INAUGURATIONS

MILTON CAMPBELL, Washington, D. C. Confederate.

I was born December 29, 1846, just over the line here in Virginia. I entered the Confederate Army while I was still in my teens and I served five days in the Signal Corps just before Lee's surrender. We had a fine time while it lasted. My prime regret is that I only got to serve five days.

All I had to do was stand up on a high mountain, with a pair of field glasses and a couple of flags, and watch what was going on. I was supposed to use the flags to signal with, but I think the war was over before I got on how to wave them so they would mean anything. I could look down the valley on both armies, but no one ever tried to shoot me because I was too high up.

When Lincoln was inaugurated, I was so close I could hear him kiss the Bible. I've attended all the presidential inaugurations since he took office. As a boy, I wasn't so strong on actually seeing the inaugurations as I was on going to town. With several other lads I would go to Washington, ostensibly for the ceremonies, but we always wound up by riding around on the street cars all day.

CAPTURES FIFTEEN HUNDRED YANKS THREE DAYS AFTER LEE'S SURRENDER

MAJOR ALFRED A. CANNON, Childress, Texas.
Confederate. B. May 22, 1847, Jacksonville,
Ala., Stephens Div., 30th Ala., Chattanooga, Tenn.

When I think of the fine specimens of manhood, fighting right alongside of me, whose lives were snuffed out in a split-second, I realize how kind the Supreme Power was to me when I missed by a bare fraction of an inch having my head split by a bullet. It happened like this. Near Atlanta, I had captured a horse. Four comrades and I were taking turn-about riding him. Lieut. Powers and four companions came along and we joined them. After we had traveled a few miles, we noticed a man making frequent and regular trips in and out of a house, about a quarter of a mile distant. Lieut. Powers and four of us went to investigate. We crawled on hand and knees through the briars and thickets. I tell you, every minute hung over our heads like an hour. Finally we crossed a small creek, just a short distance from the house. We crept steathily, parting the thickets to force an inroad, when all of a sudden we found ourselves staring right into the main line of a Yankee camp. We all turned and took to our heels. I ran so fast that I became exhausted and had to grasp a tree for support while I recovered my breath. Powers rushed by at that moment and yelled, "Come on Major, there's a fellow on a mule after us." About this time a bullet came sizzling above my head. It took my hat right along with it. My heels didn't hesitate any longer, but started "biting the dust" faster than ever. Since that time, I have never seen a single one of the comrades who were with me, nor did I recover my horse. Passing through one of the enemy's deserted camps,' I found an old, red hat which I salvaged and wore until the end of the war.

When foraging proved unfruitful, corn which we picked up from where the horses were fed tasted mighty good to hungry soldiers. There were times when we had to exist for several days on a mere few kernels of corn. We parched the corn as we sat around the camp fires at night. Once, two of my comrades and I found a sheep. It didn't go very far in satisfying the hunger of the whole camp, but at least most of us found out what mutton tasted like once again.

When General Johnston resumed charge of our regiment at Charleston, we had been marching four days without food, except parched corn. Despite the famished condition of our boys, we went into battle at Salisburg and captured fifteen hundred Yanks. But we learned three days later that Lee had already surrendered. I divided my portion of food with one of our Yankee prisoners, and at the Gettysburg Reunion, I met this same Yank and he recalled my kind action toward him.

HALTS LINCOLN AND GRANT

JOSEPH CHISAM, ROME, New York. Union.
B. Nov. 10, 1845, Tabert, N. Y. 24th N. Y.
Cav., Co. F, Taberg, N. Y. Jan. 2, 1864.
Dis. July 4, 1865, Cloud Mills, Va.

I did something for which I was made a sergeant, at the Battle of the Wilderness, but I don't remember what it was. But there is one thing I do remember. Just before the close of the war, I was placed on guard in a very important position, on the main road leading from Petersburg to City Point. It was just before the last battle and I had strict orders not to let anybody pass without giving the countersign. Who should come along but President Lincoln and General Grant! They were making a review of the whole army. It would have been all right but they had an escort with them and I didn't hardly know what to do. I halted them. I said, "Advance one and give the countersign!" The orderly advanced and obeyed the command. Then I motioned to them to pass on. Grant rode up to me, his eyes fairly spitting fire, and said, "Young man, do you know who we are?" I said, "Yes, Sir, I think I do." He demanded, "Who are we?" About this time I could feel my whole body trembling and I almost knew if I tried to speak that my voice would crack, but I answered, "General Grant, the Commander-in-Chief of the Great Army of the Potomac." He said, "Do you know who the other gentleman is?" I took a look at the gentleman referred to and said, "Yes, Sir, I think I do." He ordered, "Who?" I said, "Abraham Lincoln, President of the United States." I felt like the next moment I might be caught by the throat and whisked away. General Grant said, "Knowing us as you do, what made you halt us?" I said, "General Grant, I was simply obeying your orders." By that time my knees were so weak I didn't know whether they were going to hold me up or not. But

President Lincoln rode up to me, patted me on the back, and said, "You did right," and, turning to General Grant he remarked, "If all our men and officers obeyed orders like this young man did this war would have been over two years ago."

We were located for awhile at Camp Stoman, across the river from Alexandria. For nine months we acted as infantry before we drew our horses. Then it was our job to go ahead and rout the enemy and let the infantry finish up the job.

Before the slaughter at Cold Harbor, the soldiers felt the hopelessness of the battle. But at four-thirty in the morning of June 3, 1864, Grant threw his entire army into the fight. The attack lasted only an hour and was known as the shortest important battle of the entire war. It was reported that we lost seven thousand men, while the South lost less than a thousand. The Confederates caused me to lose my breakfast that morning. A shell came along and whisked my frying pan of hardtack away.

My regiment was at Petersburg when the news of Lee's surrender reached us. We were drawn in line of battle at the time, but having gone through the battles of the Wilderness, Spottsylvania, White House landing, and a lot of other sieges and skirmishes, we were ready for the end of the war. I was anxious to get home and see my two brothers who had been in the Union army too.

I wish to pay tribute to my officers, Colonel Rawlson, Captain Coventry, and Lieutenant Tucker.

I belong to the J. Parson Stone Post, G.A.R., in Camden. My boys and I went up there from Tagberg because there were so few of us left.

COLONEL BEARING FAMILY NAME
CAPTURES HIM

DAVID MADISON CLOUD, Benton, Ark. Confederate
B. June 14, 1848, Benton, Ark. Co. M.
Crawford's Ark. Cav., Camden, Ark.

I ran away from home twice to join the Confederate Army. The first time my mother came after me, but that didn't break my spirit. I was inspired by my uncle, Tim Cloud, who joined as a private. A braver man wasn't to be found in the whole Confederate army than Uncle Tim. Then there was Uncle John Cloud, who was a lieutenant in the 11th Arkansas, Company B, as well as my two cousins, James and Tillman Cloud, all good soldiers.

I was first assigned as a messenger to carry letters through the Federal lines from Confederate soldiers to their families in Little Rock, Arkansas. As soon as I was old enough I joined Company M and got into actual battle.

On April 17, 1864, at the Battle of Poison Springs, I was detailed, with four others, to the Second Arkansas Company. We were ordered forward, across a hollow into a field, to join them while they were under fire. Hufstutler, one of the four referred to, started to jump a fence and met instant death. The next thing I remember we were in possession of a three gun battery. We captured all the cannons, wagons, mules, and everything they had. There was a heavy loss of soldiers and horses. I know I must have observed four or five hundred men, white and black, dead upon the field. It was a horrible sight, such as propagators of war should have to witness before making a decision that fighting is more necessary than arbitration.

I was in the Battle of Marks Mill on April 25, 1864, when over five hundred of our men were killed and an even greater number of the Federal's.

On May 4, 1864, I was sent on a scouting trip to Little Rock. It was so near my home that I slipped over to see mother. The Seventh United States Cavalry of Little Rock came there on a scouting trip too. I was scared that they might catch me, so I tried to slip away. I had gotten down to the railroad when their scouts came so near that I tried to hide behind a rather small log. I couldn't keep my head from protruding. I knew they would get me so I decided to open fire first. It was useless, I had to give myself up. The man who captured me was also named Cloud, but he was an enemy colonel. He sent me to Little Rock and, on my sixteenth birthday, put me in the penitentiary. The State Capitol now stands on that old prison site.

I remained in the penitentiary for one month and nineteen days. Then, with two hundred and eighty-seven Confederate prisoners, I was taken on a cattle car to Devall Bluff on the White River. When we arrived I was required to unload cargo from the boat. I was so small that I could hardly carry the heavy loads.

We went down the White River into the Mississippi and on up to St. Louis. From there we were transported on cars to the Rockland, Illinois, Federal prison. We stayed there six months and were to be exchanged for Federal prisoners, but something went wrong with the contract. As prisoners we were taken to Cairo and then to New Orleans via steamboat and again imprisoned. After a month they took us up the Mississippi to the mouth of the Red River and exchanged us for Federal prisoners.

I was put on a steamboat bound for Shreveport, Louisiana, and put in charge of the commissary. Two of our men broke out with smallpox, so I was ordered to issue rations to them and put them off at the first landing. I never heard of them again.

It was the first of March when we arrived in Shreveport where we were encamped a month. We received the first real food we had seen since leaving Arkansas some ten months previous. Rations consisted of two pontoons daily. We had real coffee, meat, flour, sugar, and molasses. I took a pound of coffee to New Orleans and sold it for $27.00.

Shreveport was a quarantine camp at this time, so we were soon released. I started out on foot to my home in Benton, Arkansas. It was a long, lonely trek, but I was a happy man to be released. Outstanding in my memories of my officers was one Brigadier General, Cabell. He was as tough a customer as one could find and for that reason we all called him "Old Tige". I deliberately refused to extricate his horse from a mud hole, though I received the second order to do so.

The Gettysburg Reunion is going strong, so are the old soldiers.

MOHAWK RANGER-1861-1865

LT. CHARLES CLINTON COVELL, Fish Creek Landing,
Co. E, Dec. 14, 1861, Rome, N. Y. Died, Sept. 17,
Landing, N. Y. Sgt. N. Y. State Inf. Vol.,
N. Y. Union. B. Nov. 30, 1938, Fish Creek, 1925.

I relate here some of the trials and experiences of myself in the Civil War- and this is not the half.

It was in the fall of 1861 that I enlisted in the army to help put down the rebellion. The regiment I joined, after a short time of drilling, was consolidated with the Oswego Regiment, or the 81st Reg. N.Y. Vols. Colonel Rose commanded this regiment though he was never with my particular division. My immediate officer was Lt. Col. Jacob J. DeForest. In a reorganization the 81st Regiment was divided into eight companies and the Mohawk Rangers grew out of this division. Our regiment comprised Companies C, E, and I. I was a member of Company C. Each company was comprised of about four hundred men and ours was the largest in the group. It was a grand regiment. I studied Hardee's Tactics and was made sergeant, so I never had to stand guard, except as an officer.

In November we were taken to Staten Island for a couple of days, then we were taken to Kalorama Heights, a suburb of Washington. We stayed there a week or two then marched to Alexandria and encamped. Our first initiation into the hardships of war began there. The first night we had about three inches of snow and sleet which lasted thirteen hours, and we were without our little A tents.

Submitted from the diary of Lt. Charles Clinton Covell by Mrs. Margaret Covell Nero, daughter by a later marriage to Mrs. Ida Covell.

In Washington I visited the Marshal House and saw the spot where Col. Ellsworth fell, while he was in the act of hauling down the rebel flag and for which act he lost his life.

The next day we embarked on the Vanderbilt for Fortress Monroe. We landed the next day, April 1st, and marched to Newport News, where we stayed about a week. We then started up the peninsula after the rebels. We had to march and fight under a scorching sun. We drove the Johnnies every day until we arrived at Yorktown on the York River, where we halted and besieged the city. As we charged the breastworks the rebels ran.

I will say that while we were at Yorktown it was the first time in about five months that we had time to cook a meal.

After Yorktown we were ordered out again and engaged the rebels at Williamsburg and a bloody battle it was. Our regiment was held in reserve and just as we were ordered to charge the rebels ran and our regiment lost only a few men, but to look over the battlefield was something awful. The ground was almost covered with bodies clad in blue and gray who had made the supreme sacrifice. We kept right on chasing the rebels until we fought the battle of Seven Pines, where we were not so fortunate; it was here that we lost a lot of officers and men.

Then came the battle of White Oak Swamp and Malvern Hill, where we fought continuously for seven days and lost a lot of officers and men. At Malvern Hill, McClellan ordered a retreat to Harrison's Landing and General Phil Karney rode up to McClellan and said: "I, Philip Karney, an old soldier, enter my solemn protest against this order for retreat. We ought, instead, to follow up the enemy and take Richmond, and, in full view of all responsibility, I solemnly declare this order for retreat is prompted by cowardice or treason." McClellan placed Karney under arrest and would have court-martialed him, but Abraham Lincoln ordered him to Washington, promoted him to Major-General, and gave him a command under General Pope. He was reconnoitering in the front lines before the battle of Chantilly and was killed. He was one of the bravest officers the north had, despite the fact that he had lost an arm in the Mexican war.

It was at Harrison's Landing that Prince DeJainville was captured outside our lines by our men and taken to McClellan's headquarters. We thought he had been conferring with the rebels, but McClellan knew better. He was a volunteer aide from France, in fact, he belonged to McClellan's staff.

On the 19th of August we were ordered to Yorktown. We hardly had enough clothes to cover us and were a ragged looking lot. We had left home with one thousand and forty men, all fit for duty, now we could muster only about four hundred men.

I was sick with jaundice when this march to Yorktown started and I was advised to go to the hospital, but I would not go. I suffered so terribly that a soldier in Company A got an old plug of a horse that I rode the second day. That night we camped in a large corn field and I ate so much roasted corn that the next day I was entirely cured-felt as good as ever.

At Yorktown we were issued clothes and shoes, for which we were thankful as we were destitute.

The latter part of December 1862 we were ordered on transports. We encountered a severe storm on the ocean and the captain said that we were blown six hundred miles out to sea.

The 1st of January, 1863, we landed at Beaufort, N.C. We found recruits enough to make our regiment six hundred strong. While we were awaiting further orders the general in command gave us this address:

"All will remember with regret the deadly effects of the swamps before Yorktown. You were the first in advance upon Williamsburg, and ordered by General McClellan to support General Hancock. The enemy gave up the contest on the 19th of May at Bottoms Bridge, and you waded waist deep in the swamps of the Chickahominy and drove away the enemy, and were first to cross the stream on the 23rd. One hundred and seventy of your number made a reconnaissance from Bottoms Bridge to the James River, near Drury Bluff and returned, bringing valuable information. On the 24th, 25th, and 26th, after other troops had failed, you made a dashing reconnaissance of the Seven Pines, driving a superior force of Gen. Stuart's, from Bottoms Bridge to within four miles of Richmond, the position nearest that city ever occupied by our troops. On the 31st day of May at Fair Oaks or Seven Pines, you occupied the above advance position. Your brigade made the most bloody and obstinate fight of the war and while we mourn one half of your command, you have the consolation of knowing that by your heroic and stubborn resistance you saved the army of the Potomac from great disaster.

"On the 27th, 28th, and 29th of June, the rebel general, Jackson, hurled his immense force upon our right and passed that flank of the army and turned with extreme solicitude toward the rear at Bottoms Bridge, which if crossed would result in irretrievable ruin. 'It ran through the army that Neglee's Brigade had destroyed the bridge.' You stood night and day, for three days, in the middle of the Chickahominy, successfully and continuously resisting its passage. This is yours, the honor of being the first to pass and the last to leave the Chickahominy, and while you led the advance to near Richmond you were the last in the retreating column, when after seven days of constant fighting you received a place of security and rest at Harrison's Landing."

We remained at this place but a short time when we took part in a score of engagements, marches, and raids; and finally took transports for Newport News and camped on the same ground we occupied in 1862. This was in October 1863.

On the 15th of November we were ordered to Northwest Landing, twenty-five miles south of Norfolk, in the vicinity of Dismal Swamp. While in this place, I was ordered to pick fifty of the best men in the regiment and to go in the night to a place about four or five miles away to capture a band of bushwhackers who were shooting our men every time they could catch them out of camp. We got there about the break of day and surrounded the place, but the officer in charge had got notice of our approach, so we only captured a lot of guns, ammunition, and three prisoners. These three men were sent to a northern prison until the end of the war. I was highly praised in the newspapers for the way I conducted the raid.

On the 1st of January the men of the regiment having less than one year to serve were solicited to re-enlist for three years more under a call from the War Department. On the 23rd of February two-thirds of the men had re-enlisted, which made the 81st a veteran regiment and entitled them to a furlough of thirty days. So on the 23rd the 81st left camp at Northwest Landing for home.

On February 27th at four o'clock in the morning, we went aboard the steamer Prometheus homeward bound. The weather was pleasant and all on board enjoyed the voyage. At two o'clock in the afternoon of the 29th we arrived in New York.

On the 1st of March the regiment was mustered for pay in the City Hall Park. On the 2nd day of March we were reviewed by the Mayor. General Burnside also received our regiment. We were escorted to the railroad station by the 8th and 37th regiments of the National Guard, and we took the night train for Albany where we arrived at seven o'clock on the 9th for a three-day visit. Here we were reviewed by Governor Seymour and members of the Legislature, after which we took a car for Oswego. But Rome had greater attractions for me and on the 3rd day of March, I was at West Branch, where I met the girl I left behind me, and on the 22nd day of March we were married.

On the 12th of April the regiment assembled and on the 16th we embarked on the steamer Ericson, arriving at Yorktown, Va., on the 18th of April, 1864.

On the 9th of May the 81st Regiment was deployed as skirmishers and during the entire day continued as such in the advance, marching in the direction of Petersburg where we engaged the troops of Beauregard. Constant skirmishing was kept up until nightfall, when an engagement took place in which the rebels were routed at Violet Station on the Richmond and Petersburg railroad. During the night the rebels tried to regain their position, but without success.

On the 10th of May we were ordered to our entrenchments at Bermuda Hundred. On the 12th another advance was made toward Richmond. The regiment being temporarily attached to the 10th Corp, under command of Major General Gilmore; and on the 13th we engaged the enemy at Kingsland Creek, capturing a strong position on the enemy's right. The loss was quite severe on both sides, the enemy being driven out, a long line of works was taken, together with many prisoners. Fighting continued until midnight as the rebels made several charges to retake the works.

On the morning of the battle at Drury Bluff, the enemy took advantage of a fog and smoke and succeeded in forcing through the right of our lines. We had hard fighting and lots of it. The enemy captured many of our men, including our commander, General Heckman-a mighty good officer. The day was saved by the 81st Regiment and we were complimented by General Butler and General Gilmore for gallantry.

During the day, on two occasions, we repulsed charges of the enemy. The brigade sustained a loss of three thousand in killed, wounded, and missing.

On the 31st of May, we moved forward to join the Army of the Potomac. We rested at New Castle overnight. At daylight we continued our march through a day so suffocating hot that many of our men fell by the roadside.

We reached the Army of the Potomac on the 1st day of June, 1864, at Cold Harbor. Although we were almost exhausted from excessive marching in the burning sun, with the thermometer at a hundred and over, the 18th Army Corps was ordered to engage the enemy and to take their position on the left of the 6th Corps. The men did not murmur but went into the fight with a determination seldom witnessed, capturing a strong line of works before nightfall. The 81st with the rest of the brigade was selected to hold the works during the night and the enemy was repulsed several times in trying to retake them. We lost about seventy men.

On the 2nd of June the 81st was to be withdrawn owing to hardships undergone.

The 3rd of June will long be remembered as the date of one of the bloodiest battles of all history. It was participated in by the entire Army of the Potomac, under General Grant, not excepting the gallant 81st, whose men were worn out from four days of constant duty with little food and practically no sleep. About four o'clock in the afternoon I received a gunshot wound in my right wrist joint and a shell struck me on the skull, glanced and wounded my shoulder. That wound made me black and blue from the top of my head to my toes. Of course, it put me out of business for a while. I got the boat that night at White House Landing and in fifty-two hours was at home with my wife. It was lucky for me that I got home, for I was probably as near to answering the last roll call as a boy ever was to live. A number of times the relatives were called in to see me die, but I was spared for some unaccountable reason and I recovered enough to go back and join my company and the boys.

I got back to them on the 27th day of September and the battle of Fort Harrison was fought on the 29th. Here we lost a lot of good men. One of my sergeants, who was wounded at Cold Harbor on the same day I was and who returned with me on the 27th, was shot dead. On the 29th we took the Fort. The 81st was the first to plant their flag-Old Glory-on the ramparts of Fort Harrison. In this engagement we lost Captain Rix, Lt. Dolbier, Lt. Porter, Lt. Copeland, and many sergeants and private soldiers.

This was the last fighting the 81st did, for the war was virtually over. The 81st was the first regiment to go into Richmond and the first to open Libby Prison, and the first to plant Old Glory on Libby Prison and the courthouse.

The 81st Regiment was ordered to hold the Fort and here we rested until we went into Richmond. There was no more fighting except a little raid near the old battleground of Fair Oaks and Seven Pines, but the Fort was ours by virtue of taking it.

After doing duty in Richmond for several weeks, we were ordered to Williamsburg. I will say here that the 81st Regiment entered Richmond on the 3rd day of April, 1865, and several weeks afterwards went to Williamsburg. There we stayed until the last of July, then we were ordered to Fortress Monroe where we were mustered out of the service on the 31st day of August and ordered to Albany, N. Y.

This is an incomplete history of myself during the Civil War of 1861-1865, incomplete because pen cannot describe the hardships and privations that I and my comrades experienced. I was always with my regiment except when incapacitated by wounds and I always returned to my regiment as soon as I was able.

When my service ended, I was First Lieutenant of Company E, 81st Regiment, New York State Veteran Volunteers. At the time of writing this story, I am Adjutant of J. Parson Stone Post No. 482, Department of New York G. A. R.

Brother Warriors

WITH HINES FAMOUS RAIDERS

NEWLAND MOFFITT CRUTCHER, Midway, Ky.
Confederate. B. Sept. 3, 1840, Franklin Co., Ky. Co. E.
9th Ky. Reg. White Sulphur, Ky.

I went with Captain Hines on his famous raid through Indiana. We were in the saddle nine days and nights without food, except ears of corn snatched from the stalks; or rest, except for moments of unconsciousness that occasionally overtook us as we rode along.

Near a small town in Indiana our little band of fifty men ran into three thousand Union soldiers and were forced to turn back. Arriving at the Ohio River, we formed a line of battle, stood our ground until we had fired our last round of ammunition, threw our guns in the river and surrendered. We were not told why we were sent on this raid until the close of the war. General Basil Duke told me that they had expected this little band might be sacrificed to save the command.

At Elizabethtown, Kentucky, we were given new shirts and told to make a hurried change. We found a creek, plunged in for a bath, having stationed pickets to prevent a surprise from the enemy. Our pickets fell asleep and the Yankees came. Our men could only snatch their clothes, mount, and ride.

Captain Hines told us to fall in as rear videttes. We rode from three o'clock until dark. On the trip, the company passed through a gate, closed, and fastened it in front of me. I thought the end had come. I fired my gun at the gate lock and to my delight found that it opened easily. I passed through to safety. Captain Hines tried to rally his men, but failed, and we made for the Ohio River.

I served with Morgan's Raiders and we often captured many times our number. I also served under the command of Colonel John Cabell Breckenridge and Captain Thomas H. Jones.

Brother Warriors

Excerpt from a war diary. Submitted by Mrs. Clara C. Smith, who states: "I have the fond memory that my father, Newland Moffit Crutcher, who died February 18, 1931, was a true soldier to the last.

BLOCKADE RUNNER

ELI SCOTT DANCE, Towson, Md. Confederate
B. Jan. 5, 1843, Delaney, Md. Co. C. 1st
Bat. Md. Cav., Richmond, Va.

My sympathy was with the Southland, so I fought for the Cause I believed in. I served my entire time in the cavalry. My officers were General Wm. E. Jones, General Rosser, and General J. E. B. Stuart.

My experiences included skirmishes and numerous engagements in the Shenandoah Valley, Maryland, and West Virginia. At night I ran the blockade.

In April, 1863, General W. E. Jones, with a cavalry brigade, started from Woodstock, Virginia. He had horsemen, but no wagons. We encountered the enemy at Greenland Gap. They were occupying a block house. This encounter proved a victory for us. We took all the Yankees prisoners. We paid dearly though as our colonel, major, and adjutant were wounded, as well as many privates.

We proceeded to Oakland, Maryland; Morgan-town, Fairmont, Clarksburg, and Bridgeport, West Virginia. I participated in all the activities in this area. During this time my good friend, Bob Whitley, was killed right alongside of me.

In June, I helped capture General Milroy's army just outside of Winchester. I participated in the battle of Gettysburg, proceeded to the Rapidan, and was in the battle of Spottsylvania, where the Union forces lost 15,722 men.

At Moorfield, on August 7, 1864, I was taken a prisoner and sent to Lookout, Maryland.

I have no wish to boast of my record, more than to say that I am glad I came out safe. I especially appreciate the good health that has been mine when I think of many of my friends who passed out in the prime of life. At the age of ninety-three I still attend business every day and maintain an active life.

I attended the Gettysburg reunion. Had a good time and came home feeling as fine as ever.

A CAVALRYMAN

JOHN S. DAVISSON, Omaha Neb. Union.
B. Aug. 4, 1845, Clarksburg, Va.
Co. I, 9th Reg. Cav. Vol., Davenport, Ia.
Sept. 22, 1863, Dis. Mar. 15, 1866, Little Rock, Ark.

Long life is largely a matter of good health and alert interests. Though I am nearing the century mark, I find a great deal in life to actively engage my time. I have a garden where I grow virtually every variety of vegetables and many flowers. I, of course, am interested in all activities of the G. A. R., and I was Commander of their post.

My war service started in 1863, but I was never in any great battles- you see, the cavalry always managed to keep out of them.

NARROW ESCAPES IN SHENANDOAH CONFLICTS

G. W. DELLINGER, Winchester, Va. Confederate
B. Nov. 11, 1845, Co. I, 23rd Va. Cav.
Emboden's Brigade, Com. by Col. Charles T. O'Ferrell.

On May 15, 1864, I was in the Battle of New Market, in which the cadets of the Virginia Military Institute were engaged. Commanded by their officers, they took their objective, but suffered heavy casualties. My company camped on the battlefield that night. The next morning I reviewed some of the scenes of hardest conflict. Standing in any one place, I could see from forty to fifty dead soldiers in every direction. On my return to camp a wounded Yankee boy, hearing my footsteps, threw up his hand, beckoning me to his side. He had been shot through the body and was badly wounded. I had a canteen of water, which I gave the poor, suffering lad. I talked with him and learned that he had a wife and children up North, but he knew he was dying and would never be able to see them again.

That evening a Yankee soldier-a courageous soul-came walking by himself to our hospital. His entire lower jaw was shot away. He received treatment but died soon afterwards. An old barn served as our hospital.

In the battle of Piedmont, Virginia, my coat was peppered with shots. But the closest call I had was when a shell came whizzing along and clipped my sword belt, right off, at the hip line.

The battle of Lynchburg, Virginia, occurred the last of June and was one I have never been able to forget. It was here that I became separated from my company for awhile. The Confederates were in a skirmish line on top of the hill, while the Federals were lodged in the woods. Colonel O'Ferrell instructed our company to cross the road. My comrade and I were the only ones who obeyed the command. I scrambled in behind the breastworks and got down on my knees. My comrade told me to lie flat if I didn't want to get shot down. To make matters worse, I found that I was out of ammunition, but he tossed some to me. Crouching on my knees, I proceeded to load and fire. Then the Yankees started coming over the hill, four abreast, until we were forced to leave the breastworks and take refuge behind trees, which were so small that they were not much protection. I turned to tell my comrade that we should seek the shelter of a nearby house, when to my horror, I saw him felled by the enemy guns, falling forward on his face-dead. Bullets were coming thick and so were the Yankees. I thought I would never get out alive. I hid behind a tree, jumping from one to the other, until I reached the house. Fortifying myself behind the house, I inched my way along until I finally reached my company. They, of course, had given me up as killed. That night reenforcements came from Richmond, and by morning the Yankees had vanished.

We had a hospital on the present site of the old Taylor Hotel, in Winchester. In the back yard it was not an uncommon sight to see wheelbarrows stacked with amputated arms and legs. I have seen a Confederate's leg amputated without the use of any anesthesia.

In the battle of Cedar Creek, on October 19, 1864, our General marched his men on, and the Yankees beat a hasty retreat. This is one time the Yankee will never forget, for it was on this day that we got their breakfast. If they hadn't retreated they would have suffered greater losses. We worked hard preparing for that battle. All night long we carried brick to build our breastworks. Without stopping for dinner or supper, we worked until we were weak and hungry. I told the Captain that I would have to stop as I felt I could not go on. He replied coolly, "Better not, one brick may save your head." I continued to carry brick.

On October 20, 1864, at Fisher Hill, General Early stampeded the Union army. Sheridan, who was staying in Winchester, heard the cannons and rode with his men twenty miles, without stopping to rally his men, and attacked Early. This was General Early's last stand.

Before this battle, I was designated to hold horses. Now, the one job I disliked was holding horses. But we always counted the men and every fourth one was designated to take charge of the mounts. There happened to be an old fellow in our company who scoffed at young blood being used for such a simple duty. Hearing him grumble, I bargained to change places with him, which he gladly accepted. Taking his place in line of battle, once again luck was in my favor. The Yankees spotted our horses and threw shells among them, killing or capturing every man and beast.

When I attended the Gettysburg Reunion, July 1938, I found two Union veterans who had fought in the battles of New Market and Fisher Hill. One of them distinctly remembered having to leave his breakfast hurriedly.

On January 21, 1939, I was guest of honor at a reception held in Stonewall Jackson's headquarters, in Winchester. Although my folks were worried about my staying up so late at night, I never felt better in my life, nor had so much fun. I arise every morning at daybreak and enjoy a walk, whenever the weather permits, so you see I am still a gay old gander.

PRISON WALLS COULD NOT HOLD THIS MORGAN RAIDER

CAPTAIN JOHN DOWDY (alias John Evans), Seagoville, Texas. Confederate,
B. Dec. 20, 1848, Lincoln Co., Tenn. Co. C, 7th Texas Cav. Gen. Sibley's Div., Alto, Texas, Apr. 5, 1862.

I was among sixty-three who were transferred to General Albert Sidney Johnson's division in Tennessee. Then three of us were transferred to General Forrest's division. I also served under General Robert E. Lee, and I was turned loose at Appomattox Courthouse, where Lee and Grant met.

My greatest activity was when I belonged to Morgan's Raiders. There was a $1,000 reward offered for me, dead or alive. So I was glad when the war was over and I could go home. There was $1,000 reward offered for my buddy, Frank Fletcher, and also for General Morgan.

General Morgan was killed near Greeneville, Tennessee, while resting up at the William's home. Mrs. Thompson betrayed him and got the $1,000 reward. I was with General Morgan at four o'clock on the morning he was killed. My camp was located two miles southeast of Greeneville, and I had gone to receive orders as to what we should do. General Morgan told me to tell the troops to dry their guns and clothes and not to move before seven o'clock. That morning at six o'clock the Yankees came with eighty men from Bull Gap and surrounded the William's home. When General Morgan realized what had happened he grabbed his pants and boots and ran, still in his night clothes, out into the garden. The William's woman shouted, "There he goes." He hid behind some lumber in the shrubbery and the Yankees ran in and shot him through the chest. It was a mistake that the General hadn't placed a picket line on the north side of the house. While

Mrs. Thompson was the one that disappeared the night before and notified the Yankees, those William's were in the plot.

I and Frank Fletcher were captured twenty miles south of Greeneville. We were sent to an Ohio prison and tried as spies. They didn't get any papers off me, but I was convicted and sentenced to die. In pleading my case, I asked for thirty days grace to prove my innocence, but November 30, 1864, was set as the date for my execution. I told Fletcher I would gain out. He said, "You are in for it this time; there ain't no chance."

Ten days before the date set for my execution, I made a trade with the guards to eat cake and coffee with me on my last morning. I had them bring me one-half gallon of coffee. Into this I slipped some cayenne pepper. At the proper moment, I took the cakes in my left hand and a pint cup of boiling coffee in my right. Just as they reached for some cake, I dashed the coffee in their eyes, blinding them. I grabbed my gun, knocked them in the head, snatched their pistols, and went for the back derrick. I jumped over and made for the Ohio River. I found a small boat and rowed across. I walked two miles before I could find a barn, then I stole a horse and saddle and rode for dear life, all that night and next day. Then I hid in a creek bayou and rested one whole day; stole a fresh horse and left for Tennessee. In three days I was back safe to the scene of my capture and General Morgan's death.

On December 25th, early in the morning, I went to visit the lady who betrayed General Morgan. I met her coming from the cow pen. I spoke to her and she exclaimed, "Oh Captain Dowdy!" I said, "Correct Ma'm." We engaged in a little heated argument. She told me that she thought I was in prison and admitted getting the thousand dollars. She said, "Captain, don't kill me, I'll give you the thousand dollars." But I told her, "No, no, not me. If you have anything to say, you have five minutes to talk." She knelt down and prayed. When the five minutes were up, my gun went off-she was dead. I laid her on the porch, crossed her hands, rode off, and I ain't been back there since.

I and Frank, and nine other fellows, were in the Blue Caves, in Tennessee. We lived there three days and nights on six crackers a day each. I told Frank we would gain out. I went to the mouth of the cave and called,

"Surrender!" Frank and the boys stood in back of me. When the Yanks came up, I stepped out and knelt down to them. The boys behind me fired, killed the whole passel of them, got their grub, we left and ain't been back there since. Fletcher was true to heart, never missed a shot.

On my birthday, I and Frank spotted forty-five Yankees encamped. We got some nitro-glycerine and crawled to within twenty-five yards of their camp. Four men were sitting on their guns, others were lying around the fire, rolled up in blankets. When I said, "Ready!" I and Frank let go and blew them into thunderation. Then we celebrated my birthday by feasting on the Yankees' supper. Frank said "Let's pile them up." I said, "No, they wanted to kill us, let them go." We got everything we could use, left there and ain't been back since.

We were captured at Willow Springs, twenty miles east of Memphis, and turned over to two husky Yankees. I wore boots with large legs, in each of which I carried a derringer. As we were going along, Frank told the guards I was subject to epileptic fits and if I should take one and fall off my horse not to shoot me. "Oh no," they said. When I got to a convenient place, I pitched off, head foremost, rolled over on my back and drew up my legs, to give free access to my derringers. They jumped down and came running to help me up. Just as they got near me, I was ready, I fired both guns, killed the two guards, stripped them of their guns. I left them and I haven't been back there since. As I have said, Grant wanted Captain John Dowdy.

I was with General Lee when he surrendered. I did not dare go as John Dowdy. I used the name James Evans.

I never had any hard feelings for the North, but I killed every man I could as I figured they would do the same. Four horses were shot right from under me, but I didn't get a scratch.

I've made my peace with the enemy, and at the Gettysburg Reunion all their daughters kissed me; and that's one place I want to go back to.

SOLDIERS KILL MEMBERS OF OWN ARMY

WILLIAM H. DOWELL, Kahoka, Mo. Union. B. June 16, 1846, Zanesville, Ohio. Co. I, 66th Reg. Ohio Vol. July 26, 1862, Mechanicsburg, Ohio. Trans. Co. E, 20th Reg. Vet. Res. Corps. Dis. July 26, 1865, Philadelphia, Pa.

It must have been the saddest day in my mother's life when she watched her six boys march off to war. There was George W., James M., Thomas J., Lorenzo J. and Senas W., beside myself.

On August 9, 1862, my regiment was engaged in the Battle of Slaughter Mountain, south of Culpeper, Virginia. During this battle some of our men got killed by our own army. I think I was the first to discover the mistake. I reported it immediately to our commanding general and he called, "Cease Firing!"

About September 14th, we arrived at Frederick, Maryland, just after the Confederates had marched through. We went into camp about dark and had orders to stay in line as it was expected that we might be attacked at any moment. We had been on a straining march for four days and nights and the men were so fatigued that the command of human nature overcame military orders. The men gradually eased out of line and by midnight the entire camp was asleep. The night was as silent as a deserted cemetery. Then suddenly a loud noise rang out like the thud of a thunderburst. Our commanding officer thought the Rebels were upon us and ordered, "Fall in Line!" The half-asleep men wearily tried to rise to the command. A deep sigh of relief resounded throughout the camp when we learned that it was only the capers of two mules that had gotten loose and overturned a wagon. The vehicle was on a ledge and had rolled down the hill.

On September 17, 1862, my regiment entered the Battle of Antietam. We started early in the morning and fought desperately. I was wounded in the left arm, near the shoulder socket, and almost lost my arm. That ended my service for I was transferred to the Invalid Corps at Baltimore for treatment. The Federal's loss in this battle was twelve thousand and five hundred in killed and wounded, while the Confederate's was over eight thousand.

The Gettysburg Reunion is an inspiring and enjoyable occasion. There is plenty of entertainment for every hour of the day and we all well cared for.

PLEASE REMEMBER MY COMRADE

CHARLES DOTY, Valparaiso, Ind. Union.

Charles Doty was born November 30, 1846, in Kendall County, Illinois. He enlisted in the Union army March 2, 1865, as a private in Company I, 23rd Illinois Infantry, and was honorably discharged July 24, 1865. Charles Doty married Minnie McNary, January 1, 1870, at Ashkum, Illinois. His children are: Charles A., Lucy E., Howard G., Ida M., and Wayne.

The above record is that of the only comrade I have left. He cannot write a story, but please do not forget him."-Jacob Mooker

BATTLES ELUDED HIM

JAMES S. DUNCAN, Taylor, Texas. Confederate.
B. Feb. 7, 1848, Anderson, S. C. Confederate
State Militia, Tom Russel's Co., Anderson, S. C.

I was never in any battles as they managed to keep out of my way. During my entire enlistment I was never out of the State of South Carolina. I suppose my father, Captain Benjamin Franklin Duncan, did enough fighting for the rest of the family. He served two years in Company C, First Regiment, South Carolina State Troops, and was in a great deal of action.

When a fellow volunteers to fight for a Cause it means that his heart is in it. Whether he makes the supreme sacrifice or merely rides through is the influence of a power beyond his own.

The Gettysburg Reunion of the North and South is an occasion that will go down in history, for the spirit here is that of one people serving one country. I am glad I am a Confederate soldier and I am glad I am an American.

FAITHFUL HORSE SAVES HIS LIFE

CHARLES FREEMAN DUNN, Omaha, Neb. Union.
B. Nov. 14, 1847, Robbinston, Maine.
Co. B, 9th Reg., Io. Cav. Aug. 20, 1863,
Cedar Rapids, Io. Com. by Captain John
Flick. Dis. Mar. 23, 1866, Little Rock, Ark.

War is not merely a conflict that is carried through to a glorious victory
or defeat. It is a hideous means of matching strength against strength, and
the results of it live so long as there is a man who carries its scars. Not in
bitterness toward the enemy, for mental woes are usually reconciled with
time, but in physical sufferings inflicted in one way or another.

I did not suffer the deep and lasting bodily wounds as did some of my
comrades, but I was pretty badly hurt at Brownville, Ark. General Price
and General Marmaduke were leading a raid up White River. I had to cross
a ditch. My horse could not quite make the jump. His feet struck the soft
embankment and, as it caved in, he fell and rolled over on top of me.

One of my vivid experiences was when I was assigned to picket duty,
with only one day's rations. For three days and two nights I was not given
any relief. At times it seemed as though I could not stand the fatigue a
moment longer, but I could not give up. I did a lot of sham fighting to keep
myself awake. Though near collapse, I am proud that I performed my duty
with all the strength I had.

Then there was the time I had to cross through a portion of the enemy's
picket lines to deliver a message to our army. The night was dark and I
had to proceed with great caution. A Rebel sentinel challenged me. I
plunged into a deep, thick brush and kept going. The Rebel pickets,
stationed on the sides of the mountain, set fire to a lot of weeds and brush
to light the valley where I was hiding. Lost from the trail, I led my horse

while I crawled on hands and knees, feeling my way through the darkness. Somehow, I got through and I always figured it was the darkness that saved my life.

My faithful horse saved my life once. I was out reconnoitering and a bushwhacker took a shot at me. Before I was aware of what was happening, my horse sensed a movement in the thicket and made a quick turn just as a shot was fired. Instead of piercing my body, the shell struck along my left side and lodged in the hip. I carry that bullet to this day. The bushwhacker thought he had me, but I was able to give him the chase of his life and then make it back to camp.

The dividing of the paths of comrades is something that has always interested me. I know of one man who belonged to the same company that I did. Though he lived in Omaha, I never saw him after the war ended until a few years ago.

COUSIN FIRES AT THE STAR OF THE WEST

JOSEPH HAYNSWORTH EARLE, Greenville, S. C.
(By his son, Dr. Baylis H. Earle, Commander-in-Chief, Army
of Northern Va., S. C. V., Greenville, S. C.)

Joseph Haynsworth Earle was born April 30, 1847, at Greenville, S. C. He enlisted in the Confederate Army, Charles' Battery, Kemper's Regiment, Johnston's Army, Florence. He died May 20, 1897, at the age of fifty.

Relative to my father's service in the War Between the States:

He was the youngest child of Colonel Elias Drayton Earle, of Mexican War fame. His mother died when he was three years old, and his father died when he was five years old. Thus orphaned, he was reared by his mother's sister at "Ingleside," a large plantation near Sumter, S. C. The ample fortune bequeathed him at the death of his parents was squandered by the executor of his father's estate.

Father was taken by his maternal aunt, Mary Heriot, wife of Major John Ouldfield Heriot, Q.M.C., C.S.A., who was commissary at Sumter, S. C. The little boy worked with his foster father from the time he was thirteen to fourteen years of age. He then ran away with two older brothers and joined Charles' Battery, Del Kemper's Regiment, Johnston's Army, at Florence, S. C. To escape parole he and his brothers slipped through the lines the night before the surrender at Greensboro, N. C., and made their way back to "Ingleside".

Father's five brothers who went through the four years of the War Between the States as active participants were: Major George W. Earle, Cadet Elias Drayton Earle, Cadet Baylis John Earle, Sergeant-Major and sharpshooter Thomas T. Earle, and Orderly Sergeant Joseph H. Earle. A noted cousin was George Edward "Tucker" Haynsworth, who was among the first to fire a shot at the "Star of the West" in Charleston Harbor. These six men become noted, high rankers in their respective professions, and were among the handsomest men I have ever seen. All are dead now.

My father, the late United States Senator Joseph Haynsworth Earle, had a most adventurous life. He was a great personal friend of General Wade Hampton, General John Bratton, General M. C. Butler and General Mart Gary; also of Presidents Arthur, Cleveland, and McKinley, as well as many of the notables, military and political, of his time.

Fort Sumter, located at the entrance of Charlestown Harbor, was under the command of Major Robert Anderson, with seventy-five Union soldiers. It was one of the few within the limits of the seceded states that had not been seized. An effort was made to send men and supplies to Major Anderson by the merchant steamer "Star of the West." She sailed on January 5. 1861, from New York, with two hundred and fifty soldiers and an ample supply of stores, provisions, and ammunition. On January 9, 1861, the people of Charleston fired upon the steamer and compelled her to put back to sea. On April 12-13, 1861, the Confederates bombarded the fort and forced Anderson to evacuate it, thus inaugurating the Civil War.

A FAMILY DIVIDED

HENRY A. EVANS, Washington, D. C. Union.
B. July 23, 1840, Washington, D. C. 2nd Reg.
D. C. Vols., Washington, D. C. 1861. Dis.
Washington, 1865.

During the war of '61 my family was divided between the North and the South. My father, Travers Evans, and his sons (except one) lived in Maryland, so were in the Union Army; my brother, John T', was in Florida, and had to enlist in the Confederacy. My uncle, William Evans, and his sons were in the Confederate Army, as it so happened that his family lived in Virginia, just about a mile from our home. All our Evans relatives in Manassas enlisted in the Union Army.

Once I made the painful mistake of capturing one of my first cousins. I had been helping to push an old truck to the top of a hill along our skirmish line. When we got to the top we saw a man on a horse come dashing through the woods. Well, I and my comrade, Ed, were sent down there to catch him. After we caught him, Ed noticed that the boy seemed pretty close to me, so, after awhile, he began to sorta wander off. Finally, he said, "Hen, you stay here and guard that fellow for awhile and if he tries to escape shoot him." I said, "I've got seven shells in my gun and if he tries to get away, I'll let 'im have every last one of 'em." After Ed got out of sight, I and Will were a-setting there on an old box, and he says to me, "Hen, I know you've got a gun and can shoot me, but I'm a-going to try to make a break." I said, sorta quiet like, "You'r damn right. Boy, go, get from here-run like hell!" And he did. When he got about fifty yards away, I raised my gun and shot in the air seven times. I don't know who was scareder, I or Will. I went to Fairfax then and reported that I had captured a prisoner who got away from me. Poor ole Will, he didn't live so very long after that.

Do I remember Belle Boyd! Yes, ma'm, I should say I do. She was one dashing, pretty woman, and gave us plenty of trouble. She was famous as a Confederate spy. I'll never forget when I received orders, through Lt. Edward Duvant, to report at New Market, Va., to take charge of Belle when she was captured at Orange Court House. I was to take her to Alexandria and there board a boat for Washington to deliver her to the Provost Guard's headquarters at Eighteenth and Eye Streets. Well, I and Belle were a-riding down King Street in Alexandria, within about two squares of the dock, when Belle smiled shyly and said, "Mr. Evans, I would like to go in a store down here to see a lady about a rather delicate, private matter that I hesitate to speak to you about, would you mind?" "Of course not," I said, "that will be all right." So Belle conversed with the storekeeper, in a whisper, for a moment, and then followed her to the back, in the general direction of the ladies room. I waited and waited, till a customer went into the store, and I could see that they all got excited. So, I asked the storekeeper if there was a back entrance to the store and she said that there was. Well, I walked out that way, and, lo and behold, Belle had done gone. Yes, sir, had flew the coop! I hurried to Lieut. Duvant and reported my dilemma. He laughed and said, "Henry, my boy, you're up against it, so sure as you're born." I knew it, but I asked him to please help me out. He had about a hundred men on guard duty, so sent them a-scurrying in all directions, and by twelve o'clock that night we had Belle in his guardhouse. She had been hiding, crouched in a corner, near the jail, and thought she was snug and safe till we run across her. Believe me, that gal was like wild fire to keep up with. Well, the next morning, I and a detachment of Lieut. Duvant's men took her on the boat and brought her to Washington. When I started to leave, I couldn't help feeling sorry for Belle-she looked so defenseless. She smiled at me sorta sad and cute-like, and said, "Goodbye, Mr. Evans, I hope you will come back to Washington to see me sometime." I made up my mind that I was surely going back to see her, but I never did get the chance. Gosh, she just had a way about her that was irresistible. Belle was captured three times and condemned to be executed, but got by somehow. The third time she was captured by Lieut. Sam Wylde Haringe, a Union officer, then she turned around and captured him-they were married in New York, where they lived for many years.

There used to be a family by the name of Americus, who lived half way between the Union and Confederate lines. They were mighty fine people and we liked to call on the girls there. The Johnnies liked them too, so we had a time trying to see them and avoid being captured by the Johnnies. If the girls saw us a-coming up there and Johnnies were in the house, they would warn us to turn back; but if we were there first, they would warn the Rebs not to come.

I certainly had a pretty close call one time. It happened like this: You've heard tell of shelter tents. Well, each one is made in two pieces and shelters two men. When on march each man carries half of it. I and Ed Page were camped about where Fort Myers, Va., now stands. After we had gone to bed, we decided to get up and mix some buckwheat batter for cakes the next morning. We got a kettle, put in the flour and other stuff, mixed in six yeast cakes, and covered it over with blankets to make it rise. The next morning, the dough had run out all over everything-there was enough to sink a boat. I got up to look the situation over, and, when my eyes beheld Ed, the boy was covered with splotches. I run and got a doctor and he wasn't long in deciding that Ed had a bad case of smallpox; and there I had slept with him all night, and together we had mixed buck-wheat dough over the kettle. Well, they sent poor ole Ed to the hospital up here at Meridan Hill and he got all right. In 1937 Ed was attending the G.A.R. reunion in Washington and came to see me. You can bet we were glad to see each other after these seventy-four years.

I fought in most every county in the Shenandoah Valley, and I remained there during the entire campaign, so naturally was in more skirmishes than real battles. The Battle of Antietam was what the Rebs considered the "nail to win the war". That was my first big battle. The rebels made three charges, but we drove them back every time.

We were pretty well fed as the government was taking care of us, but most of the time we didn't have a tent to sleep under. Many is the time I have lain down in a corn furrow and slept with nothing overhead but the sky.

I was at Orange Court House when Lee surrendered. I remember him well. He and General McClellan, though opposing each other, had been great friends when they were together at West Point.

I took a drum all through the war and brought it home with me. I have presented it to my great-grandson, Jackie Evans.

A PATRIOT

RICHARD EVANS, Hillsboro, MD., Union.
Born March 7, 1843, Philadelphia, Pa. ,
Co. D,1st Reg. E. S. Md. Inf. Vol.,
Newton, Va.; Co. D, 2nd Md. Vol. Inf.;
and Co. G, 11th Md. Vol. Hon. Dis.
1865, Port Delaware, Del. Married
Amanda Cohee, who died at Hillsboro,
Md., 1881. Married Annie Elizabeth
Evans, Aug. 27, 1888, Caroline Co., Md.

"In memory of Richard Evans, who died in 1922. He loved his comrades and was loyal to his country. It would be his desire to be represented here with his comrades."

Submitted by his widow, Mrs. Annie E. Evans, a veteran's attendant at the Gettysburg Reunion.

WASN'T BRAVE, BUT GOT INTO MORE DEVILTRY

JAMES O. FAY, Syracuse, N. Y. Union.
B. Jan. 27, 1848, Onondaga, N. Y. Co. G,
3rd N. Y. Light Art. Sept. 5, 1864, Syracuse, N. Y.

How did I come to enlist? Well, it was like this: In those days, people got their hired help by taking boys fourteen years old and caring for them until they became twenty-one. Then they gave the boys $100 and two suits of clothes, one for every-day wear and one for Sunday-go-to-meeting. Well, my family was poor and I had to live with a Mrs. Dayton. But, when I was sixteen and the last call for volunteers came, I went down and enlisted and got myself a pretty blue suit and a hat with a cord on it-didn't have to wait until I was twenty-one.

Captain Aberdeen was my first officer. He got discharged, and, if you must know, it was for getting drunk. Well, Captain Kelsey took his place.

I went with a detachment to New Bern and Kingston, N. C. We did heavy artillery duty for awhile-then were out on picket duty and things like that, until we got our cannons and then we became a part of Company G. I couldn't go to work and tell you all the deviltry I was in, but I never hurt anybody, nor killed anyone that I know of.

When encamped, we used dog tents-a piece of canvas spread over a pole and supported by two crotched sticks. When we cooked a little hardtack, we dug a hole in the ground to hide the fire from the enemy; and to make coffee, we held a tin cup over the fire with a forked stick. Yes, sir, we did all of our own cooking and it seemed mighty good eating at times.

On a march, we always had orders to burn houses and destroy everything in them. You know, I've seen many a fine painting slit to pieces and many a nice piano and other furniture chopped up and set fire to. We burned up all the fences, often using them for camp fires.

I was lead teamster for the cannon carts. You see, there were three teams that went together. Now, the biggest guns we had were just like these brass Napoleon pieces down here at the armory. These little two-wheelers used about a two-pound shot, you know, or like that. Now then, when we went into a fight we marched along until the bugle blowed, "Action front!" Then we counter-marched, swung right-about-face, and placed the gun facing the enemy, don't you see?

When the 149th Syracuse came to Kingston, I and a comrade stole a couple of mules off the picket ropes and went down to see if we knew any of the boys from home. We lay over at Fort Anderson until late the next day. Well, the next morning the orderly sergeant got ready to call the roll. Our sergeant took his usual stand in front of his detachment and when my name was called, he reported, "Fay is away without leave." This sergeant was a snappy little bugger, some rich fellow's son, you know, and just an up-start. Well, he reported all his men present but me. So, I was sent before the captain. He asked me my name and I said, "Fay when I'm home, but I don't know what you would call me down here." Now, he usually punished me by making me stand on a barrel. This time, he said, "You can sit on the hub of the fifth wheel for three hours." Well, the hub projected five or six inches and I was tied onto it; my hands and feet were spread-eagle and tied to the wheel. There I stayed for about an hour, when Lt. Billy Patterson happened by. He said, "Hello, Jim, you're in rather an awkward position for a soldier." I told him the circumstances, so he cut the ropes and told me, "Go to your tent and when the roll calls for boots and horses don't you answer, but stay in your tent." He was a great fellow, Billy was.

Now, let me tell you how the girls use to dip snuff. They put it in a handkerchief, wound the handkerchief around their finger and sucked on it-yes, sir, that's the truth, real young ones did that too.

Well, after the war was over I was anxious to get back home and see my brothers, Frank and Norris, who fought for the Union too.

I am one of the few last survivors of Root Post G.A.R., located in Syracuse, New York.

CLIMATE OF SOUTH SUITS NEW YORKER BUT NOT THE WAY THEY SERVE COFFEE

HENRY FIKE, Rome, N. Y. Union.
B. June 7, 1846, Germany. Came to the U. S.
in 1848. Oct. 26, 1864, Co. A, 12th N. Y.
Cav., com. A. D. Corteuse, Buffalo, N. Y.
Dis. May 29, 1865, Beaufort, N C. Member
G. A. R. Post No. 47, Rome, N. Y.

I wasn't in any battles - just a skirmish down near New Bern, N. C., but I'll never forget that. We were just getting ready for breakfast. The first thing I knew a bullet came whizzing right by my ear and took another fellow's coffee right out of the fire. You can bet we all lit out of there. The fighting lasted about an hour or two and then it all quieted down again.

You see, I usually drove two horses hitched to an ammunition cart. I always rode the horse on the left-hand side-those were orders. Well, during a skirmish, I stood between my two horses, holding them, and along came a bullet and cut two inches off the mane of the horse that I usually rode.

Once, I was riding a-well, I always called him a "wild" horse. He would rear up and then jump right out. Well, this horse started a-rearing back and forth and wrenched my back. I didn't mind it much until I got off. I couldn't stand up and wasn't able to follow my command, so they left me there and told me to "take care of the pony." Well, I was there nine days, alone, until Sergeant Duffy came along and said, "Why in the world did they leave you like that?" I told him that they went off and left me to take care of the pony that I stole from the Rebs, until I got better. Sergeant Duffy ordered an ambulance and sent me to the hospital at New Bern, then later to Beaufort; from there I was sent to Washington, where I got my discharge.

We use to take turn-about doing guard duty, it came my turn two nights during the winter. One night, some fellows stole a pig and the next morning they began to get scared. They came to me and wanted to know if I had seen anybody around the night before, but I told them, "No, I didn't see anybody."

It was nice and warm where I was, and not being in any hard battles, I couldn't say that I saw much hardship.

I went down to the Gettysburg Reunion, visited with the Johnnies and my old comrades, and had a nice trip. Jonas Fike was my attendant.

FROZEN PUMPKINS ONLY FOOD OBTAINABLE

SYLVESTER FLUMMER, Council Bluffs, Io. Union.
B. Sept. 19, 1845, Grant Co., Ind. Co. K.
118th Ind. Vol. July 27, 1863; Co. B, Battery
Reg. Ind. Light Art. Vol., Somerset, Ind.
Dis. Mar. 5, 1864, Indianapolis, Ind.

My first enlistment was for six months. I was on the march most of the time. I served under the command of Captain W. R. Coldren. My last three years' service was under the command of Captain Ben S. Nicklins. My war experience is unusual in that I was never in an active battle.

During my first enlistment, provisions were cut-off from us numerous times and on occasions our only rations consisted of parched corn. Sometimes, for as long as three days we only had one ear of corn daily. This gave me chronic dysentery. Many times our only food consisted of frozen raw pumpkins which we found in the fields.

After my health became very bad, I was left behind with some patients, at Cumberland Gap, Tenn. We were practically uncared for. Men were dying all around us. Every morning we would take out two or three dead men, wrap them in their blankets, and, because of the ground was frozen hard, we had to dig holes in piles of refuse from the barns to bury them.

Sick, discouraged, and homesick, I left alone, on foot struggling along to 1 did not know where. I was looking for any sort of help I might find. I came to a log cabin, the home of a Mr. and Mrs. Ballard, and they took me in. They had to hide me to protect themselves, as well as me. They put me in the attic, reached by climbing a ladder. It was a dark place with no furnishings of any sort. I rolled up in blankets to sleep. This kind family took good care of me and I began to improve, but I lost all trace of time.

One day, a company of Indiana troops stopped there as they were marching through. Mr. Ballard told them that a boy of their state was in the attic. Who should come up to investigate, who might it be, but my own brother, Ebb Flummer! To look upon his face was like seeing the sun's rays after a storm. I had given up all hope of living, but now I wanted to pull through and go home. Ebb was allowed to stay there with me until I was strong enough to accompany him home.

I re-enlisted immediately upon my discharge, but I was not strong enough for the hard life and became sick, though I served until the end of the war.

As I look back upon the time when I was in Gallation, Tenn., I still laugh at an experience I had when I was detailed with a squad to guard a general's home. I was awakened from a deep sleep to take my turn to go on duty. More asleep than awake, I dropped my big revolver and it accidently discharged. Luckily, no one got hit, but it gave a general alarm that aroused the boys all over the camp. My embarrassment was beyond words, I had a lot of explaining to do to the officers, and also took a lot of razzing from the boys.

I am thankful from the bottom of my heart for the kindness of the government in giving me the trip to Gettysburg. Mrs. G. P. Grosvenor was my attendant.

Sylvester Flummer

Thomas Metzger

Jacob Mooker

Homer S. Woodworth

UNION VETERANS

A COURIER FOR GENERAL COURLEY

J. D. FOOSHE, Augusta, Ga. Confederate.
B. Mar. 29, 1844, Abbeville, Co., S. C.
James Bat., Laurens, S. C.

At the age of seventeen I was in the battle of South Mountain, Md. I ran as fast as I could, retreating, with the enemy just a-shooting at me. Finally, I had to throw down my gun and surrender. They sent me off to a hospital in Fredericksburg to be treated for a foot wound.

Soon after my arrival at Fredericksburg, the kindest lady came in. She said that if any of us wanted to write letters home, she would bring writing material and deliver the letters to a spy who would slip through the Union army the next day. I was glad of this opportunity to let my people know that I was still alive. They were tickled to hear from me too, for they had heard that I was killed. The northern army occupied Fredericksburg, the day after we evacuated it. From that time on all southern sympathizers were barred from further intercourse with the Confederates.

One rather unusual coincident, I and my brother were never in the same conflict, though both of us were wounded; our mess mates were brothers, fought in several battles and neither of them was wounded, and all four of us got home safe after the war.

When we reached Petersburg, before Lee's surrender, I was promoted to courier at Colonel Corley's headquarters, being assigned to Dr. Baruch. However, another brigade surgeon, who was promoted to take Dr. Baruch's place, tried to prevent my assignment to this position. At this instance, Dr. Baruch did me a most agreeable favor by taking my part and persuading the doctor to take me.

About ten days after Lee's surrender, I and Williams, also a courier for Colonel Corley, decided to make it home on the horses that were assigned to us as couriers. General Grant sent over to General Lee's headquarters a barrel of whiskey for a present. I drew a canteen full before starting for home, but I am a teetotaler, so the whiskey came in handy to celebrate the end of the war. We gave it to people all along the way. When we arrived home, Father gave me $65 in gold for my horse. This was the first money I had after the surrender.

It was a lot of fun swapping stories with the Yanks at Gettysburg during the reunion of the Blue and Gray.

THOMAS TAKES MISSIONARY RIDGE

FRANK D. FRENCH, Johnston, Ohio. Union.
B. May 21, 1844, Granville, Ohio. Co. B,
76th Reg. Ohio Foot Vol. Com. Col. Wm. B.
Woods and Capt. J. T. Wintrode. Re-enlisted
Co. B, Ohio Vet. Vol., Jan. 4, 1864,
Alexandria, Ohio. Dis. Jan. 5, 1865.

I barely escaped being killed in Atlanta, Ga., on July 22, 1864. After a day's heavy fighting, I was helping a wounded comrade when a stray shot from the picket line caught me in the thigh. I recovered from my wound just in time to answer Grant's call for re-enforcements to go to Lookout Mountain and rescue Rosecrans's men. The Confederates had them hemmed in the valley at Chattanooga and they were on the verge of starvation. Their food supply was so exhausted they were eating their horses and mules. We arrived in time to see Thomas' men go out of Chattanooga and take Missionary Ridge. Magnificent! We watched the whole procedure from a mountain cliff. The overwhelming success of this battle was based on the fact that the soldiers acted on their own judgment. After successfully executing the orders of their officers, they did not stop but proceeded on to a victorious finish.

My saddest experience was perhaps at Ringgold, Va., where my brother, Captain Ira French, was killed. I had a close call in that battle, too. I and two of my mess-mates were lying together flat on the ground. Shots were a-flying wild and fast. Both of my mess-mates were killed instantly. All the color guards were killed or injured, and that Arkansas regiment got our flag too.

Humorous and ridiculous incidents go hand in hand. One fine day near the city of Rome, I, as sergeant, had posted a picket line. I spread my rubber poncho on the ground, using my cartridge belt for a head rest, and was delightfully basking in the sunshine and perusing a dime novel. Just when the story reached a pretty interesting pitch, a hissing noise at the edge of my blanket disturbed me. I lazily glanced around and there, about a foot above my head, a huge snake about the length of a rail was swaying to and fro, its tongue going at lightning speed. I lit on my feet about three yards from my bed, but by this time the frightened snake was about twenty feet away. I am quite sure he must have been laughing at me as he trailed away.

At the Gettysburg reunion, I enjoyed Veterans' Day and Governors' Day. They had a parade and re-view of veterans of all wars in the college stadium. An address was made by Secretary of War, Harry H. Woodring, Governor George H. Earle, of Pennsylvania, and the Commanders of the Grand Army of the Republic and the United Confederate Veterans.

SERVICE OF JOHN W. FURR IN THE CONFEDERATE STATES ARMY-1863-1865

In October 1863, my father, John W. Furr, eighteen years of age, living near Bloomfield, Loudoun County, Virginia, left home to join Company A, 6th Virginia Cavalry Regiment, Confederate States Army, on the Rapidan River, in Orange County, Virginia. The high tide of the Confederacy had been reached the previous July at Gettysburg. The easy, joy-riding days of Stuart's Cavalry were over, for the Union Cavalry now outnumbered the Confederates two to one. In addition it was splendidly equipped, the horses were well-fed, and the men, in many cases, were hand-picked after they had performed some act of bravery in other branches of the service.

The 6th Cavalry Regiment already bore a distinguished record, having served with Stonewall Jackson in the Valley Campaign, and with Lee from Richmond to Gettysburg and return. It consisted of ten companies from Loudoun, Fauquier, Clarke and Prince Williams Counties. The Regiment was commanded by Colonel Henry W. Flournoy until his capture, July 12th, 1863, near Hagerstown, Maryland. He was succeeded by his son, Thomas S. Flournoy, who was killed at Cold Harbor. Colonel Daniel T. Richards, of Clarke, succeeded, but thereafter it was commanded most of the time by Major Daniel A. Grimsley, of Culpepper County.

The Brigade of which the regiment was a part was commanded by Brigadier General Lundsford. Lindsay Lomax, a graduate of West Point. This brigade consisted of the 5th, 6th, and 15th Virginia Regiments and the 1st Maryland Regiment. Later on the 8th Virginia and the 35th Virginia Battalion, commanded by Colonel Lige White, of Leesburg, were added to the brigade. This brigade, together with Wickham's Brigade, made up Fitz Lee's Division of Cavalry.

My Father's company was commanded by Captain Bruce Gibson, whose home was on the Paris Road, just above Upperville. This company had originally been organized and commanded by Colonel Richard H. Dulaney. In it were many of the young men of Loudoun whom Father knew, including (Dr.) Richard Hoge, Luther Hopkins, Dallas Leith, Fauntleroy Neal, Frank Peak, and Bill Sours.

Father's decision to join this particular command was arrived at after careful consideration. Many of the young men of his neighborhood joined Mosby's, Rangers who operated throughout that section. Al-though he could have been at home a large part of the time had he served with Mosby, he preferred to join, and my grandfather, Fenton Furr, favored his joining, the regular Confederate Army.

Before leaving home he had already secured his uniform, consisting of a gray woolen shirt, with small brass buttons and pleated-down the front, jacket and breeches made of gray homespun, and cavalry boots made to order by the local shoemaker. Upon joining the company he was issued: one Colt six-shooter, carbine, cavalry saber with scabbard, cavalry saddle and bridle, one leather haversack, leather belt, and a bullet carrier. The weapons bore the stamp of the United States Government, having been captured from the Union Army in a battle.

His father gave him two horses-one to keep at home, to be groomed and conditioned by Dennis Williams, a young slave and constant companion of Father's when growing up. This horse was to replace the one in service when the first one should become disabled or worn down by hard duty. One of these horses was a blooded mare called "Fox." She was a prized animal, and was so named because of her resemblance in color to a fox. When I was a boy, I have often heard Uncle Dennis say that "Fox" had a sad ending. After a tour of duty with Father in the Confederate Army, and Dennis had fattened and groomed her ready for duty again, a "Yankee" patrol came through and carried her off into the wrong army.

Father's other war horse was a dark bay named "Bob." He was a tall horse with a long neck-not much on beauty, but for speed and endurance an ideal cavalry horse. Father had a great affection for this horse. It was Bob he was riding when stunned by a bullet at Five Forks; it was Bob who carried him through those last terrible seven days of retreating from Petersburg; and on that last morning of fighting out on the Lynchburg road at Appomattox, it was this gallant old horse which stood out in front, literally as a breastwork, as Father fired over his back at the enemy point-blank. Finally, it was "Old Bob," tired, worn, and thin, who was his companion on that last long march home from Lynchburg to Loudoun.

Almost immediately after Father enlisted, the 6th Regiment, along with the other regiments of Fitz Lee's Divisions, was engaged in a series of encounters and skirmishes from the Rapidan River to the town of Manassas. On October 11, 1863, Fitz Lee's Division was at the river near Rapidan Station when the Union General, John Burford, advanced from

Stevensburg and crossed the Rapidan. Fitz Lee attacked, driving Burford across Raccoon Ford and following him until he struck him again at Stevensburg. Burford retreated to Brandy Station where he joined General Kilpatrick with the rest of the Union Cavalry. General J. E. B. Stuart came from the direction of Madison Court House with Hampton's Division of Confederate Cavalry, and with Fitz Lee, attacked the Union Cavalry around Brandy Station.

Five times that day the 6th Virginia Regiment charged. Lieutenant Colonel Harrision was wounded in one of these charges. A Union cavalry general with his troopers charged head long into Father's company. He was a large man and was fighting fiercely with his sword when Lieutenant Armstead spurred his horse, "Long Tom," up until his pistol almost touched his side and shot him. This stand was made by the Union cavalry to cover General Meade's retreat toward Manassas; by nightfall the Union cavalry had also retreated. In this fight, Lomax's brigade, in which was my Father's regiment, was on the right until late in the afternoon when the brigade was sent to the left of the line, past the Barbour house, to get between the Union cavalry and the Rappahannock River.

Fitz Lee led his troopers across the Rappahannock at Foxville Ford. The next day, October 13th, Lomax's brigade was sent to reconnoiter toward Catlett Station. Reaching the little village of Auburn, beyond Warrenton, they found Warrenton Junction occupied in force by the Federals. Lomax remained in Auburn until in the night he was driven back toward Warrenton by the main body of Meade's army.

On October 19th, Fitz Lee united his brigades and attacked General Custer in a hot fight at Buckland Mills, driving him back toward Washington. On the 20th, the cavalry was ordered back with Lee's army. Father's company went into camp near Brandy Station, but, on November 7, 1863, moved back one-half mile south of the Rapidan River near Orange Court House. On November 27th, Meade crossed the Rapidan and advanced against Lee's army in what is known as the "Mine Run" campaign. The enemy's cavalry crossed at Morton's Ferry but were driven back by Fitz Lee's division. Soon after Meade retired with his whole army, having accomplished nothing.

The army went into winter quarters, but for the cavalry this meant no particular change. They lived in the open without tents. In order to keep warm seven or eight men would sleep close together in groups on the ground, and the men on the end pulled logs up beside them for protection.

Branches of pine trees and leaves made mattresses, and saddles were used as pillows.

The middle of January, 1864, the Union cavalry came on again to see if the Confederates were planning any winter surprises. The Southern regiments quickly crossed to the north side of the Rapidan, and soon both forces were dismounted, lying flat on the ground fighting as infantry. The 6th Regiment was forced back to the river by heavier forces, and some of Father's company did not have time to mount their horses, but plunged into the freezing river to avoid capture. With the help of some artillery, the 6th Regiment was ordered right back again across the river to try conclusions again with the Yankee cavalry. In the same field they dismounted and fought again, their battle continuing long after dark, until the Union troops retired toward the Rappahannock.

Several weeks after this, late in January, while the company was on picket duty, further up the river and detached from the main body, on a foggy morning before daylight, the Union cavalry got in the rear of the company. Captain Gibson and his men had to do some hard riding to avert capture, and at that one member of the company was captured. Father was awakened that morning by a bullet whistling past his ear.

About the first of February, 1864, it was decided to let Father's company go on furlough. Loudoun and Faquier Counties at that time were in enemy territory. Captain Gibson thought that they could elude the enemy, so he gave his pledge to the regimental commander that his men would return to duty at the end of the furlough. In the Confederate service each cavalryman owned his own horse, and a furlough was necessary occasionally in order to get a fresh horse.

Early in March, Captain Bruce Gibson summoned his men to meet him in Upperville. Mounted on "Fox", Father bade home folks goodbye and joined his comrades for the march back. His regiment was then at Staunton and thither Bruce Gibson and his men marched. The first night out they were covered with six inches of snow. This was quite a change from warm beds at home.

Upon their arrival at Staunton, without a day's rest the regiment started on to Richmond. After remaining at the Capitol city for two weeks, they were ordered to Fredericksburg. There was plenty of forage here for the horses in the grassy meadows south of the town. Here, too, the men had a pleasant stay. The fresh fish taken daily out of the Rappahannock came as "manna from Heaven" to vary the one-quarter pound of fat pork and a little corn meal, (the unvarying ration now issued—except that often this meager allowance did not come). For once, too, the company was not called upon for constant contact with the enemy's cavalry.

Then on a bright May morning in '64 came Grant's great push for Richmond. The young troopers of the 6th Cavalry were glad of action. Quiet camp life had grown monotonous. Bugles sounded, each company formed into line, counted by fours, wheeled into column, and marched for the Wilderness battlefield. Here Fitz Lee's division dismounted and formed the extreme right of the Confederate battle line.

The fighting was heavy and a number of men in Company A, which was in front, were killed or wounded, among them Dallas Leith. He was shot in the head and thought dead, but nevertheless lived ten days, thus giving his father time to come to see him from Loudoun County before he died. Father was wounded by a bullet in his side. It passed through some of his leather equipment and clothing. Being in great pain and seeing blood trickling into his boot, Father thought it was a mortal wound. His comrades opened his clothing and when they saw it was only a flesh wound, they laughed loudly at Father's concern.

On the night of May 7th, Fitz Lee threw his regiments in front of Warren's Union Infantry Corps and fought dismounted from Todd's Tavern back towards Spottsylvania Court House. This was to prevent Grant's getting Spottsylvania Court House and thus getting in between Lee and Richmond. Kershaw's Infantry of Longstreet Corps, after a night march, arrived early in the morning of the 8th and formed quietly in the rear of Fitz Lee's dismounted cavalry. Warren's heavy column came on. The cavalry retired rapidly through the concealed infantry line, which remained concealed on the ground, until the Union line was within one hundred yards. Then Kershaw's troops rose to their feet and poured a hot volley into the faces of the Blue infantry; many were killed, wounded or captured.

The cavalry moved farther to the right and became engaged with Wilson's Union Cavalry. One of the Union officers described the Confederate Cavalry in the Wilderness battle as "swarming in the woods like angry bees."

At daylight, on the morning of May 9th, Sheridan, with twelve thousand cavalry, cut loose from Grant's army, passed around the right flank of Lee's army and started toward Richmond. A few hours later all available cavalrymen, about four thousand and five hundred, being Fitz Lee's two brigades and Robert-son's brigade, headed by General J. E. B. Stuart, started after Sheridan. After marching all that day and far into the night, with no food for men or horses, General Fitz Lee went to General Stuart and begged him to let his worn-out men and horses rest a few hours. General Stuart reluctantly consented to this at Hanover Junction, but at one o'clock that morning he roused his sleeping cavalrymen and again pushed forward to beat Sheridan, who was marching on another road into Richmond.

At one place Father stopped to let his horse drink at a river crossing when General Stuart came riding up and said, "You must not stop for even a minute; let your horse drink a little as he walks through, like mine." The head of the column reached Yellow Tavern about 10 A.M., on June 11th, where the two roads the opposing forces were marching on converged. This was more than sixty miles from their starting point. The order was, "Dismount and prepare for battle!" Father's company was in the road north of Yellow Tavern, facing west, and he was soon firing at Sheridan's advancing line across a field to the west side of the road. Sheridan's line, by rushing, falling on their stomachs, and then rushing again, kept coming. Being greatly outnumbered, it was soon apparent that the Confederates, if they stayed in the road, would be killed or captured.

Father said that he heard no command to retreat, but he saw Major Grimsley jump his horse over a fence into a field and start across it. Father, on foot, followed the Major in the nick of time, for a few minutes later about twelve of his company, including his nearest neighbor in Loudoun, Luther Hopkins, were captured in the road. The ones who got out of this mounted their horses and were ordered back for a charge. As they advanced up the road, at a trot, they met an ambulance bringing back a wounded officer. Father recognized this wounded officer as General Stuart and said that he saw the General turn his head so his eyes could follow them in the charge. A few minutes before General Stuart had called to' some of his men, "Go back and do your duty; I had rather die than be whipped."

In this battle it became apparent to the Southerners that the Yankee cavalry had a new weapon. It was the Spencer Carbine breech-loading repeater. From now on the Confederate cavalry realized it was not alone a disparity in numbers they would face, but also a great superiority in fire arms.

The next day General Fitz Lee, now in command, followed Sheridan, who went to Malvern Hill, on the James River below Richmond, and did not get back to Grant until May 25th. In the meantime the Confederate cavalry returned to General Lee's army on May 18th, and once more took up the work of guarding the flanks and advising Lee of Grant's movements.

General Wade Hampton succeeded Stuart as commander of the cavalry corps, and, on May 26th, he and Sheridan met at Hawe's Shop, near Cold Harbor, in a fierce combat which lasted all day. The Confederate cavalry got the worst of it in this combat. There followed quickly now the great battle of Cold Harbor, where Colonel Thomas Flournoy, commanding the 6th Regiment, was killed. About this time my grandfather, Fenton Furr, having business in Richmond, decided to visit Father in the field on his way there. He arrived on horseback from Loudoun and Captain Bruce Gibson gave Father leave for a day and night to accompany Grandfather into Richmond.

Sheridan now started out with his great body of cavalry on his Trevilian's raid. His object was to capture Charlottesville, destroy Confederate supplies, and tear up the tracks of the Virginia Central Railroad. General Wade Hampton, after seventy miles of hard riding, headed him off at Trevilian's Station, in Louise County, on June 11th, 1864. Sheridan claimed a victory. He struck Hampton before Fitz Lee's division got up, and in a fierce fight forced the Confederates back.

Upon arrival of Fitz Lee's two brigades (Lomax's and Wickham's), Hampton sent them (the next day) on a flank movement to charge Sheridan from his right flank. Sheridan gave ground then and turned back instead of doing what he had set out to do. The result was a distinct victory for the Confederates. Hampton lost six hundred men in the two days fighting; Sheridan lost about the same number. On the ride around Sheridan's right flank, Father was riding close to General Fitz Lee and remembered very well that when they rode out a Confederate officer called to General Lee, "Where are you going, Fitz?" and he replied, "I am going to attack them on their right flank."

On June 13th, Sheridan circled north to Spottsylvania Court House, thence southeast by Bowling Green to West Point on the York River. Here he placed prisoners he had captured at Trevihan's on ships sailing for the North. On June 20th, on his way back to Grant, he was shelled by Hampton's horse artillery at The White House. Four days later Hampton and Fitz Lee attacked and defeated Gregg's cavalry at St. Mary's Church, eight miles east of Malvern Hill. They pursued him nearly to Charles City Court House. Gregg left his dead and wounded on the field.

In the meantime Lee and Grant were facing each other at Petersburg. Word came to the Confederate cavalry leaders that another famous Yankee raid was on. This time it was General Wilson with fifty-five hundred cavalrymen in Southside, Virginia. He started out on June 22nd, towards Burkville, for the purpose of tearing up the tracks of the Danville and Southern Railroad, and to collect all possible plunder.

The Confederate cavalry crossed quickly on the south side of the James. Hampton with fifteen hundred men hurried to intercept Wilson at Stony Creek. Fitz Lee "trotted" his division thirty miles south of Petersburg to strike Wilson on his return march. As Wilson approached Ream's Station, on June 29th, Mahone's infantry stopped him. Fitz Lee, at the point of a six shooter, forced a burly negro living in the neighborhood to guide his cavalry over an obscure route to Wilson's rear. Father's brigade was dismounted and made the attack. Wilson was completely routed. He lost "everything on wheels," including wagon trains, twelve pieces of artillery, one thousand negro slaves, and a large amount of other plunder he had taken from private homes. In addition, he lost fifteen hundred of his soldiers. Chased by Fitz Lee, he fled across the Nottaway River, and, with foaming and exhausted horses, regained the Federal lines near Prince George Court House. This was a great day for the 6th Virginia Cavalry. It had been roughly handled at Yellow Tavern and at Hawes' Shop; and its Colonel had been killed at Cold Harbor, but this day they had more than evened up the score with the Yankees.

The regiment remained around Petersburg, and between Petersburg and Richmond on the north side of the James River, guarding the flanks and doing scout work until early in August, when it was ordered on a long march to the Valley of Virginia. Thence, Sheridan had already gone with a large force of cavalry and infantry to crush General Jubal Early, who had advanced a Confederate army to the very outer defenses of the City of Washington.

At this time several changes in commanding officers were made. General Lunsford L. Lomax was promoted to command the brigade my father was in. General Payne was as gallant a cavalry leader as ever led a charge. By this time the brigade had been reduced by hard fighting and riding to less than four hundred men. General William C. Wickham now commanded Fitz Lee's division; and General Fitzhugh Lee was promoted to command all the cavalry in the valley expedition.

On the morning of August 12, 1864 Fitz Lee led his troopers into the capitol city of Richmond, thence west along Main Street, and quickly the long, hot march started to the valley by way of Culpepper Court House. They arrived on the Front Royal road August 15th. Advancing toward

Winchester, the Confederate cavalry had a sharp engagement with some of Sheridan's forces at Cedarville. They camped that night on the cool banks of the Opequon. On August 18th, Fitz Lee advanced to Winchester and Sheridan retreated. He was driven through Charlestown on August 22nd. General Early established a battle line in front of Charlestown with Fitz Lee's cavalry on the right. On August 25th, Fitz Lee advanced to Leetown, by way of Smithfield, and on to the Potomac at Williamsport. He had a brisk engagement with the enemy's cavalry at Williamsport, marched to Shepherdstown, had sharp clashes with the Union cavalry on the 28th and 29th, and retired to Brucetown.

On September 2nd, the cavalry moved towards Berryville intending to march back to Richmond. General Robert E. Lee had sent word that it was sorely needed to help him at Petersburg, but, on September 3rd, Fitz Lee came in contact with Sheridan's cavalry at White Post and retired to Newtown in order to protect Early's right flank. On August 7th and 8th, there were cavalry skirmishes, and General Early, seeing that a battle was imminent, retained the cavalry of Fitz Lee's division.

Sheridan massed his army west of Berryville, facing toward Winchester, and started a heavy attack on September 19th. Fitz Lee's division was transferred from the right to left flank on the Martinsville road north of Winchester. Early was greatly outnumbered, both as to cavalry and infantry. The relative forces were approximately ten thousand and thirty thousand, and, after an all-day fight, the gallant old Confederate, Jubal Early, still hoped he would be able to maintain his positions. However, at four P. M. a great body of Union cavalry descended like a "cloud of locusts" on the Confederate forces on the Martinsville road, north of Winchester, and by sheer force of numbers broke through to Early's rear.

In order to save his army from capture, it was necessary for General Early to make a rapid retreat south on the Valley turnpike. The 6th Regiment made a number of charges in the north end of Winchester, trying to hold back the Union cavalry until Early could extricate his infantry. In receding from one of these charges, Father noticed a young Federal cavalryman lying wounded in the road. He jumped from his horse and carried the wounded boy in blue into the protection of a nearby yard. He was rewarded for this knightly act by the wounded lad opening his eyes and gratefully saying, almost in a whisper, "You helped me-you helped me!" That night the cavalry covered the retreat of the army to Fisher's Hill, south of Strasburg. General Fitz Lee was severely wounded at Winchester and was unable to return to his command for several months.

Fitz Lee's cavalry was sent to the Luray Valley, and Payne's brigade was stationed at Millwood to prevent Torbert's Union cavalry from advancing up the Luray Valley and getting in the rear of Early's troops. In the meantime, Early had met a terrible reverse at Fisher's Hill, and General Payne, after holding the Union cavalry at Millwood as long as possible, retired and joined Early down the Valley between Port Republic and Brown's Gap.

On August 28th, Payne's brigade covered Early's right flank on a march towards Waynesboro. Or. September 29th and 30th, they rested at Waynesboro, after having driven out a body of Union cavalry. On October 1st, the whole force moved to Mt. Sidney on the Valley turnpike, remaining there until October 6th.

On October 5th, General Thomas Rosser arrived from Richmond with his brigade of cavalry and was given command of Fitz Lee's division, succeeding Brigadier General William C. Wickham. Sheridan now retired followed by Early, still the Confederate cavalry became entirely too bold and venturesome. On October 9th, General Torbert turned on Rosser at Tom's Brook with his whole force and drove him back to Columbia Furnace, with a loss of nine pieces of artillery.

On October 12th, Early advanced, with cavalry in front, and, on the morning of the 13th, reached Fisher's Hill. He remained there until the night of the 18th of October, when he fought the famous battle of Cedar Creek. In this battle General Payne's little brigade of cavalry, now reduced to three hundred men, including my father's regiment, bore a conspicuous part.

On the night of the 18th, General John B. Gordon's infantry, preceded by Payne's cavalry, crossed the Shenandoah River, followed a narrow path around a mountain trail, recrossed the river at a point farther north, and, at daylight, attacked the rear of Sheridan's army. General Payne was instructed by General Early to endeavor to capture General Sheridan himself. The attack was a complete surprise and Sheridan's army was routed.

The 6th Cavalry Regiment that day had the unique experience of charging Union infantry behind a stone wall on the edge of Middletown. Sheridan, coming from Winchester on his famous ride, rallied his army and near nightfall defeated Early, driving him from the field. The temptation to gather food and other supplies from Sheridan's captured camp was too much for the hungry, destitute Confederates. General Early attributes his disaster to this. Father got a very fine old-fashioned razor out of one of the captured camps. He gave his razor to my oldest brother, Fenton Furr, when he became of shaving age.

Major Jed Hotchkiss, Stonewall Jackson's famous engineer and staff officer, and later with Early, said of this fight, "Fitz Lee's division saved Early's army in the battle of Cedar Creek, holding the line and checking the enemy's pursuit until 9:30 P.M."

As Father's company retreated from the field, after Early's infantry had gone, they stopped just before entering Strasburg, and Captain Gibson sent a lieutenant and two men (Father and Dick Hoge) to enter the town to see if the Yankees had beaten them to it. Father said, "When we arrived on the edge of the town we discovered it was full of Yankees, and we withdrew and so reported to Captain Gibson." In order to extricate themselves from inside the Union lines, it was necessary for them to make a long circuitous night march and join the rest of the army at Mt. Jackson, which was twenty miles up the Valley. In this Valley campaign Sheridan's cavalry alone outnumbered Early's whole army.

General Early, though defeated, always returned for more fighting. On November 10th, Payne's cavalry was marched north on the Valley turnpike; on the 11th it drove the Union cavalry through Middletown to Newtown; on the 12th a sharp cavalry battle took place.

In this fighting, Company A was galloping hotly after the retreating Union cavalry. Father and Bill Sours' horses outran the others. A large Yankee cavalryman, on a small horse, was several yards behind the others. Bill Sours and Father caught up with him at the same time. Father withheld his shot but Bill Sours was not so merciful. He placed his pistol almost against the cavalryman's back and shot him, as both he and Father galloped on after the others without stopping.

Early in his career as a cavalryman Father had learned to rely on his pistol in the charges rather than his saber. When they were ordered to charge with drawn sabers, Father said that he would start that way, but as soon as Captain Gibson was not looking, into the scabbard would go his saber and out of the holster would come the six-shooter. Thus he became a crack shot with the pistol. After the war he could easily knock over a running rabbit with his army six-shooter.

On November 27th, Rosser, with his own and Payne's brigades, crossed Great North Mountain into Hardy County, West Virginia; on the 29th they surprised and captured the fortified post at New Creek, on the B.

& 0. Railroad, taking eight hundred prisoners, eight pieces of artillery, and a large number of commissary stores, sorely needed by the Confederates. Shortly after the cavalry returned from the New Creek expedition, Early moved back toward Staunton.

On December 16th, General Custer, with the Union Cavalry, advanced up the Valley turnpike from Winchester. On December 20th, before daylight, on a snowy morning, Rosser and Payne's brigades attacked Custer's command at Lacey Spring, just nine miles north of Harrisonburg, and drove it back. The cavalry returned to near Staunton on December 22nd.

Active operations being over for the time being, Father was given a leave of absence to visit his home in Loudoun, but he returned to his regiment, stationed near Staunton, early in the year 1865. When he was nearing the camp, he met one of the older soldiers in his company, who said to him, "Boy, why did you come back up here; the war is nearly over; we can't hold out much longer. If you want to turn back now and go home, I'll never report it." Of course, Father refused to listen to such advice, but rejoined his company to "stick it out" to the bitter end.

On February 3rd, General Payne was near Lexington when he was ordered to march with his brigade to General Lee at Petersburg. This was the fourth time since Father had joined the 6th Cavalry that it made the long march to and from the Valley.

Brigadier General Thomas Taylor Munford now commanded Fitz Lee's division of cavalry. General Fitz Lee had returned to duty, but he was now placed in command of all the cavalry in Lee's army.

Company A, while on the north side of the James River, in front of Richmond, was dismounted and sent to help hold trenches— a new experience for cavalrymen. The company was put out in front of the trenches in a thin line of skirmishers, close up to the Union line. The Union infantry advanced to the charge. Father was in one of the tightest places he had ever been in. In all probability this thin line would have all been killed or captured but for the fact that the Union charge, for some unknown reason, stopped. It was certainly not stopped by the thin line of dismounted cavalry.

On March 29th General Grant's final movement around General Lee's right flank began. General Sheridan, who had also come back from the Valley with his army, advanced towards Five Forks, twelve miles southwest of Petersburg. The Confederate cavalry was quickly transferred from the left flank on the north side of the James River in front of

Richmond, to the right flank southwest of Petersburg. It now consisted of three divisions, of about five thousand men in all, mounted on skeletons of horses. Under Fitz Lee this cavalry was supported by Pickett's infantry and drove Sheridan back towards Dinwiddie Court House.

The next day Sheridan, reinforced by the 5th Corps of Infantry, advanced against Pickett and Fitz Lee at Five Forks. It was a mean fight, and the Confederates, as had been the case in most every fight Father was in, were outnumbered. Father's company was on the left of the line, one mile northeast of Five Forks. His brigade commander, General Wm. Fitzhugh Payne, was wounded and captured. Father was hit. The bullet, passing through his overcoat and other clothing, bruised but did not penetrate the flesh. Though stunned (he said that it "felt like a sledge hammer"), it did not incapacitate him for duty. He dismounted and sat on a rock until he was able to ride again.

The Confederates were driven back and the seven-day retreat to Appomattox began on April 2, 1865. To the cavalry this retreat was a nightmare. On their poor, jaded horses, with scarcely any food for man or beast, before daylight each morning until after nightfall, the cavalry was in a running fight trying to protect Lee's army from Grant's heavy columns.

At High Bridge, near Farmville, the Confederate cavalry attacked and captured seven hundred and eighty prisoners, and on April 7th, in another fight, the Union general was captured. In the meantime General Lee had had one corps cut off and captured at Sailors Creek.

On the morning of the surrender, April 9th, Fitz Lee's cavalry made an attack and cleared the Lynchburg Road of Federal cavalry. Fitz Lee had told General Lee, at the night conference with the higher officers, that if the army surrendered, he with his cavalry would endeavor to cut their way through. He feared the men would all lose their privately owned horses if they surrendered. This last fight which Fitz Lee's gallant cavalrymen took part in was made at sunrise. Father's command was on the extreme right. The Yankee cavalry was driven back, with the loss of two pieces of artillery and some prisoners.

So far as Father personally was concerned, this last fight proved to be one of the most dangerous he was in. He saw several of his comrades, who had been in the war four years, killed here in the last hour. Being hard pressed, at close quarters, he sprang to the ground and, with his carbine across "Old Bob's back, he fired as rapidly as he could. Things were hot all around him. Later on in life, he always felt that he was very lucky to have come out alive on that last morning at Appomattox.

So the cavalry did break through, as promised by Fitz Lee. It went on to Lynchburg. Officers and men realized that the war was over. The companies broke up and the men started for home. General Fitz Lee, in his final report, dated April 22, 1865, had this to say of the gallant behavior of his heroic cavalry in its last campaign: "They fought every day from the 29th of March to the 9th of April, inclusive, with a valor as steady as of yore, and whose brightness was not dimmed by the increasing clouds of adversity."

The hardships of this war were great, but it must not be thought that Father and his young comrades did not get fun out of it. Many times he referred to the lighter side. The good times, playing and singing around camp fires, the comradeship on the long rides, the 'ragging" they always got from the infantry, and the excitement of the cavalry actions-all had their appeal.

From Lynchburg, Father started on the long ride to Loudoun, going by way of Charlottesville. Near Upperville, he saw approaching four mounted soldiers in blue uniforms. He neither wanted to be captured, nor did he want to start a fight, but it was too late to run, so he rode right up to them and to his great surprise found them to be Mosby's men dressed in Yankee uniforms. He gave them the sad news of Lee's surrender.

When he arrived near home his father and two of his sisters (Agnes and Ella) were standing on the front porch. They saw him leading "Old Bob" down the hill from the direction of Unison. "Old Bob" was so tired and worn out that his head drooped nearly to the ground as he followed along. Of course, Grandmother cried, and the girls thought it strange that she was crying instead of rejoicing.

After waiting three months, when he and my grandfather were satisfied that the war was over, he rode to Winchester, the nearest army post, where he surrendered and was paroled.

Our family will never forget "Uncle" Dennis Williams. My grandfather bought him from a slave block when he was four years old. He did this at the earnest solicitation of Dennis' mother, who lived in the neighborhood but was not owned by Grandfather. Dennis remained in the family after the war. He was loyal, trustworthy, and efficient. He acted as overseer at my grandfather's homestead. When Grandfather died, Dennis, on horseback, was assigned a place in the funeral line, but immediately when the start was made he pressed forward and rode along beside the hearse. Dennis said afterwards that the best friend he had ever had was passing on and he felt that he must ride as close to him as possible.

Herman R. Furr,
1st Lieut., 314 Machine Gun Bat.
80th Division-1917-1919.

THANKFUL WE SERVE ONE FLAG

DANIEL GENHOW, Tecumseh, Okla. Confederate
B. Oct. 27, 1846, Newton, N. C. Major Younts Bat.

Those Yankees caught me right after I enlisted, so most of my time was served in prison. I will thank the government so long as I live for the great privilege of attending the Gettysburg Reunion. It was mighty thoughtful of the government to send someone to look out for the welfare and comfort of the old soldiers.

My attendant, R. C. Hurst, didn't let me want for anything.

I want to say, I appreciate the President's sentiments when he said, "All of them we honor, not asking under which flag they fought then, thankful that they stand together under one flag now."

I am the father of seven children. I have thirty grandchildren and three great grandchildren. How many men of this age do you think will keep up with me?

A PRISONER AFTER THE FALL OF RICHMOND

JOHN J. GEORGE, Washington, D. C. Confederate.
B. Aug. 27, 1846, Fredricksburg, Va. Inf.,
2nd Bat., Fredericksburg, Va. Trans. to Navy,
James River Fleet.

The story of my experiences in the War Between the States begins long before my actual enlistment. My father, Moses George, served as a pilot in the Confederate Navy, devoting most of his time to blockade running, and an older brother, Moses Lee George, was a member of Thomas Battery, Confederate Artillery, later serving in the Navy.

I was only fifteen at the outbreak of the war, and, consequently, too young to enlist. But how well I recall the horrors of battles fought near Fredericksburg, the first one in December of 1862. The city was under fire for three days, and after the battle I did my bit toward helping to bring in the wounded. I shall never forget the soul-sickening sights of the dead and dying men as I wandered over the battlefield. Needless to say, many homes were entirely destroyed, and, as I recall, about five shells went through our own home, one of them demolishing the inside stairway.

How many times I was shot at while running the blockade, I don't remember, but my Guardian Angel didn't desert me, and, as soon as I reached the age of seventeen, I enlisted with the Provost Guard and helped transfer captured northern soldiers to Richmond. After a short period of service with the Provost Guard I was transferred to the Second Battalion, Confederate Infantry, under Captain Bradley, and, after about six months' service, due to a shortage of seamen, I was transferred to the James River Fleet.

My most vivid recollection and outstanding experience was, of course, the Fall of Richmond. Never have I witnessed such a bedlam. The tobacco warehouses were set on fire, and the flames spread rapidly, so that the heart of the business portion of the city was destroyed, leaving her literally "in sackcloth and ashes." The people were wild.

It was at this time I was captured, the city now being in the hands of the Federals, and I was put in old Libby Prison. I shan't go into the horrors of that old prison. Suffice it to say that our rations consisted, at most, of two pieces of hardtack a day, and sleep was nearly impossible because of the presence of all sorts of vermin. Our few remaining garments were in tatters, and shoes were such a luxury as to be almost unknown. When released from prison I had only a threadbare pair of trousers. Each soldier was given a small portion of cornmeal and bacon to be eaten on the journey homeward. Soldiers living a considerable distance from Richmond were, of course, given larger portions, and it was surprising suddenly to discover how many were going to Alabama, Mississippi, and other distant States.

Another Confederate and I set out for Fredericksburg, and on the way we met a soldier returning home who, somehow or other, had obtained a ham. We built a fire, cooked the ham and bacon, and cornmeal, but were unable to eat the meal. After three days of walking, sleeping under the stars, and very little food, I arrived in Fredericksburg, a distance of fifty-six miles.

There was great happiness when I at last reached home. The hunger and hardships suffered in the war were quickly forgotten in the joy of our happy family reunion, and in the conviction that no sacrifices were too great for the Glorious Southern Cause.

BATTLES AND MEMOIRS, 1861-1865

O. R. GILLETTE, Commander-in-Chief La.
Div. U.C.V., Bossier, La.

April 30, 1861, we, the Second Mississippi Regiment, left Corinth, Miss., under Captain J. M. Stone. We went to Lynchburg, Va., where we remained for a short time before moving to Harpers Ferry, where we became a part of the Third Brigade, under the command of Brigadier General Bee.

Our first engagement was the First Battle of Manassas, where we suffered heavily in killed, wounded, and missing. After this battle we moved to Fredericksburg, where we rested before going to Humphreys, at which place we went into winter quarters. In the early spring we were ordered to Fredericksburg, and, after some maneuvering about there, moved on to Yorktown. There the troops were organized, and on April 10, 1862, Captain Stone was elected colonel of the Mississippi Regiment. Soon after, the command moved up to Richmond from which place we were ordered to Staunton, Va., to join Jackson, who was moving around to the rear of McClellan.

Our next engagement was at Gaines Mill, June 27th, where we rested after the battle of Malvern Hill, in which we participated. The command marched to near Richmond, where we went into camp.

Movement of the armies brought on another battle at Manassas, August 30, 1862, in which we were hotly engaged. After this fight we moved back to camp, near Richmond, where the troops were rebrigaded and Joseph R. Davis placed in command. We then became known as the Davis Brigade. Before returning to Richmond we were engaged at Boonsboro and Sharpsburg (or Antietam).

In the early spring, we were in the field in active movement to meet the advances of the federal troops and were in several actions, among which was that of Bristoe Station. For a time we were on detached service.

When General Lee began his movement northward into Maryland, our Brigade, under command of Brigadier General Heath, was ordered to join him. This offensive movement of the Confederate army brought on the memorable Battle of Gettysburg, July 1st, 2nd and 3rd, in which the Second Mississippi Regiment was hotly engaged. Our regiment was stationed on the left and was opposed by General Reynold's forces. We lost heavily in killed, wounded, and missing.

On the third day our regiment was in constant action. We, being placed immediately to the left of Pickett's division, were conspicuous in the famous charge.

On the return of Lee's army, from the fatal field of Gettysburg, we were engaged in a sharp fight at Falling Waters. Returning, the army went into winter quarters at Mine Run, where it remained until the spring of 1864. When activities commenced, we participated in the battle of the Wilderness, fighting with General Longstreet.

We were also in the battle of Spottsylvania and all the engagements of that campaign. We were then ordered to the defense of Petersburg, where we remained until the evacuation of that place, except when we were called out to meet a feint of General Grant. That was at the time the grub mine was sprung. We went into winter quarters at Hatcher's Run.

In January 1865, I and several others, among them Colonel Stone, were granted leaves of absence to return to our homes in Mississippi. Upon our return to join our regiment, which was then near Salisbury, N. C., we were taken prisoners by General Stoneman's forces, and taken to Johnson's Island. We were discharged from there on July 25th, 1865.

On May 2nd, 1863, General Thomas J. Jackson was mistaken for the enemy and was shot by his own men. He was carried by the writer and others of his staff to the field hospital and given first aid by C. 0. Gillette, Jr., and the lance which was used in giving first aid to his wounds was given to me. I am giving this surgical instrument to my good friend Major E. R. Wiles, Commander in. Chief, S. C. V., Little Rock, Ark.

FINDS SWORD AFTER SEVENTY YEARS

CAPTAIN DAVID COFFMAN GRAYSON, Chevy Chase,
D. C., Confederate. B. May 29, 1838, Luray,
Page Co., Va. Co. K, 10th Reg., Luray, Va.

My sword was given to me by a relative who had been a colonel of militia, and I used it while serving as Third Lieutenant, A. N. V. During the first battle of Manassas, July 21, 1861, I was advancing with my company and carrying my sword. After the battle, I noticed that the scabbard had been hit by a bullet, which probably saved me from being wounded. Due to the injury to the scabbard, I could no longer carry the sword in battle, so I sent it home to my father in Luray, Virginia, Being afraid to keep it about the house for fear the enemy might find it, he sent it to a relative who lived up in the mountains close by. That relative was also afraid to keep the sword in his house, so he hid it in his barn. Shortly afterwards the enemy passed that way and burned the barn.

I suppose the sword must have been found in the ruins of the barn; at any rate, it was taken to the home of a neighbor, and there it lay in the attic for many years. Shortly before this Christmas, the sword was found in the attic, and the finder, a son of the neighbor living there during the war, not knowing anything about it, sold it to an antique dealer in Luray. The Luray paper carried an article about the interesting old sword in the antique shop, and I wrote to a niece in Luray to bring the sword to me, which she did on Christmas Day, and I knew it was mine, But it cost me seven dollars to buy it back.

OPPOSES FARRAGUT AT PORT HUDSON

R. D. HARDESTER, Yellville, Ark. Confederate.
B. Feb. 1, 1840, Washington Co., Ark. Co. B.
14th Ark. Reg., Yellville, Ark.

At the age of ninety-nine and a half years my philosophy remains the same as when I was twenty-one. The greatest happiness to be found is at the fireside of a happy home. I knew that joy so well that I regretted the necessity of going to war. The hearth that my boyhood memories cherished was swept away by the scalawags while I was fighting for Civil Rights. The negroes, whom we had always known as peaceful, happy creatures, and had provided for according to our means, were given a freedom which they did not know how to cope with. They were turned loose without adequate provision being made for their future or training to assume the responsibilities of livelihood. That is why a good many of them turned to stealing. It was the only means they could devise when struggling under such handicaps. They were a pitiful race to behold. If the nation is any better off today than it was before the war, I can't see it. Now we are all slaves to commerce and the situation hasn't changed much.

I went through four years of the war. I was wounded three times, but I never went to a hospital. Men in those days bore the strain of hardships and suffering like men. Of course, we lived an easy, natural life and were a sturdy people,

On March 15, 1863, Admiral Farragut commanded a fleet of gunboats against Port Hudson. General Frank Gardner was in command of the port. This attack was from land and water. Cannon balls were driven from battleships while shells were bursting overhead. Farragut was forced back shattered and torn. The Mississippi, one of the largest vessels of the Federal Navy, was lost in this battle. The federals were using a lot of Negro troops so it was easy to whip them. Vicksburg was surrendered on July 4, 1863, and we were forced to surrender on July 8th. Our loss amounted to about one hundred and fifty men, while the federal's loss was fifteen hundred.

At Iuka, Miss., everything was quiet and peaceful until the enemy came upon us unexpectedly about one o'clock. Rapid fighting started and continued until dark. General Price was the Confederate commander. It has been so long since all this happened that I can't remember the details.

If anyone wants to know how come I liked staying at home-I had a faithful wife, and eight children who lived to be grown. The oldest is now seventy-five years old. I have twenty-seven grandchildren, seventy great-grandchildren and eighteen great-great-grandchildren. How's that for an old soldier, eh?

I'm as hardy as my name would suggest. I came all the way from Arkansas to Gettysburg to attend the reunion and I'm having a mighty fine time.

John J. George

David M. Cloud

John W. Harris

Belle Boyd

CONFEDERATE HEROES

CAPTURES CAVALRYMAN WITH EMPTY PISTOL

JOHN W. HARRIS, Oklahoma City, Okla.
B. Nov. 24, 1848. 20th Tenn. Cav. Jackson, Term.

In OCTOBER 1863, my regiment made a raid in the rear of Thomas' army, south of Nashville. Tenn. We captured one thousand prisoners and five hundred head of beef cattle. Then the problem had to be met of crossing the Tennessee River with the gains of our victory,

My particular regiment was sent to hold ten thousand Yankees in check. We had to swim our horses across the river under a fusillade of fire from the enemy. They chased us for three days, but General Forrest was too foxy for them. We turned about, capturing a wagon train with eighteen hundred mules. We could not handle the wagons, so burned them. We made use of the mules and ammunition. We burned the trestle and tore up the railroad south of Nashville that had served to freight post supplies to Thomas' army.

I belonged to a light battery consisting of two thousand men. For thirty days we were in the enemy lines, with only one full night's encampment.

While war-time is no time for humor, it did tickle me when I captured a cavalry man with an empty pistol.

The reunion at Gettysburg is a phenomenal success.

139

ORGANIZES FLORIDA INFANTRY

E. J. HILLARD, Frostproof, Fla. Confederate.
B. Dec. 22, 1842, Ware Co., Ga. Capt. Wm. I.
Turner's Co. Mounted Vol., Turkey Creek, Fla.

After six months with the mounted volunteers, I went to Tallahassee, Fla., where I organized the 8th Florida Infantry, then I went to Richmond, Va.

When I was a prisoner, I saw a Mississippi soldier, who was a prisoner, hit a Union sergeant in an altercation over the issue of meat rations. They court martialed the prisoner and took him before the high officers, but when he told his story they sent him away without punishment.

At ninety-six, I stood the trip to Gettysburg with-out a mishap. We were generously provided for. Our tents were comfortable and we had camp chairs where we could sit in the sun. The mess hall was large and provided good meals for us. I want to extend my heartfelt thanks to the good people who gave us this opportunity to meet our old buddies and to visit with our former enemy. It was a touching scene when two veterans-one in blue and one in gray-pulled a cord that unveiled the monument to peace; as President Roosevelt said, "Immortal deeds and immortal words have created here a shrine of American patriotism," and then he referred to "the last full measure of devotion," and "the simple faith for which they died." It was all something long to be remembered.

Roderick Donald McLeod, U. C. V.

Julius Franklin Howell, U. C. V.

IN THE RANK AND FILE OF FITZHUGH LEE

JULIUS FRANKLIN HOWELL, National Commander-in-Chief,
U. C. V. (1937-1938), Bristol, Va.

I was born on January 17, 1846. I enlisted in the Confederate army in
1862, as a private, and later became a corporal in Company K, 24th Va.
Cavalry, Gary's Brigade, Custis Lee's Division.

Until about May, 1864, I served in southeast Virginia and northeast
North Carolina. Much of this time I was a courier on the staffs of General
Roger A. Pryor, of Virginia, and General John Bratton, of South Carolina.

My regiment was occupying a position near the James River when
General Grant began the siege of Petersburg. We could see, across the
James River, a part of his infantry marching toward the pontoons below
the mouth of the Appomattox River to surround Petersburg.

About August 1, '64, we were sent to guard the lines northwest of
Richmond. We camped during the winter near the Old York River railroad
which was not in use.

About October 1, '64, we were engaged in a minor battle near the
Darbytown road, leading out of Richmond. In this fight I was wounded in
the right leg-the only hurt I had during the war. It laid me up for some
weeks. We did picket duty near the Federal lines, but had no contests with
the enemy.

On the night of April 1, '65, we broke camp, marched nearer
Richmond and remained quietly in camp all day Sunday. April 2nd, early
in the morning, we marched through Richmond, crossed old Mayo's bridge
to the south and could see the city in flames. For three days we marched
southeast, probably with the intention of uniting with General Lee, who
had abandoned Petersburg on the 2nd. On the 6th, the federals overtook us
in large forces and after fighting much of the day, General Ewell, who was
in command, surrendered with nearly three thousand of us. This was at

Sayler's Creek, about twelve miles from Farmville. Thus, we did not surrender with General Lee at Appomattox Court House.

We were sent to prison at Point Lookout, Md. I remember the bad water, the Negro soldiers guarding us, Major Brady, and General Barnes, who was in command part of the time.

On one of General Barnes' visits, he was riding along a street so near my quarters that I witnessed a regrettable occurrence. A soldier in one of the tents uttered aloud a remark possibly intended to insult the general, who had been kind and considerate of us. General Barnes stopped in front of the tent and ordered all the occupants to come out, but with no results. He repeated the order, drawing his pistol and threatening to shoot through the tent. All of them came out then, but no one would confess the guilt or deny the charge. So the general selected one of the men and ordered him to march up the street along in front of him. We never heard of any other punishment, if any that was inflicted. A rumor passed along that the general reprimanded him mildly and sent him back to his quarters. We liked the general and did not approve of the prisoner's slack remark.

Going back a little-we arrived at Point Lookout prison about April 13th. The flags at half-mast on the 15th, early at sunrise, aroused our curiosity. We soon learned from a Federal sergeant of the guard that President Lincoln had been shot by Booth. Of course, we knew nothing of the great excitement outside the prison, but a variety of opinions were given voice among us. Various reports, surmises, and grapevine telegrams, came to our ears. One of these was that the United States government intended to select by lot every tenth man among the Confederate prisoners and shoot them in retaliation for the President's death. While this report brought gloom among us, I took consolation in the fact that my sixty-seven year old father lived on a large farm and had many loyal slaves who would remain with him and that I had no dependents. I felt sorry for the men who had families back home-wives and children, fervently wishing for the war to cease. I resolved to accept the situation with courage and if need be to die like a man for my beloved Southern Cause.

About June 7, 1865, orders were posted on the bulletin board for all prisoners whose surnames began with the letter "A" to report for discharge.

There being many thousands of us, I wondered how many days would elapse before the letter "H," my initial, would be reached. Finally, it was posted and hundreds of us reported early at the gates. Thirty-two men were passed through the turnstile at one time. We were marched into a long house where a United States flag was suspended, literally, above us. Our height, complexion, color of eyes and hair were recorded. Then every fourth one of us held a Bible while Federal officers read the Oath of Allegiance. Each of us was required to kiss the Bible which the fourth fellow was holding. When it came my turn, I kissed it with much earnestness-just as the Confederates kissed the Bible when they enlisted. I did not think of any possible germs or microbes that might be on the Bible. It had been so long since I had kissed a pretty girl at a dance, I did not call to mind how a real kiss tasted.

After this ceremonial was over, we marched to a steamer at the wharf but were not allowed to go above the lowest floor. We noted, with chagrin, several well-dressed negroes, who were allowed free access to all parts of the boat "The bottom rail was on top!" We were transferred to Fortress Monroe and our paroles were signed and returned to us. Then over to Norfolk, where we landed without guards. I crossed the river to Portsmouth, spent the night with friends, and next day went by rail to Suffolk, twenty miles from home. From there, I rode with friends in carts until I reached home, just before sunset. All were delighted to greet me.

Deeply discouraged and looking forward with little interest to my future, I suggested to my father that I remain at home and work on the farm. With a better outlook than I had, he encouraged me to return to school. This I did, and in a few years I began the life of a pedagogue. I had some ambition to succeed in this line. I studied at normal schools, Harvard, and the University of Pennsylvania. I was superintendent of public schools, a professor in a State university, and President of two colleges. I was given an A. M. degree by a State university and an LL. D. by a chartered college.

My record with the United Confederate Veteran's organization extends back to 1898. I have filled the positions of First Lieutenant, Captain (skipped the rank of Major), Lieutenant-Colonel, Colonel,

Brigadier General, General Commanding the Army of Northern Virginia, as well as National Commander-in-Chief.

I am actively engaged in the insurance business; treasurer of my church of over eight hundred members; member of the State Pension Board of Tennessee; and trying to grow old gracefully.

I never miss a Confederate Reunion. I think it is a great privilege to grant us the pleasure of an occasional joint Celebration with the Union soldiers.

FINDS ROMANCE AT AGE OF EIGHTY-TWO

AARON L. HURT, Honaker, Va., Confederate.

A romance which had its inception at the Confederate Reunion at Birmingham in 1926, resulted in the marriage, at the reunion held in Tampa, Florida, April, 1927, of 82 year old Aaron L. Hurt, of Honaker, Virginia, and Mrs. Fannie Graves, 59, of Chattanooga.

Mr. Hurt first saw his bride when they were introduced at the Birmingham reunion. A correspondence was kept up and they agreed to meet at the reunion in Tampa and have the knot tied.

The ceremony was performed in the courtroom of Judge Cornelius, from whom the license was obtained. W. D. F. Snipes, a Presbyterian minister and superintendent of the Tampa schools, officiated.

It had been planned to have the wedding ceremony performed by the Reverend J. M. Smith, also a Confederate veteran, of Marshall, Texas, but there was some delay in the appointment and the couple found themselves with a license and no minister. They wanted the ceremony performed by a minister, preferably one of the Presbyterian faith, to which church the bride belonged.

Inquiries were made about the courthouse and at last someone suggested Mr. Snipes. He was sent for and at once agreed to officiate.

By the time Mr. Snipes reached Judge Cornelius's courtroom it was nearly two o'clock and a large crowd had assembled. The bride, while a little bashful, was not disconcerted and faced the concentrated fire of many pairs of eyes without flinching. The bridegroom also professed great courage.

"Well," he said, as he looked over the gathering, "I've faced worse crowds than this one and lived through it. I guess I'll   survive   this." However, there was a slight quiver in his voice just as there probably was a perceptible quaking of his knees as he charged up the hill with Pickett at Gettysburg.

Mr. Hurt is a veteran of many of the most desperate battles of the war. Though the snows of eighty-two winters have whitened his hair, his spirit is undimmed and his carriage is as soldierly as that of a West Pointer. He was attired in a faultlessly tailored uniform of Gray and with his fierce mustache and pointed goatee he was a perfect military picture from the pages of Confederate history.

The bride is a small, brown-eyed, woman with face unlined and hair still vigorously colored. After the reunion they will go to the home of Mr. Hurt in Virginia. The stepfather of the bride was the only relative of either at the ceremony.

Tampa Tribune-1927

YOUNGEST SOLDIER SERVING THE COMPANY

FRANK M. IRONMONGER, Jacksonville, Fla.
Confederate. B. Mar. 4, 1853, Portsmouth,
Va. 16th Va. Reg. Petersburg, Va.

My heart throbbed for the cause of the Confederacy, so in February 1864, I made my Way from the old plantation in the Blue Ridge section of Virginia to Petersburg where I offered my services.

I was assigned to duty as brigade quartermaster's courier and served in this capacity up to April 9, 1865, when my command surrendered with the Army of Northern Virginia. My parole, giving me permission to go to my home and there to remain undisturbed, was given me on April 10, 1865.

The Daughters of Confederacy presented me with a handsome gold medal about forty-five years ago as the youngest soldier serving the Confederate Army. I wear it with a great deal of pride.

I am now Commander-in-Chief of the R. E. Lee Camp, No. 58, U. C. V., Jacksonville, Florida.

YANKEES TOOK HIS RATIONS

JAMES J. JAMES, Augusta, Ga. Confederate.
B. Richard Co., Ga. Co., B. Jefferson Co. Ga.

Time heals all wounds. It also erases from the memory moments that at one time or another seemed very vital. So often, we build up an ideal. We worship and cherish it. No sacrifice on earth is too great to offer in order to maintain its original form. In later years, that ideal has been demolished, but we survive just the same. Though we suffer a lot of hardships in trying to cling to something that seems very vital, after awhile, even the hardships suffered slip into the background of our forgetfulness. So it is with war.

I was wounded during the war by a shell that struck me in the side. It was pretty serious for awhile. Then another experience I had was when the Yankee cavalry dashed in on us and made us leave the rations we were cooking. My, I was hungry, but had to make my escape right away in a wagon.

About the queerest sensation I experienced was in 1865. I came to Augusta on furlough and found the town infested with Yankees. It looked like I had walked into a nest of wasps, until I learned that peace had been declared. So, I was safe and happy to know the war was over.

GOT "HITCHED" DESPITE WAR

HENRY M. JEFFREY, Syracuse, N. Y. Union.
B. Sept. 23, 1841, Truxton, N. Y. Co. D
185th N. Y. Inf. Sept. 15, 1864.

I am 98 years old and my memory is fading, but I do remember that Colonel Sniper was my colonel, and I use to like to look at the grand statue of him here in Syracuse.

When the war came on, I was engaged to be married, and I didn't hardly know what to do. But Mrs. Blakeman, my fiancé's mother, gave her consent and we went right out that night and got "hitched up." Two days later I marched away. I was in the battle of Gettysburg, and at Appomattox Court House when Lee surrendered. We went down there and closed up the war in 1865.

The medal I wear on my chain was presented to me by the G. A. R. Post I've filled every office they have, and I will probably be their quartermaster as long as I live, even though I can't get out much, George Cathers attends to all the duties of the offices I hold, and he even went down to Gettysburg so he could come back and tell me all about the reunion.

NONAGENARIAN

MRS. MARY FRANCES JOHNS, Schoolfield, Va.
B. Nov. 28, 1839, Trevilians Station, Va.

I am nearly 100 years old, but I recall June 11, 1864, as a bright and sticky-hot dawn, in the vales of Louisa County, Va., when my heart hammered harder than did Scarlett O'Hara's, at Tara, at the words, "The Yankees are coming!" I grabbed a gun and crouched, waiting for the dangerous moment. Soon they came into Trevilians and burned the depot. I was in our little home a few miles away waiting for them, but they never came that far because our soldiers stopped them. Their line of battle did not quite reach to our home.

Lee knew that Sheridan was coming and he sent Wade Hampton and Fitzhugh Lee to stop him, and they did. This was the biggest engagement I saw and I remember it perfectly, just as I remember seeing Abe Lincoln and General Grant. After the battle one of our soldier boys came galloping by yelling that the Yankees had been stopped.

My, husband, Henry Clay Johns, was wounded at Chancellorsville and again at Manassas. He was as fighting a man as there was in the Army of Northern Virginia. I met and married him while he was a soldier. He died in 1903.

When I look back over my long life, everything has changed so much it doesn't seem like the same world I was raised in. Once about seventy-five years ago, a young man wanted to smoke and he said to me, "Do you object to the smell of tobacco smoke?" I told him I didn't know whether I did or not, because no gentleman had ever smoked in my presence.

FENCE SHOT FROM UNDER HIM, HE KEEPS ON FIRING

ELIJAH JONES, Springfield, Ill. Union.
B. Jan. 1, 1842, Barren Co. Ky. Co. C, 1st
Ill. Cav. Vol., Mattoon, Ill. July 13, 1861;
Co. A, 54th Reg. Ill. Inf. Vol. Jan 1, 1864.
Dis. as corporal, Oct. 15, 1865.

Down in Arkansas, we were combating a strong resistance from the rebels. Crawling through a wheat field toward the banks of a river, we were using everything available for the little protection it might lend. I was lying behind the roots of a tree and did not see a rebel who had got pretty close to me. He fired and the bullets hit the roots about six inches from my head.

Later we were advancing on Little Rock. I was lying on a fence, just a-firing away. The rebels were using small cannons then. One of the cannon balls came a-flying along and knocked the fence right out from under me. I found myself deposited flat on the ground, unhurt, so I kept on firing.

In one fight, we were moving southward, pushing the rebels back. The comrade next to me noticed a carbine, sort of musket or rifle, laying on the ground where the enemy had retreated. He told me that he wanted to keep it as a souvenir of the fight, and just as he bent over to pick it up a cannon ball landed a short distance from it, tearing up the ground and the gun. With a bewildered expression, he said, "I didn't want it anyway."

About the 28th of May, 1864, while encamped at Little Rock, I had charge of a squad that was ordered to clean up its arms. I was sitting on a box with my feet dangling. A gun was handed me to examine and I laid it across my right leg, with the muzzle pointing downward. I raised the hammer and from some defect in the lock the shell exploded. The ball struck my left foot just below the ankle joint. It passed through the foot and came out just in front of the hollow part, crushing the bones. I was sent to St. John's Hospital and treated for about four months. As a result, my leg had to be amputated. I wear a leg now that shots can't hurt—it's wooden.

I was right with the boys at Gettysburg to attend the reunion. I swapped yarns with them and kicked my heels as high as the rest, despite my wooden leg.

ON THE MARCH WITH SHERMAN

DWIGHT T. LANDON, Marcellus, N. Y. Union
B. Aug. 17, 1845, Marcellus, N. Y. Co. D.
105th Ill. Inf. Aug. 13, 1862, Bloomingdale, Ill.

A war meeting was called in the church of our town. All the neighbors turned out to hear the stirring speeches. It was all so exciting that I enlisted right then and there. My brother Charles also enlisted.

I spent the first two years of my service in the hospital, but I got well enough to go on the march with Sherman. We took everything we could get our hands on and burned everything we could not take with us. Of course, we were only obeying orders in doing so. I got hold of a bundle that looked like a bale of cotton. I took it with me and when I opened it up, it contained women's clothing. I sold one of the dresses for $5.

I was in the hospital in Atlanta while my regiment was stationed about three miles from town. I joined them as soon as I was able to do so. One cold, rainy day several of us were detailed to go on a wagon for supplies. We were so miserable we decided to stop for awhile and warm up by a camp fire. We soon had one built and were gathered around it. I'll never forget my chagrin when an old nigger wench came up to us. I had on a new hat and coat. She looked up at me and said "Whut a mighty purty Yankee."

When we left Atlanta, I don't believe there was a building left standing. We warned all the citizens to leave and they were swarming over the country roads like bees. The city officials protested and Sherman told them that he was going to burn the town. A torch destroyed what cannon balls and shells had left. Sherman's idea was to make it a pure military garrison with no civil population to influence military measures.

The first night I had to stand picket the minutes passed like hours. I was on duty two hours that seemed like two weeks. The rain was pouring so that I could not see my hand before my face. Then there was a time when we had to guard a railroad tunnel all day, slushing in mud up to our ankles. A lot of the fellows were taken sick, a lot died, and some deserted. I disliked guard duty so much that one time I tried playing sick when the bugle called. Well, that worked, but I was ordered to take some medicine. I wouldn't have minded quinine, but it turned out to be a half-cup of castor oil. Oh, I was sorry that I hadn't gone on duty.

We were supposed to live on the country, but we had pretty poor pickings, except, when we now and then struck up against a bit of luck. Once, we struck a nice plantation where we filled up the family wagon with sweet potatoes, fresh beef, and were on our way.

Once, we found the nicest new log house with all the family gone. So we went in, opened up the cupboard, and right before us was a platter of chicken. No nigger parson was ever happier than I. I ate my fill and left the bones so that they would know company had been there.

The next time I entered a house for food, I didn't get such a fine welcome. There was a six-quart pail of milk on the table. My comrade and I drank all we could. As we turned to go, the lady of the house picked up the pail and threw the rest of the milk out. She said, "I don't want any of it after the damned Yankees have drunk out of it." That didn't bother us none.

Well, I've had my good times and I've lived to a ripe, old age. At one time there were 540 members at the Lilly Post of the Grand Army of the Republic. I am the last survivor.

MADE GUNPOWDER OUT OF DIRT AND CHARCOAL

H. K. LAUHTER, Edneyville, N. C. Confederate.
B. Feb. 15, 1847, Buncombe, Co., N. C. Co. G,
56th Reg. N. C. S. T., Asheville, N. C.

It all seems more like a dream to me now. I would rather have love and joy any time than man matching vengeance against man. It always ends in disasters and hinders the progress of mankind.

I did not enlist until the last year of the war when I saw that I was going to be drafted. I had a pretty easy time, except when we got out of rations a few times. We were out for three days once and there was little or nothing around to forage. We gathered anything we could find that might have a little sustenance in it, and made out as best we could. The Northern army had taken stock, rations, and everything they could get hold of as they passed through.

As to duties I performed, I had no say-so about anything I did. My main duty was to obey orders and do what I was told. My active part in the war was making gun powder for the Southern army. This was done by collecting dirt from under houses and in smoke houses where the, drippings from salt meat made the dirt rich with saltpeter. This dirt was put through a sifter to extract the grit. The fine powder left was then mixed with charcoal and boiled, and then poured into big troughs to dry.

This prepared the main ingredient for making cartridges. We took dirt from under this very house I am living in and shipped it to, I disremember where.

General Lee was a fine, portly-looking man and I saw him many times when he passed through North Carolina, but I never spoke to him.

I am a home loving man and so I have never attended any reunion. Not even when the government wanted to pay my way and all expenses. The hillsides of Sugar Loaf Mountain are good enough for me anytime. I was born here, have always lived here, and expect to be buried here.

THE STORY'S END

FRANKLIN W. LORD, Plano, Ill. Union.
B. Aug. 30, 1848, Colchester, Conn.
Co. I, 23rd Inf. Ill. Vol., Little Rock, Ill.

The most exciting moment I experienced was when Lee surrendered, the joy of the Army of the Potomac knew no bounds.

This beloved veteran visited with his buddies and comrades at the Last Meeting of the Blue and the Gray at Gettysburg, July 1938, and answered the last roll call on August 28, 1938. The few lines of his unfinished story is submitted as he left it on his desk, by his son Maurice F. Lord, Aurora, Ill.

MANNED A CANNON

WARREN M. LORE, Charlotte, Mich. Union
B. Jan. 2, 1846, Cayuga, Cayuga Co., N. Y.
Co. G, 3rd Reg. N. Y. Light Art., Auburn, N. Y.
Dis. June 24, 1865, New York, N. Y.

I was engaged in the last battle fought in North Carolina. That was at
Kingston in March 1865. It lasted for practically three days. I was No. 2
man in charge of a cannon and when my number was called, I knew it
meant to step to the front and face the fire. I usually sheltered myself
behind a tree to await my turn. I felt sure that I would be killed sooner or
later, so it was easier fighting than awaiting my turn, because the moment
I took my place at the cannon I stopped thinking and went to work.

After the battle we marched to Goldsboro. There we met Sherman's
army and with them advanced to Raleigh. We crossed the Dismal Swamp
canal, which was dug under the supervision of General Washington. It was
dismal too. The boat following ours across the canal had Jeff Davis aboard
as a prisoner and was taking him to Fortress Monroe.

As a little pastime, our sergeant once took four of us privates to a darky
revival near New Bern, N. C. The pastor said he couldn't read, but he knew
a Bible when he saw it. As the services proceeded, the darkies began
getting the "power." They waived their hands in wild gesticulation,
shouted their prayers in loud and mournful tones, and rolled and tumbled
over the ground. One large fat woman was so entranced with the spirit that
she was oblivious of all earthliness. In her convulsion she struck our
sergeant across the face. It tickled us, but we decided to leave then. We
were so surrounded by the worshipful bodies tumbling on the ground that
we had great difficulty in getting past them.

I was hospitalized once during the war. That was at Elmira, N. Y., in
1864.

Gettysburg has turned out a fine reunion for us. I'll take the reunions
anytime in preference to the fighting at Gettysburg.

JUST A SOLDIER

JAMES P. MARTIN, Sutherland, Io. Union
B. Nov. 10, 1847, Aberdeen Scotland,
Co. H, 1st Reg. Wisc. Art., Milwaukee, Wisc.
Dis. June 26, 1865 Port Lyon, Va.

I was born November 10, 1847, at Aberdeen, Scotland. At the age of sixteen I was enlisted in Company H, First Regiment of the Wisconsin Heavy Artillery, on September 22, 1863, at Milwaukee, Wisconsin. I served under the command of Captain Charles S. Taylor. My discharge is dated June 26, 1865, Port Lyon, Virginia.

I have no story to relate, but I want to be remembered with my comrades attending the Last Meeting of the Blue and Gray at Gettysburg, July 1938.

HIDES IN LOG FOR SAFETY

NATHANIEL RICHARD MARTIN, Leach, Okla. Union
B. Oct. 27, 1845, Wayne Co. Tenn. Co. A, 2nd
Tenn. Mounted Inf., Nashville, Tenn.

We got hemmed in between a bluff and a farm, so we left our horses and went by foot. I hid in a big chestnut log and stayed there until the Johnnies left. When I got out, the place looked deserted and I thought all my comrades had been killed, but it was not long before they started coming out of their hiding places too. We were all safe.

The modern warfare exhibitions at Gettysburg are one of the most interesting at the reunion. Of course, it is a thrill to see the President too.

COMRADES CHEER HEROIC DEEDS

WILLIAM M. MATHEW, Birmingham, Ala.
Confederate. B. May 8, 1843, at Warrace, Tenn.
Co. A, 37th Tenn. Inf., Tullahoma, Tenn.

My first fight was with Dan Becknal over the question of where our mess tent should be placed. We got chop axes and started at each other, but both quickly ended up in the guard house. Just before daylight the next day, we found the guard asleep and made our escape. Not knowing where to go, we rambled off into the woods. Soon hunger overtook us and we forgot all about our quarrel and began a search for food. Some cows came along, so we looked around until we found some gourds, hanging near some old wash pots. We took these and milked the cows. We felt rather mature to be starting on such a soft diet, but it beat nothing. We finally decided it would be better to return to camp and face the music. When we got back, everybody ragged us about it, and the funniest part was that we were not punished for escaping, but the guard who fell asleep was punished.

After the battle of Monticello (Fishing Creek), the Confederate army retreated, and in order to get back to camp it had to cross the Cumberland River. It was a dark, stormy night and everything was in confusion. We missed Pete Anderton, and someone remembered that we had left a man of our company in a ditch, who was seriously wounded in the hip. Captain Hunt asked who would volunteer to take a wagon across the river and return with Pete. I volunteered, not knowing that the Federal army had pursued and already taken possession of the boat in which we had crossed the river. On returning, before I knew it, I had arrived at the foot of a hill on the bank of the river right in the midst of the Federal army, and it was impossible to turn the wagon around. I drove on to the boat, which was ready to return to the other side for more Federal soldiers. I observed that everything was in confusion and that no one spoke above a whisper. I concealed my identity by keeping quiet and under cover of intense darkness. I had no trouble in finding Pete and getting him in the wagon, but when I returned to the river I was again confronted with the problem of getting across on the enemy's boat. I expected to be discovered and arrested at any moment, but instead I arrived safely at camp and was cheered by my comrades. Besides, I was given a two weeks' furlough for accomplishing this hazardous task. Pete was so ill that I took him home in the wagon. He was suffering terribly as he had received no medical attention and had nothing to ease his pains on the one hundred and fifty mile trip. He died two or three years later because of these wounds.

Once, when the Confederates were travelling to Knoxville for a battle, the train came to a sudden stop. Men were pitched across the seats and headlong into the aisles. We investigated the cause and learned that a bridge crossing the river had been burned by northern sympathizers. The train had stopped short within three feet of plunging into the river. We made a search for the incendiary and found an old man with his two sons hiding in a tree. They confessed the crime and were sentenced to be hanged. A scaffold was hastily constructed and they were asked to decide which one should be hanged first. I shall never forget my feelings on seeing that old man and his two sons, heads together, deciding which one of them should go first.

I bear no malice toward my old foes and enjoyed meeting with them at Gettysburg. Lavish entertainment was provided for us, as well as every means for our comfort and welfare.

REMINISCENCE OF THE LIFE AND SERVICE OF CAPTAIN WILLIAM THADDEUS McCARTY

Just one hundred years ago on December 15, 1938, Captain William Thaddeus McCarty was born in Warrenton, Fauquier County, Virginia. As the daughter of Captain McCarty, I am both proud and happy to give a short account of his life and War Between the States record.

Captain McCarty was the son of William Thaddeus McCarty, descendant of an exiled Irish nobleman, and Hannah Fox, a daughter of Captain John Fox of Prince William County, Virginia. While attending a seminary at Fredericksburg, Virginia, Hannah Fox was presented to Lafayette, who expressed his pleasure in meeting a relative of his personal friend, Charles James Fox, the English statesman. Before leaving, he called upon her.

When Lafayette and John Quincy Adams visited President Monroe in Leesburg, they were entertained on August 9, 1825 at "Newington," a stone mansion overlooking the Little River near Middleburg in Loudoun County, Virginia. This was the home of Captain McCarty's grandfather, George Washington McCarty, who bore the name of his illustrious cousin. The relationship between the McCarty and Washington families was bound by the ties of friendship as well as marriage. In George Washington's diary, the original of which is in the Congressional Library, he often speaks of the McCarty's being entertained at his home and he at theirs. Such was also the case with regard to the Lee family with which the McCartys intermarried several times.

Captain McCarty attended the old Field School of Virginia. In 1858 and 1859, he was a student at Bloomfield Academy, in Albemarle County, a preparatory school for the University of Virginia, which he entered the following year.

Captain McCarty states in his diary:

"In the fall of 1860, at the University of Virginia, we formed a company of students called the University Volunteers. We drilled during the school year. On July 1, 1861, the company went to West Virginia and enlisted in the brigade of General Henry A. Wise, who had been Governor of Old Virginia. That fall (1861) we were at the Junction of the Gauley and New rivers (in what is now West Virginia). These rivers are tributaries of the great Kanawha. While at this place, General Rosecrans' Union army of one thousand men marched up the Kanawha Valley to attack us (we had an army of about five thousand men). General Wise entrenched his command on a high mountain across the valley. Skirmishing and small attacks were kept up until early in January, 1862, when one morning we found that the Union army had retreated down the Kanawha Valley. It was said that our position on this mountain was naturally so strong (and had been made doubly so by fortifications) that Rosecrans was afraid to risk a general engagement.

"Our company was composed of many graduates, and the War Department at Richmond issued an order disbanding us so we could go to our homes and aid in raising companies and regiments for the South. This was in January, 1862.

"I went back to my old county and helped raise the battery called the Fauquier Artillery.

"I was in this company the balance of the war; first, as a non-commissioned officer, then as lieutenant and finally as a captain.

"We saw much service and participated in the Seven Day's Battles around Richmond, Fredericksburg, Chancellorsville, the battles of the Wilderness, the sieges of Petersburg and Richmond, and many minor engagements. At Fredericksburg and Spottsylvania, the horse I rode was shot from under me, but I never received a wound in battle and never was absent from duty.

"At the battle of Gettysburg, we were engaged in a terrific artillery duel. General Pickett's celebrated division was just in our rear during the bombardment, and passed between our guns when they made the charge. We were attached to Poague Artillery Battalion composed of batteries as follows: from North Carolina, from Mississippi, from Albemarle County, Virginia, Stanton, Virginia, and our Fauquier Battery of Virginia. When the fight first opened the commander of our battery was badly wounded, and I had command of the battery during the balance of the engagement. Our artillery battalion was with Stonewall Jackson's division in most of the battles that Jackson engaged in. After the Gettysburg fight, our Colonel, W. T. Poague, wrote me a letter of congratulations on the manner in which I handled our battery.

"Some years after the war ended, Colonel Poague wrote me a letter saying he had just been over the battlefield, at the request of the Virginia authorities, in order to locate the place where his batteries fought, and he told me that Virginia was about to erect a monument on that field to her soldiers who fought in this battle, and that my name as Commander would appear on the monument.

"At the battle of Fredericksburg, Virginia, in December 1862, our battalion was placed on a high point called Hamilton's Crossing. We had a fine view of the enemy's three lines of battle in the bottom on the Rappahannock River. Stonewall Jackson and staff came up this hill and used their glasses to inspect the Federal lines. While they were thus inspecting the Union Army at the bottom, a number of the enemy's battery opened on this hill and we induced Jackson's staff to go to the left out of the range of shot and shell. Jackson sent his courier back to our commander with word not to reply to the Federal artillery but let our men lie flat on the ground to protect themselves. It was expected that the Yankee infantry would attack this fine position when their artillery ceased firing. Many of our infantry and artillery men were killed or wounded by this terrific bombardment. One of our guns was knocked off its carriage. We waited all that afternoon expecting the enemy's infantry to charge us. To our left, they made many assaults on the Confederate line but they were, in each case, driven back with great slaughter. During this fire on our position many of our artillery horses were killed or wounded.

"The next morning, after this fighting, we looked down over the bottom and found that the entire Union army had retreated during the night across the river. We went into winter quarters in the timber south of this battlefield.

"One of the southern soldiers got up a minstrel show in a large tent. He composed a song on the battle of Fredericksburg and sang it to the big crowd of soldiers. I remember a few verses of this song as follows:

The Yankees came to Fredericksburg
To whip each Southern Rebel,
But Lee and Jackson turned the joke
And thrashed them like the devil.

Chorus

Then let them bum, let them bum,
The way is always clear.
But while they are a-bumming,

We'll flank them in the rear.

You talk about your horses fast,
And about your four-mile heater,
But when you let a Yankee loose,
He is much the fastest creater.

T'was then Burnside rode up the lines,
And stood up in his saddle,
He waved his sword and gave command,
Right-about and skeedaddle.

"Our battalion was at Chancellorsville in Virginia where Stonewall Jackson was wounded and died. We were with his troops.

"Some people think that General Jackson fought behind a stone wall and that is the reason he was called "Stonewall" Jackson. It is not true. It is as follows:

"At the battle of Bull Run, near Manassas in Old Virginia, General Jackson was supporting General Bee in the Valley of Virginia (Shenandoah Valley). The southern army was falling back in disorder and Jackson's brigade marched to the front and took a position on an elevated place. The Yankees attacked him at once and he repulsed them time and again. General Bee's men were falling back, I think, to Jackson's right. General Bee drew his sword, waved it in front of his men, pointed to the ridge and said: "Rally men, rally around Jackson; there he stands like a stone wall." A few moments later Bee was killed. Jackson ordered his forces: "Reserve your fire till they come within fifty yards; then fire and give them the bayonet; and when they charge, yell like the furies." This is where the "Rebel Yell" originated.

"Jackson's bravery saved the day. The Union army was defeated with heavy losses. A fine regiment of Confederate cavalry from Loudoun County, Virginia, charged the enemy and many were killed. My first cousin, Enoch McCarty, who was about twenty years old, was in this regiment and was killed. A bullet went through his forehead and his fine horse galloped into the Union lines.

"We fought at Appomattox Courthouse and were discharged and paroled there. Lee surrendered there to General Grant-the result of overwhelming numbers and resources.

"We went in sorrow and poverty to our homes. I returned to my father's plantation to find the home and farm ruined by fortunes of war and with no money to rebuild. The fences, barn, and sheds had been burned. I helped the family in the tasks of getting started anew; felled trees, split rails, and made fence posts. Together, we got the plantation once more under fence. As soon as possible, I resumed the study of law, this time with Allen Forbes, a noted Virginia lawyer.

"A little later, I left Virginia and started to Texas to visit relatives, with the prospect of locating in Texas, should the country appeal to me. I stopped en route to visit relatives in Oxford, Mississippi, and there delivered a letter of introduction to L. Q. C. Lamar, afterward a member of Cleveland's cabinet, then dean of the law department of the University of Mississippi. Mr. Lamar induced me to enter the University of Mississippi and to study for a degree, which I received in 1868. At Oxford, I met Miss Olivia Cecelia West, the daughter of General Absolem Madden West, a planter, politician, former member of the Mississippi State Legislature, and at that time President of the Mississippi Central Railroad, which ran from Cairo, Illinois, to New Orleans. Olivia C. West was educated at Ward's Seminary in Nashville, Tennessee. We were married October 20, 1867."

In May 1867, Captain and Mrs. McCarty went to Kansas on a prospecting trip. They liked Emporia and went no further. Emporia was then a small, but booming town. A description of the town written by Captain McCarty in 1871 gave little promise of the college town ranking, a quarter of a century later, as one of the most beautiful towns of America. Captain McCarty became interested in the town and made himself, not merely in the town, but of it. He opened a law office and, "For all the radicalism of Kansas, the manhood of Captain McCarty was too patent for folk to discriminate politically. He rose in the law profession; he filled offices of trust and honor." (Quotation from Newton Republican.)

During the first year of his practice; he was associated with the late Colonel H. C. Cross. Then he went into partnership with the late E. W. Cunningham, with whom he was associated until Judge Cunningham's election to the Supreme Court Bench of Kansas in 1891. Judge Cunningham was a Republican, but their long association served only to cement a warm and sincere friendship.

Captain McCarty carried the religious ideals of old Virginia into this new region and was one of the founders of the Episcopal Church in Emporia. He served as Vestryman for thirty years and Warden for twenty years. The fiftieth anniversary of service was unusual and received comment from the Kansas press. He was a Mason and also a member of the Knights of Pythias.

Olivia Cecelia West remained the one sweetheart of Captain McCarty for fifty-four years during which time they reared a family of four daughters and six sons, all of whom are living today, except Wirt Glover McCarty, who at the time of his death in 1911, was Editor of the Tulsa, Oklahoma, Post.

In 1917, Captain and Mrs. McCarty celebrated their Golden Wedding Anniversary and received congratulations from different sections of the country. An extract from a letter by Honorable Dudley Doolittle, member of Congress from Kansas, follows:

"I was pleased to read in the State Journal

sometime ago the fine article headed 'Married Fifty Years' concerning yourself and Mrs. McCarty, which I read at the time with a great deal of interest. I felt like writing you a letter of commendation, and I now congratulate you upon your fine pedigree, your excellent service to your country and the esteemed family you have raised to such fine maturity."

During the entire war my father kept a diary, often writing on horseback as he found a moment here and there. The diary which has been carefully preserved is priceless to his family.

In later years, he wrote an article entitled "Recollections of Gettysburg," which was published in Kansas and Virginia papers.

I close this short sketch of Captain McCarty's military record and subsequent career with a quotation from William Allen White, and published in the Emporia Gazette at the time of his death on October 30, 1925:

"Taps for the Captain"

"Some say he was a soldier to the end, a soldier and a gentleman. Tall, square, courtly, dignified, never sacrificing his square-cut military beard to the fashionable hirsute adornment of a newer day, Captain W. T. McCarty, who died this morning, remained always a soldier and a gentleman of the Old South.

"Since the bitterness of the Civil War has become only a memory, he fraternized more or less with the veterans of the G. A. R. But in his heart he remained a Confederate soldier, true to the traditions of the Confederacy. Not that he was in a whit disloyal; no more devoted

American ever stood in shoes than Captain McCarty. But he thought in terms of the Old South. Blood meant much to him. The amenities of life were important. He said "sir" more times than any ten men in town. Money spelled little in his estimate of success. He had a low opinion of all the forms and obligations and fashions that go toward the accumulation of wealth. He practiced law, but he never made out a statement of account in his life.

"Yet he and his wife reared a large family-ten in all-educated them and started them well in life. They have all done well. Some died after maturity, but they died in successful stations. How he did it was the marvel of the town. Yet there was the fact accomplished. We of these colder, northern climes could not understand how a man to whom money meant nothing could get on in a world where money was the counter in the game of success.

"But he lived his own life, the life of a Southern gentleman in his own way, quite indifferent to his environment. He was strong-stronger than our northern traditions and customs and creeds. It was rather a fine thing to do-to live up to his traditions and ideals to the last. But the Captain did it well. And as he passes in the innumerable procession out to Maplewood, we lift our hat in reverence to the passing of a fine, strong, knightly soul. And in the end he conquered; for he never lowered his flag-God bless him!-even though he laid down his sword!"

Evangeline McCarty Brunswick.

REMINISCENCES OF A CONFEDERATE SCOUT

RODERICK DONALD McLEOD, Crawfordville, Fla.
B. Jan. 15, 1848, Line Creek, Sumter Co., Ga.
Co. G, 8th Ga. Reserves Trans. to Co. G. 3rd Ga. Reserves.

I was not old enough to realize the full significance of war, but the thought had been instilled in the McLeods: "Remember that in your veins flows the blood of a true soldier who never shirked a duty. If your country is in war, Go! Indulge in no wild bravado, but go bravely where duty calls. Remember this always. Be true to your God, true to your country, and true to the traditions of those whose name you bear."

In the year 1861, when the war subject was discussed in our family circle, it was as something possible but not probable. When we got news of the big battles, it still seemed that the destructive and demoralizing effects could never reach our humble home. When Sherman's victory in Chattanooga started him on his march to the sea, the government had furnished him with everything in supplies and ammunition that he had asked for. He had one hundred thousand soldiers and two hundred and sixty pieces of artillery. Fear and terror began gnawing at the heartstrings of even the most remote families. Old men and young boys were feeling the need of their strength in the forces, and women were valiantly using their resources to help their beloved Southland. Though only fourteen, I felt strongly the fever that stirs in the veins of patriots. I told my mother I was going. She took me in her arms and wept, saying, "Oh, my child, my child!" To relieve her as much as possible, I announced my intentions and quietly slipped away. Half way between Abbeville and Hawkinsville, about twelve miles from each, a company was being formed. I joined Company G, 8th Georgia Reserves, and was later transferred to Company D, 3rd Georgia Reserves. This company was carried out of Georgia, but was still called Reserves to distinguish it from other companies.

Sherman had under his command Generals Thomas, McPherson, and Schofield. General Joseph E. Johnston commanded the Confederate forces of sixty-five thousand. While Sherman had an army almost twice as large as Johnston's, Johnston was one of the most apt generals of the war. His bravery held him as strong in the fore as it was humanly possible to stand. After the battle of Chattanooga, he was forced to retreat back gradually to Kenesaw Mountain. Here his men dug trenches and tried to fortify themselves against Sherman's approach, but daily fighting took its toll in men and Johnston was pushed back farther and farther toward Atlanta. At this time it was felt that Johnston was walking backward, so President Davis replaced him with General John B. Hood. After this experience, naturally, Hood had to be more aggressive. He attacked Sherman at Peachtree Creek and, on July 28th, when Sherman's forces were coming in full force at Ezra Church, he went out to meet them. I can remember my first impression as the Yankees began pouring over the landscape like a nest of ants, I thought "The earth is fairly belching blue coats." It seemed that every kind of ammunition was being drawn into use. I planned to use the church to fortify my position, but the enemy drove me out and pushed us back. Four thousand of our men were slaughtered. Hood was forced to abandon Atlanta on September 1st. Sherman took over the city and sent the terror-stricken inhabitants throughout the countryside seeking refuge. This is one of the saddest effects of war.

Once when the words rang out "The Yankees are coming!" Volunteers were called out to hold a bridge spanning the Chattahoochee River. I was one of the first to step forward. As the enemy made things too hot, most of the Confederates saw the time had come to surrender, that is all but twelve. It was just about dark. The ground sloped to the river bank and the fading light made progress seem easy under the spreading willows. But a hail of lead from the Fifth Michigan Cavalry cut down and killed eight of the twelve. I dashed under the bridge, dived into the river, and swam under water for a distance. When I reached the bank on the other side, there was Dink Davis, one of the quartet. We had to start out to find some comrades, but instead ran into a bunch of Yankees and they captured us. They held us two days before they learned that Lee had surrendered three days previous, then turned us loose.

Quite a coincidence came to my attention in later years. My eldest daughter, Ola, after her mother's death, spent a great deal of time with her aunt in Fort Myers, Fla. Consequently, she met and married Nathan G. Stout in that city. While I was visiting her, she invited her father-in-law to dine with us. It developed that he was in the company that captured me during the war. He boasted that he then raised a son who captured my daughter and that they were raising the finest little bunch of Yankee-Rebels you've ever seen.

Comrade J. B. Fletcher, of Chattahoochee, is one of the defenders of Natural Bridge, Fla., and the lone builder of the monument commemorating the bravery of his comrades, a group of small school boys who held it against a larger force. He is lieutenant-colonel on my staff, the First Florida Brigade George W. Scott Camp No. 1557, U. C. V.

The following is a newspaper account of my retirement from the Judgeship of the Circuit Court of Florida:

"Aged Wakulla Judge Retires from Bench After Long Service." January 12.-With the passing of the year 1928, the old year closed the political career of one of the most prominent and distinguished figures in the history of Florida, when Judge Roderick Donald McLeod retired from the office of county judge of Wakulla County after serving in that capacity for twenty-eight consecutive years, a record which perhaps no other county judge has ever held.

"Judge McLeod, generally called "Daddy" McLeod by his county people, is eighty-two, but he is as spry as the average man of sixty-five. He spends a great deal of time reading, though he has never worn spectacles in his life. He still has his own full-set of teeth and has had very little dental work done. He attributes his good health to the fact that he never indulged in tobacco in any form or intoxicating liquors; he has kept his conscience clear enough to sleep any time; and he has always eaten his wife's cooking.

"Thirty years have elapsed since Judge McLeod settled in Wakulla County, coming here from Oglethorpe, Ga., where he was owner and editor of a newspaper, and Mayor of the city. His motto has been "Honor is to be valued more than riches, and loving favour more than silver and gold." His integrity and high moral ideals have been an example for young and old. He is universally loved by all who know him. He has always held the faith and confidence of people and he was never known to be too busy to give direct and personal attention to all who needed his advice and counsel.

"Judge McLeod organized and founded the Tallahassean newspaper which has since become the Tallahassee Democrat. He is one of the organizers of the Florida Press Association at the Cotton Exposition at New Orleans. He is a veteran of three wars, having enlisted as a scout in the Civil War, he took part in all of the engagements around Atlanta, going through the entire campaign. He was a commissioned officer in the Spanish-American War, and during the World War, though age would not permit his going abroad with the A. E. F., he served as captain of the Home Guard of Wakulla County and held a record for hitting the "bull's eye" and out-shooting any man in his company. Judge McLeod is past commander of the Florida Brigade, United Confederate Veterans, and Gen. T. J. Appleyard, the present State Commander-in-Chief, was his adjutant general and chief of staff.

Judge McLeod's political career has received commendation in the Florida Legislative Blue Book, and his biography appears in many publications of histories of Florida, as well as a national history of outstanding men."

ROASTED MICE MAKE A PRISON MEAL

WILLIAM MEADOWS, Castelton, Ind. Union.
B. Oct. 20, 1844, Monroe Co., Ind. Co. B,
16th Inf. Ind. Vol. July 21, 1862, Bloomington,
Ind. Dis. June 30, 1865, New Orleans, La.

My first battle was at Richmond, Ky. On August 3, 1862, the smoke of bursting shells covered the field. All our energies were exerted toward our objective, with hardly a thought given to the dangers that awaited us. It was here that I was wounded by a ball that lodged in my leg. They sent me to a sick camp at Indianapolis, but the bullets were not removed. I carry them to this day.

We were later moved to Memphis. Landing there in the winter time, we had to lie on the wharf while about four inches of snow covered us like a blanket. Then we joined Sherman and went up the Arkansas River. We captured Arkansas Fort and fought in that section for about three months and then went down to Youngs Point and Vicksburg. We then went to New Orleans. I joined General Banks there and was in a battle at Mansfield, La. We held our stand very well until ammunition gave out and then we had to retreat.

I was captured down in Texas and held a prisoner until Peace was declared. For three hundred and ninety-four days I bore the strain of a bare existence in prison walls. Starved and weakened, we ate anything that would sustain life. The best meal I had during this time was nine mice that were roasted over a small fire.

I often ponder over the anxiety my parents must have suffered when they saw their six sons march off to war. There were six of us: John, Jake, Jim, Al, Dime, and I.

THE SLAUGHTER AT COLD HARBOR

RICHARD MEDLEY, Beachville, Md. Union
B. Nov. 27, 1847, in Scotland. Co. D.
12th Reg., Co. C, 2nd Reg. N. H. Inf.
Dis. Dec. 19, 1865, City Park, Va.

I want to say that I am bitterly opposed to war. Who wouldn't be, who has faced the shock of the mighty cannons' roar; the horrors and stench of the battlefield; the groans and cries of the wounded and dying soldiers; the raggedness, hunger and thirst of regimented men. Men who go into battle and suffer because they are the cream of the country's manhood. This is the ghastly experience that lived in my memory like a terrifying nightmare following the battle of Cold Harbor. For an hour that battle struck a high pitch, then to a lesser degree it continued until about noon. An extremely heavy loss was inflicted upon the Federal army. The battlefield looked like a wholesale slaughter pen. Then for three days Grant and Lee, in a great state of confusion, could not come to terms of a truce. During this time the men were left suffering under the scorching sun and exposed to preying insects. It is said that Grant regretted having gone into that battle as nothing was gained from it.

There were lighter moments, of course. It would be impossible for men to survive without refreshing the soul with a few pleasant experiences. I remember at Point Lookout, when the 2nd New Hampshire and 12th New Hampshire were stationed there. In April, one of the prettiest snowfalls I have ever seen covered the earth with a shimmering white blanket. Our officers all turned out and we had a big snow ball fight.

I am enjoying the Gettysburg Reunion. Mr. Roosevelt, Mr. Woodring, and Governor Earle have been here to see us. Swapping yarns seems to be the greatest pastime with the old veterans.

Brother Warriors

A BOUNTY-JUMPER TRANSPORTER

THEODORE METZGER, Miles, Mich. Union.
B. Dec. 18, 1847, Bertrand, St. Joseph Co.,
Mich. Co. H, 30th Mich. Inf., Miles, Mich.
Nov. 25, 1864. Dis June 23, 1865, Detroit, Mich.

The system of bounties was inaugurated in 1863. It did not prove a desirable means of obtaining soldiers, as these groups enlisted more for money than chivalry. They had no principle to fight for and would surrender or desert at the first opportunity. Many of them accepted the money and then tried to make their way across the border into Canada. Many of them re-enlisted and obtained bounty under various names. I was placed on guard on the border between Michigan and Canada. When these deserters or bounty-jumpers were caught, they were shipped to an island about five miles out in the bay from Baltimore. My job was to take them to Baltimore. We transported them in carloads, two at a time. On one of my trips, a prisoner jumped from the car window and made his escape. I fired and barely missed him. Guess I am glad that I didn't kill him, now I am free of the blame for taking his life.

For about two months my regiment was stationed at Trenton. Then we were brought back to Detroit to guard against a threatened invasion from Canada.

In February 1865, I got the worst end of a quarrel that occurred among my prisoners. In trying to quell the disturbance, I got shot in the left hip.

"GASSED" BEFORE IT WAS A PART OF WARFARE

LAWRENCE MICHAELIS, Omaha, Nebr. Union.
B. Dec. 6, 1840, Germany, 1st, Wis. Vol.
Inf., Co. B, Milwaukee, Wis., Apr. 20, 1861.
Dis. Aug. 25, 1861; Co. B, 3rd
Reg. Ohio Cav. Jan. 4, 1865. Dis. Aug. 1, 1865,
Nashville, Tenn.

I first enlisted for three months in the First Wisconsin Infantry, Company B, when President Lincoln called for volunteers. I served four months, was mustered out, and then was called again. This time I went into the Third Ohio Cavalry, enlisting for three years and serving two. I next went into the fray at Nashville, Tenn., serving with the same company. This time I served until the end of the war.

Several incidents of my experiences in the war stand out vividly in my memory. One was in November 1861, when, with a thousand other men, I crossed the Potomac on foot with all my clothes on. We had our choice of crossing in the nude, keeping our clothing and ammunition dry by holding it above our heads, or otherwise. I did not so much as take a cold from this experience.

Although it was a long time after the Civil War that gas became a part of warfare, I, with many of the other men of my regiment, was "gassed." One night we crept into an old church to sleep. Someone blew out the gas instead of turning it out, and the whole group had to be taken to the hospital to recuperate from the effects.

I was a pretty good dodger during the War and the only injury I sustained was when a bullet grazed my head.

I am a member of the Omaha G. A. R. Post; an honorary member of the Spanish American War Veterans: the Veterans of Foreign Wars and the World War.

UNIFORMS COULD NOT DECEIVE HIM

JOHN W. MILLER, Osseo, Wis. Union.
B. Apr. 5, 1845, Nauvoo, Ill. Co. D,
16th Reg. Wis. Vol Inf. Menominee, Wis.
Sept. 6, 1864, Dis. June 2, 1863.

The one hundred day battle during the march from Chattanooga to Atlanta was about the worst time that I went through.

One night, I was placed on picket duty and told not to let anyone pass. Two men came along who were wearing Federal uniforms. They acted indifferent toward my being on guard duty, so I thought at the time it was all right to let them pass. Later, I started thinking about what a chance I had taken. So, when they came along back, I hollered to them to come and sit on a log. They obeyed. Not long after that, another man, dressed in a Union private's uniform, came along. I stopped him too, and it proved out that I had three Confederates dressed up in our uniforms. I turned them over to our Captain and I never saw them again.

After the march to Savannah, we chose a site opposite a large dam for our post. While I was on picket duty one night, I heard a noise in the woods and became frightened. After awhile some of our men came up with a large gun, pulled by twelve pairs of horses. It was to be used to blast the gates of the dam. This gun could shoot nine miles, the exact distance from my picket post to a rebel boat on the other side of the dam. The first shot from the gun hit the boat and demolished it. The rebels left in a hurry. I was the first to get over the wall of the fort and inspect the cannons. One gun was not spiked, so I spiked it, and then started chasing rebels. I saw one peeking from behind a tree. I commanded him to come out, and he began crying. I asked for his gun and he turned it over without showing any fight. I took him prisoner and turned him over to the captain.

After we took Atlanta, we rested a month and then started north through South Carolina, going through scrimmage lines. A big negro once got in between the two firing lines and a shell hit him in the neck. He jumped about four feet in the air and yelled over and over again, "I'm shot, I'm shot, I'm shot!"

We marched up to Washington on the 24th day of May 1865, and encamped on Pennsylvania Avenue for a month. Lee had surrendered on the 7th of April, and Johnston had surrendered to Sherman a day later. We were mustered out of the army at Washington, and I, for one, was mighty glad to go home.

VETERAN 125 YEARS OLD

JAMES EDWARD MONROE, Jacksonville, Fla.
Confederate. B. July 4, 1815, Ash Lawn,
Charlottesville, Va. Stonewall Jackson's
Field Art., Charleston, S. C.

I have served in five wars in widely-separated sections of the globe. In four of them I was on the weaker side, but I emerged from all of them triumphantly safe, though bearing the scars of a score of wounds.

I fought in the Mexican War, enlisting under the leadership of General Winfield Scott. I was with him at Vera Cruz on March 27, 1847, when we battered our way in and won a victory. Robert E. Lee had just graduated from West Point and was chief of engineers on General Scott's staff. Lee was credited with the success of that victory and referred to by Scott as "gallant and indefatigable."

Then I served under Stonewall Jackson in the Confederate army. I joined in 1861, but was wounded in the battle of Long Bridge. In that battle, I was riding on a gun carriage when one of the wheels came off. Just about that time a trooper of the Brooklyn Seventh Cavalry rode up and made a pass at me with his saber. It severed the arteries in my throat, and I wear a silver tube in there to this day. I fell to the ground and the wheels of the gun carriage passed over me, breaking all my ribs. I lay on the ground, barely conscious, when the trooper returned and saw that I was still breathing. He said, "You dirty Rebel, you're not dead yet." He got down off his horse and came at me with his saber to stab me through the heart, but missed and cut my shoulder. I reached for my pistol, which was loaded and cocked, and fired it. The ball went through his throat and head and he tumbled over dead. I was bleeding to death, so I put my mouth to his open wound and sucked the blood from his body to give me sustenance. I lapsed into unconsciousness for a long while. When I came to, I was in a shallow grave beneath the bodies of two dead soldiers. Through the crude disposal of our bodies, a small current of air and light found its way to me. I thought to myself, "Well, my time hasn't come yet," and dug my way out with my bare hands. Then I collapsed. When I gained consciousness that time I was in a hospital.

One day five hundred men of my regiment were killed. A shell hit right beside me and I tried to throw it out of the way before it exploded. I barely escaped with my life and my right hand was blown off to the palm. During the Franco-German War, August 1870 to February 1871, I enlisted under Napoleon III. I saw him many times while I served under his flag. I was in the battle of Black Forest in the French Artillery, and I witnessed the defeat of our army. I lived through the murderous battle of Sedan, when the Germans shattered the pride of France and hurried Napoleon III from his throne.

When things got too quiet, I went to South Africa to work in the Kimberly Diamond Mines. I was there when the Boer War broke out in 1899. I enlisted promptly on the side of the Dutch. In one of the battles, I, alone, of my company escaped death.

I saved our flag from capture once. I bore it while the others escaped; then I tore the symbols from the flag, put them in my pocket and started for safety. For four days and nights I made my way by crawling on my hands and knees to avoid British soldiers before I reached my friends.

After that war, I turned to the sea and for a time was a sailor, making Scotland my headquarters.

After many years of dangerous adventure, I decided that I wanted to settle down in my own country. So, I returned to a tract of land in Jacksonville, Fla., to which I held "squatter's rights". I salvaged an abandoned house boat on the St. Johns River and made a sleeping room out of it. I equipped a kitchen out-of-doors by driving nails in trees to support cooking utensils, set up a stove and built a table and bench. I grow almost everything I need in my garden and I have many kinds of fruit trees. I owe my vigor to sunshine and fresh air as I am seldom in-doors.

When I first "squatted" here, I selected this location because it was primitive and afforded good hunting, fishing and outdoor adventure. Since that time the section around me has grown into an exclusive neighborhood, with residences worth thousands of dollars. These rich folks consider my camp an eyesore to the landscape and have tried every way they know how to take it away from me. They have taken most of my land and squeezed me onto a small lot back in their alley. They have tried every manner and means to uproot me completely, but I have told them, "Shot and shell will move me-that's all!"

Brother Warriors

Capt. Wm. Thaddeus McCarty

Capt. John Dowdy

Robert P. Scott

James Edward Monroe

CONFEDERATE VETERANS

201

STILL SUFFERS HEAD WOUND AT 102 YEARS OLD

DAVID MOODY, Dayton, Ohio. Union.
B. Feb. 4, 1838, Ross Co., Ohio, Co. G.
27th Ohio Inf. Vol. Oct. 15, 1862. Dis.
Sept. 21, 1865, Smithville, N. C.

At one hundred and two years, I can't remember very much about the battles. Captain 0. C. Latimer, Xenia, Ohio, was one of my officers. We went through many hot contests and dangers, but I came out alive. I still suffer with my head where that shell went in.

It was a big problem how to get food and water as both were scarce. During the cold nights we used to dig out a place in the snow and cover up.

The Gettysburg reunion was a grand meeting and I'm happy to see the North and South united in brotherly love, as they should be.

CAPTURES PRESIDENT LINCOLN'S ASSASSINATOR

JACOB MOOKER, Valpariso, Ind. Union
B. July 3, 1842, Germany. Co. H, 128th
Ind. Inf. Vols., Valpariso, Ind. Trans.
18th Vet. Res. Corps., Washington, D. C.
Dis. Nov. 15, 1865.

My regiment drew ammunition and clothing about two weeks after formation, and were sent to Chattanooga in hog cars. The first thing I did when I arrived was wash out my clothing in the river at the foot of Lookout Mountain.

We were joined by the 129th and 130th regiments, which made up General Hoovey's Brigade and then we started out to reinforce General Sherman on his march to the sea. When we overtook him, his troops were formed in line for battle, so we were kept in reserve to fill in any weak places. In the Battle of Buzzard's Roost, our whole regiment was used to strengthen the forces.

I never performed any particular acts of bravery, I just held my place in line of battle as best I could, until now and then I got knocked out. I remember when a minnie ball caught up with me and struck me in the leg, just above the knee. It was not so very serious. My sergeant removed the ball and I had to stay in the hospital about two weeks.

I was back with my regiment at Kenesaw Mountain, until a Johnnie used a short bayonet on me. He knocked out three of my teeth and inflicted a bad cheek wound. That laid me up in the Knoxville General Hospital No. 1, until November of 1864. I was then transferred to the 18th Veterans Reserve Corp, Washington, D.C.

When President Lincoln was assassinated on April 14, 1865, my regiment was called out to cross the bridge at the Navy Yard and scour the country in search of John Wilkes Booth. We were the first to cross the bridge. We divided into three squads, each alternating on a shift of eight hours' duty. We got a good layout of the country and set out to get Booth and his accomplices. It took eleven days to round them all up. Booth was captured in an old tobacco barn on the Garrett plantation near Port Royal, Va., at midnight. David Herold was with Booth and they put up a stiff fight, but Herold finally surrendered. Booth was suffering from a broken leg and no doubt realized that he hadn't a chance in the world, one way or the other, but he kept on fighting until the barn was set afire and he was completely trapped. He died of a shot through the head and the consensus of opinion was that he committed suicide, but it was also thought that a crack of the gun of Boston Corbett might have killed him.

Booth's accomplices George Atzerodt, David Herold and Mrs. Surrat were hanged. Dr. Mudd, the doctor who had set Booth's leg, Edward Spangler, Samuel Arnold, and Michael O'Laughlin were sentenced to long prison terms.

Though some of the newspapers refer to the veterans attending the Gettysburg Reunion as "the dimming eyes of '63," I am "holding my own" very well and bet I'm about as good looking as most men at sixty, eh!

DANGEROUS MOMENTS WITH A
FLAG BEARER AND COURIER

M. A. MOORE, Colony, Kans. Confederate
B. Dec. 23, 1844, Carrol Co., Va. Co. D, 37th
Va. Bat., White Hall, Tenn.

My first duties consisted of collecting supplies for Longstreet's army. I gathered livestock and had charge of it until it was butchered out, and I supervised two thrashing machines that were used to make flour for Longstreet's men.

Entering into more active service, I was appointed a courier to General William E. Jones. At one time I was assigned to a division under the command of Colonel Carnes that was sent sixty-three miles westward to hunt a regiment of the enemy. When we reached our destination the enemy had eluded us, and had wedged in between our division and General Jones' regiment. It was necessary that we report our movements to General Jones, which was difficult in our perilous position. As courier, I was given the dispatch by Colonel Carnes, and he said to me, "Now, Moore, they will very likely get you, but we have to make this effort. They will be guarding the road to pick off couriers reporting back to General Jones. For God's sake, if they get you, eat this dispatch." I said, "I can't eat it, but I'll do the best I can." There were five Yanks on picket in the mountain cut. They should have been on duty two hundred feet apart, but instead they were huddled together playing cards. When I discovered their position, it looked like I might make an easy ride across, but my horse's foot struck a rock which alarmed them. They grabbed their guns and made a dash in my direction. I could hear the click, click of their guns, but I scooted as fast as I could, protecting myself in the dark places. They knew that if they didn't kill me and it became known that they were off duty and had let me pass that they would be court martialed, so I made my getaway. I delivered the dispatch to General Jones at Saltville, Va.

I recall the sadness we felt when Stonewall Jackson was killed. At that time I was on my way to deliver a dispatch to General Longstreet, who kept me at his headquarters until General Jones' brigade was sent to the Valley of Virginia.

One of the closest calls I had was when I was carrying my Confederate Flag. I heard the Colonel of the Yanks yell three times, "Shoot down that Flag!" Thank God, I didn't surrender it. I carried the Flag the last six months of the war. While in the Battle of Fisher's Hill, Virginia, we were forced to retreat. The Yanks were hollering to me, "Throw down that Flag!" They shot off my hat and one shell went through my finger, but I carried my Confederate Flag out.

I took part in about thirty battles. They lasted from one to sixteen hours. I rode one hundred and twenty-six miles, fifteen miles through the enemy's lines, with one dispatch and was only out of the saddle twice during the trip.

Food was so scarce that ofttime we had only cracked corn to subsist on. Sometimes we did without entirely for as long as three days at a stretch. I rode from Longstreet's headquarters at Jonesboro, Tenn., to Winchester, Va., a trip of several hundred miles and subsisted on peaches and roasting ears, foraged along the way.

My daughter and attendant, Mrs. E. B. Reynolds, and I appreciate the great privilege of attending the Gettysburg Reunion and we are enjoying meeting the veterans of the North and South. But the stretch of graves before me brings back sad memories of my brother G. T. Moore, who was with the 51st Virginia Infantry, and was killed in the Battle of Gettysburg.

OLDEST OMAHA VETERAN TRAVELS EXTENSIVELY

THOMAS E. MOORE, Omaha, Nebr. Union.
B. Aug. 15, 1842, Co. C, 4th Regt. Iowa
Cav. Veterans, Oct. 12, 1861. Dis.
Aug. 8, 1865, Atlanta. Ga. Died Mar. 22, 1938.

Though I am ninety-seven years old, during the past twenty years I have travelled into every state in the Union, except two, and I have visited Canada, Cuba, and many Kentucky Derbys.

I am the oldest Civil War veteran in Omaha today. I joined and served the full duration of the war. I have fought it over and over again with friends, but I can't hear so well now and am robbed of that pleasure.

SORRY FOR THE ENEMY

JOSEPH MORGAN, Sapulpa, Okla. Union
B. Feb. 14, 1845, Overton Co., Tenn.
Co., E, 32nd Ky. Vol. Com. by Thomas
Morrow. Dis. Aug. 12, 1863, Danville, Ky.

Eternal peace between the North and South! That's what the Gettysburg Reunion meant to me. I am mighty proud of the government I helped to preserve. Though I am a dyed-in-the-wool Republican, I get a thrill out of recalling the appearance of President Roosevelt at the dedication of the Eternal Peace Monument. I was sitting about twenty feet from the President. He looked at me with those clear, blue eyes and smiled broadly. He knew who I was. He saw my big Grand Army of the Republic badge.

Standing there on the platform on the battle field where Abraham Lincoln made his famous address, President Roosevelt promised eternal peace and good will. Then a Union and a Confederate veteran pulled the cord that unveiled the big monument. An eternal flame about the size of a wash tub leaped out of the top.

There were fifteen hundred Yankees and five hundred Johnnies in camp at the Reunion of the Blue and the Gray. The tent city spread for blocks, with all facilities for their comfort at the disposal of the veteran guests, but there wasn't a single veteran I'd ever known. They're all gone, I guess.

I joined the Union army as a cook before I was fifteen years old. Then the draft for men from fifteen to forty-five years got me a little later on. I got into the heat of the activity then. I always felt sorry for our enemy, but, of course, I couldn't let that influence my actions against them.

The biggest battle I was in took place near Louisville, Ky., on the Ohio River. That was the famous battle in which Zollicopher of the Confederacy was killed. I remember, because my uncle, Captain John Hurt, shot Zollicopher off his horse. I was standing close by and saw him drop.

Scars on my forehead and neck tell the story of my encounters at Wildcat Gap, Cumberland Gap, and Somerset, Ky. Those were just skirmishes, but they held their dangerous moments too.

As I look out on the battle field of Gettysburg and see the thousands of graves, I think of the fine manhood that this country was robbed of seventy-five years ago.

SURVIVES TWO SERIOUS WOUNDS

JOHN B. MUSSER, Philadelphia, Pa. Union.
B. Dec. 12, 1838, Lancaster, Pa. Co. A,
81st Reg. Pa. Vol., Harrisburg, Pa. Dis.
July 24, 1865.

As I approach the age of 100 years, I shall attempt to tell a few things about my experiences fighting for the Union. I was with Grant through the Valley of Virginia. At the end of three years' service, my regiment had all been shot away, except four comrades and myself. We five enlisted in the 191st Regiment, Pennsylvania Volunteers, and continued in the midst of the conflict.

My left collar bone and shoulder blade were shattered in the battle of the Wilderness, but the shots were not removed until three years after the war, at Lancaster Hospital. We grimly determined to defeat General Lee, and I continued on, giving what service I could, despite my wounds. At Spottsylvania Court House, I was again wounded by a bullet that passed through my left wrist. I went to the Mount Pleasant Hospital and had this wound dressed. Today, both these wounds show deep, wide, and highly colored scars.

Onward we pressed toward Cold Harbor and almost to Richmond. That was between May 5 and June 3, 1864, and if Grant could have taken Richmond the war would have been over instead of lasting until April of the next year.

The Southerners fought like fury, contesting every inch of the way. The livid scars on my wrist and shoulder still throb when the weather is damp, continual reminders of that ferocious combat.

One of my brothers was killed in the war and another one died of wounds. I am thankful that I came through. My discharge dated July 24, 1865, bears the signatures of Major General Hancock and Captain C. S. McDowell.

I have had a lot of interviews and here is what a reporter in Philadelphia said about me, after a visit:

"Gaunt and still straight and tall despite his 99 ½ years, John B. Musser measures six feet, two and one-half inches, as he stands on the porch of the Henrys in their Larchwood Avenue home. He chews plug tobacco, has a keen eye for disposing of it, and walks around the block of Black Walnut Park twice every day to keep in trim. He hopes to celebrate his 100th birthday on December 12, 1938, with an old fashioned party.

"Musser was a Lancaster County boy when he went out with the Union army in the first part of 1863. In a short time he was in Virginia with Grant's army trying to move against Richmond. He recalls vividly the tangled thickets and ravines in which the beginning of the bloody thirty days' fighting took place below the Rapidan River. His regiment crossed the river and plunged into the wilderness proper to give aggressive battle. Musser recalls that Grant said he would 'fight it out if it took all summer.' Heavy losses were on both sides. For a time it seemed a deadlock. Grant and the Union boys were losing, but the rebels were finally driven back to Spottsylvania Court House and after the battle of Cold Harbor things were better and brighter.

"To hear a century-old veteran recall the seventy-four year old battle and to see the big scar proofs of close contact is a rare reward."

I belong to the Dauphin County G.A.R. Post, and have never bothered about being transferred to one here.

I attended the Gettysburg Reunion, June 29th to July 6th, 1938, with G. Will Henry, as my government attendant. That stay was rich in pleasure and profit and we owe permanent thanks to the administration which planned the proposal and carried it to such mutual success. Every detail for health and happiness, for safety and satisfaction, for reviving memories, reviewing the new war material, and man-equipment of the army, was completely arranged in forethought for us there. I was over 99 ½ years old before I started as a guest on that trip and I enjoyed every day there. Much of this was due to the thorough attention and personal interest that G. Will Henry, my attendant, lavished upon me. There were no idle, tiresome moments on the trip.

So on this the 15th day of August, 1938, we are all together here, grateful to the Creator for life, thankful to the Federal government for its care and provision, and glad that I have such good, kind folks, in a clean, comfortable home, to do daily personal service for me, in all seasons, as I approach the wonderful time of becoming 100 years old. I owe my present robust condition to John G. Henry and Elizabeth L. Henry, whose detailed care and attention cannot be equaled.

Mr. John B. Musser wrote his own story on August 15, 1938.

DIGS STUMPS AS PUNISHMENT FOR ABSENCES

ELBERT NUNN, Cortez, Colo. Union.
B. Apr. 25, 1845, Memphis, Tenn. Co. F,
16th Mo. Cav. Vol., Marshalfield, Mo.
Dis. July 5, 1865, Springfield, Mo.

I acted as an escort from 1863 to 1865. My camp was only six miles from Cunningham House where I grew up an orphan. I use to slip home and stay all night so I could get something good to eat now and then. I frequently returned to camp too late for roll call and had to take the punishment meted out to me. It usually consisted of digging stumps. Well, sir, that didn't keep me from going home, but I sure dug plenty of stumps.

We soldiers always kept a keen eye out for anything that could be foraged. Well, I sure got the worst end of it when I stole two bundles of oats out of a field for my horse. I tied the oats on the back of my saddle, but the old nag didn't like it so much. She sprung forward to run. Flung me on a rock and then fell on top of me. I was pretty badly hurt and Captain Allsop insisted that I go to the hospital. In those days a fellow wouldn't think of such a thing only as a last resort.

There was a stage coach to Kite Springs that carried the United States mail and passengers. It had to be accompanied by escorts or guards. I acted in this capacity once when a raid occurred. Those fellows waylaid us and after the stage coach passed they shot the rear guards. My pal, Bill Rowden, was killed. The rest of us got away pretty quick.

Well sir, everybody should be here at Gettysburg and see the goings-on. We old veterans are the spryest ones here.

215

BULLETS CURE HIM OF LAZINESS

ERASTUS PAGE, Omaha, Nebr. Union
B. Feb. 8, 1846, Brookfield, Pa.
Steuben Co. N. Y., Co. I, 50th N. Y.
Eng. Vol. June 29, 1864. Dis. June 28,
1865, Elmira, N. Y.

Well, sir, we had one heck of a time making any headway at the siege of Petersburg, June 1864 to April 1865. The Confederates were strongly fortified and we just had to keep drumming away. You see, we wanted to get hold of the railroads which were hauling Lee's supplies from the South. This would have crippled him and forced him to either leave Richmond or surrender. We felt that if we could get the capitol of the Confederacy the war would be over, but we had to take Petersburg first. General Beauregard was in charge of the Confederate forces and they only had 14,000 men, less than one-third our number.

We had to go a long way from our camp to get water. Well, one hot day, I put on a string of canteens and started out to get some water for myself and comrades. We were supposed to go by way of the "dug road," but it was a quarter of a mile farther that way. So, feeling a bit lazy, I decided to take a chance straight over the hill. I got up to the top-right in sight of the rebel pickets-then I fell on my stomach and crawled until I could see into their lines. I was about to make a run for the water, when a volley let loose and caught me in the pants leg. I wasn't hurt, but you bet I wasn't too lazy to go back by way of the "dug road."

One of the reporters at the Gettysburg Reunion said, "A handful of ancient men in old-fashioned uniforms" were camped there, but I asked them just to come out to Omaha when our G. A. R. Post gives a big party and I'll out dance any of those young squirts.

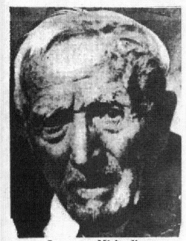

Lawrence Michaelis

Charles Barothy

Erastus Page

I. M. Wickersham

UNION VETERANS

PRISONER MISTAKES FRANKNESS FOR TRICK

MARK PATTEN, Kokomo, Ind. Union.
B. Sept. 14, 1847, Clinton County, Ind.
Co. H, 153rd Ind. Vol. Inf., Kokomo, Ind.

I fought a lot of bushwhackers during the war, but picket duty kept me busy most of the time. I guess that quick action on my part checked the enemy one time anyway. When I heard the sound of approaching hoofs, I gave the command, "Halt!" When it was not obeyed, I fired away. In a couple of seconds an excited Rebel's horse came running by without a rider, so I judged my aim must have been straight.

Then there was a time when I didn't use such good judgment, but the enemy thought I was trying to trick him and no harm was done. It happened in the middle of the night. I was sound asleep and a prisoner awakened me to take him to the bath room. The cap on my gun had been removed to keep it from accidentally discharging, in case it happened to fall, and I had taken off my cartridge belt. Well, I picked up my gun and marched the prisoner downstairs, just as diligently as could be. When we got to the first floor, I realized that I hadn't replaced the cap or put on my cartridge belt. It struck me kinda funny, so I told the prisoner about it. He said, "All right, we'll go back upstairs and get them." So he turned face-about and marched back upstairs. After he found out that my story was true, he said, "Well, I guess we're both a couple of fools."

My oldest brother, John "Cal" Patten, was wounded and captured in the battle of Chickamauga. In this battle the Union soldiers had been ordered to take the first line of Confederates, which they did. Their victory was so great that without further orders, acting entirely upon their own foresight and taking matters in their own hands, they proceeded to scale the mountain and take the second line. So rapid was the advance of troops that the wounded and dying were just trampled over by the army. This was the victory that saved Rosecrans' army when they were hemmed in the big horseshoe between Missionary Ridge and Lookout Mountain. Rosecrans' men were so starved that they were eating their mules, and they did not have enough men to fight their way out.

Brother Cal was held a prisoner for thirteen days, and he told me that during this time he did not have anything to eat but grains of corn, picked up on the ground where government mules had been fed.

Cal came out pretty lucky when he was wounded just below the knee and the doctors wanted to amputate the leg to prevent gangrene from setting in. I guess he would have consented to the operation if he hadn't caught sight of a pile of arms and legs, stacked as high as the head. The sight sickened him and he refused. The next day he was among some prisoners who were exchanged. He was able to get proper medical attention then and his leg was saved. He lived to be eighty-four years old and was mighty proud to be active all his life.

As a memento of Southern chivalry, Brother Cal brought home a walking stick that was whittled out for him by a small Rebel boy.

I met a lot of nice Confederates at the Gettysburg reunion. Yes, sir, there are both kinds, good and bad, but I never met the bad ones.

SOLDIERS "WERE NOT ALL ANGELS DOWN THERE"

HERBERT PATTERSON, Camden, N. Y. Union.
B. Apr. 25, 1841, Richmond, Yorkshire, England.
88th Pa. Vet. Vol. Inf., July 1864, Scranton, Pa.
Dis. June 1, 1865, Philadelphia, Pa.

Sometimes a soldier is so anxious to prove his valor that he over-does the job. That's just what happened to me down at the "yellow house," as we called it. I heard a rustling noise outside, and I wasn't going to let any enemy come slipping up on me if I could help it. I hauled off and let a load of lead go right through the darkness. After everything had quieted down, I slipped around to see what had happened, and there lay a fine cow-dead. My heroic intentions were rewarded by our having fresh beef that day.

During that time each man had to look after himself and do his own cooking. A canteen was the usual utensil provided for preparing our food. It had a hole bored in the side, where a stick could be inserted to hold it over the fire. A little hardtack and pork cooked this way wasn't bad eating, and the appetite got whetted up quite sharp while it was cooking. We substituted a kind of root for coffee, and our other main staple food was beans. We'd take a handful of beans, throw them in a quart cup and boil them up. Sometimes, they wouldn't get done before we'd get orders to "Fall in!" We never left the beans behind though. We just crammed them down, half-done.

You never heard of a good soldier tell about killing anybody, did you? If I killed a hundred or more, I wouldn't own it, but I wouldn't know it anyway. No, sir, I wouldn't know anything. Oh, we had lots of such things happen, you know; but I have forgotten them, we were not all angels down there.

ALL IS FORGIVEN IN FORGETFULNESS

DANIEL PERSHING, Ogallah, Kans. Union
B. July 15, 1846, Rogersville, Ohio.
Co. C, 196th Reg. Inf. Vol., Mar. 15, 1865,
Barnesville, Ohio. Dis. Sept. 11, 1865, Baltimore, Md.

It has been so long ago that I can't remember my war experiences. So my advice to the coming generation is to forget all bitterness and strife and stand united for the betterment of mankind and our country. Great strength comes from unison, and I am proud that I helped preserve the union.

This trip to Gettysburg is the last chance the old veterans of the North and South will have to join hands in brotherhood on this earth. May this message carry down through the years to the coming generation our bequest to them of forgiveness of heart, understanding, and reason.

My attendant is my daughter, Mrs. George F. Rhodes. I guess a lot of people coming here to see us were surprised that so many men nearly a century old could travel half way across this continent and camp outdoors. You see, we lived right when we were growing up.

A CAVALRYMAN

WILLIAM PIERCE, Omaha, Neb. Union.
B. June 14, 1846, Manion, N. Y. Co. H.
N. Y. Vol. Cav. Sept. 3, 1864, Fayetteville, N. Y.
Dis. June 15, 1865, Alexandria, Va.

I joined the cavalry to fight the Confederates and I gave them plenty to think about for one year and nine months.

I went through the war all right and waited until I was nearly a century old to get hurt. Two years ago I fell and broke my hip. Since that time I've been bedfast. My main interest through all the years prior to the accident was attending the annual State G.A.R. conventions.

William Pierce died Nov. 26, 1936. The above interview is one submitted by his comrade Erastus Page, member of the Omaha G. A. R. Post. Mr. Page requested that, "It will be my pleasure to have the army service and sentiments of my close friend and comrade remembered."

THE PETTICOAT SPY

FRANK ELI POWELL, New Orleans, La.
Confederate. B. Jan. 15, 1838,
Winchester, N. C. Joined Louisiana
Tigers, New Orleans, La.

When gold was struck in California and people started rushing out there, the idea of a land of promise was an obsession with my father. He tried to persuade my mother to go out there, but she stood firm and said, "No, I will not take my children over the plain. We do not know how they might be taken care of. If you want to go, go by yourself, but I will not subject my children to unknown hazards." That question was settled, but father moved from Winchester to New Orleans to ply his trade as a shoemaker. I learned the trade from him and followed it throughout my active years.

When I was between five and six years old, I was presented with a gun and taught how to shoot. I went down on the bayous almost every day to hunt turtles. Their small heads made good targets for sharp shooting. By the time I was ten years old I could compete with the best of men who were around forty years old. This experience came in handy when I later became a soldier.

The death of Stonewall Jackson was one of the greatest misfortunes to befall the Confederacy. Jackson was running against Hooker, who had almost three companies to his one. The night before Jackson was shot I had been out all night scouting and spying on the Union army. I learned that it was Hooker's intention to corral Jackson in the jungle. Hooker had concentrated on Chancellorsville, located ten miles southwest of Fredericksburg and connected to it by a corduroy road and macadamized turnpike. The country towards Fredericksburg was somewhat open, but in every other direction it was covered with thickets of dwarf pine and stunted oak. On the south end of Chancellorsville there was a corduroy road crossing toward Gordonsville, which the federals had orders to capture first. Hooker was plotting to throw his front column to a place about four miles toward Gordonsville where there was a small ford, then swing around with a fish-hook grip and await orders. His front column was divided into two columns. The rear end was to go back to Culpepper's grist mill and swing around at the point of Seven Forks. I told Jackson what Hooker was plotting and he was overjoyed at knowing his plans. Jackson consulted his road engineer, who told him there was only one way to get beyond the jungle and that was by a cow trail. Jackson took two men of his staff and six couriers and started out to explore the lay of the land. Before leaving he gave orders not to fire unless cavalry should approach from the direction of the enemy. One and a half miles from Chancellorsville Jackson left the plank road. Unfortunately, he approached his men from the direction of the enemy and was killed by them. Both men of his staff were wounded. No one knew anything about his being shot until it was over. Mayes, one of the couriers, and I had crossed the road about fifteen to twenty feet from Jackson and were so near when the shots were fired that they almost got us. I helped carry Jackson on a stretcher and I watched over him after he was shot. He might have lived if he hadn't insisted on putting cold applications to his wound, which caused pneumonia to set in.

Being small of stature and delicate of features, all I had to do to fool the enemy was dress up like a dame. I use to get around a lot of places in this way and spy on the Union army. That is how happened to be dubbed the "Petticoat Spy." I was in many dangerous places that the other men would not dare to go. I had some fine dresses and pretty bonnets and it was hard for them to detect me from a girl.

The nearest I ever came to being recognized as a spy was during the surrender. I was standing on the courthouse steps at Appomattox, all dressed up in the finest ladies clothing you've ever seen. Lee was consulting with Grant and I tried to give him a signal. One of the men saw me and thought I was flirting. I dropped my head so the bonnet would shelter my face and he mistook this gesture for shyness. Then Grant came so close to me that I was afraid he might detect some part of my make-up. I was never recognized as a spy and I usually got the information I went after without being bothered.

Frank Eli Powell, one of the two last survivors of the Louisiana Tigers, was decorated at the Confederate Reunion held at Columbia, S. C. August 1938, for being the oldest veteran attending the reunion and for travelling the farthest distance.

"GRAY BACKS," FIRST ENEMIES ENCOUNTERED

W. J. PRICE, Aiken, S. C. Confederate.
B. Jan., 21, 1848, Aiken, S. C. Co. D, 2nd
S. C. S. T., Bamberg, S. C.

In August 1864, the Governor of South Carolina issued a call for all boys between seventeen and eighteen years of age to meet at Bamberg. Lacking several months of being seventeen, I had to shove up my age in order to enlist.

Colonel William Duncan, of Barnwell, and Captain Robert Willis, of Williston, were my officers. After we organized, I was sent home and told to be ready when the call came to serve. In November, we were ordered to report for duty at Bamberg. After being there for a while, we were put in box cars and sent to Charleston and later to Grahamville.

No provision had been made for feeding us and for nearly two days we didn't have anything. We decided one night to see what we could find. Discovering a turnip patch, we gathered all we could lug back to camp. Our mouths watered with the thought of having a tasty meal, but when we got back to camp, we found that the turnip tops were in bloom and the stalks were old and dry. They had about as much flavor as chewing a grape vine, but at least we could tease ourselves into feeling that we had eaten.

We were moved, after a day or so, to an old camp site, where we met our first enemies, known to us as gray backs, but called cooties in the World War.

We were kept in this camp for several weeks, during which time a great many of us broke out with measles. Our company was ordered to march on and leave the sick behind. We were later moved to Charleston and housed in the Citadel; kept there for a while and then sent to a hospital in Cheraw, and, finally, to a convalescent camp.

While in this camp, we got word that an army would pass one day, so we went down to the road to see the boys. Along came my old company, and the urge to fall in line with them overcame me. I ran back to the tent, gathered up my few belongings and took my place in the ranks. The next day I was detailed to regular guard duty. By that time, I was feeling exhausted from marching in my weakened condition and so tried to get excused, but received no sympathy at all. They told me that if I was too weak to go on duty I should have remained in the convalescent camp.

On a march to Raleigh, N. C., we were halted to rest. I lay down in a fence jamb and dozed off to sleep. When we were ordered to proceed, I immediately obeyed, marching on some distance before realizing that I had left my gun behind. I had to do some tall sprinting to recover it and catch up with my company.

From Raleigh we were sent to Spartanburg in cattle cars which had not been cleaned since the cattle had occupied them. We drilled at Spartanburg for weeks until it was growing monotonous. We noticed that officers seemed to be gradually disappearing, but did not learn until later that the war was over. Finally, we were told to go home, but to report in twenty days at Orangeburg. We told our story to the conductor of the first train that came along and he took us to Ninety-Six, the nearest station to our home. From there we hiked the rest of the way. We passed through territory where Sherman's army had demolished everything.

At the beginning of the war, Wheeler's company pitched camp about four hundred yards from my present home. They stripped us of everything they could utilize, even using our fence rails for camp fires. The ravages of hunger and cold drove his men to such extreme action in their own southland.

I like to think and talk about the War between the States, because the most unusual happenings of my life occurred during that time; but I feel today that we are one nation with one great interest which we would all fight to defend.

CANNON BALL DECAPITATES HIS BUDDY

JOSEPH F. QUILLIN, Whitener, Ark. Confederate.
B. July 5, 1847, Centerville, Tenn. Co. D.
34th Ark. Cav., Fayetteville, Ark.

At the age of sixteen I was engaged in a battle at Poison Springs. When a fellow is in battle he hasn't time to think of danger, but acts instinctively. He has made up his mind to enter the fight and, once in it, he pushes forward with all his might without regard for life. During this battle it seemed that shots and shells were falling around us like pepper from a shaker. I and my buddy were fighting right alongside of each other. A cannon ball came whizzing along and clipped off his head and it rolled over, falling right at my feet. Every inch of fight in my body went into full action. I thought my time would come next and I gave them plenty of contest.

There was right smart to eat most of the time in my company. Once, we had to go on a march for about thirty hours and hadn't a thing to eat until some corn came for the horses. Then an ear was apportioned to each of us. I was thankful to get it and thought it tasted mighty good and sweet. Later on, we got some flour, but didn't have any salt or lard to make up a dough. We mixed the flour with water and stuck it on a stick to bake over the fire.

One night a bunch of us from the main army were within about fifty miles of the enemy. We put pickets out on all the roads to guard us from a surprise invasion.

Thus, at ease, we prepared for a night's rest. The town's citizens got their guns and, approaching from the side toward the enemy starting firing. We hopped into our saddles like a bunch of cowboys, rode twenty miles, stayed in line and held our horses until morning. Then, next day, we learned that we were seventy miles from the Yanks. Our leader said, "A good run beats a bad stand."

I am ninety-two years young and can't see so very well anymore. But I saw plenty on the trip to the Gettysburg reunion of the Blue and Gray, and I'll always be ready to go back there again.

SAVES OLD GLORY

DANIEL REAMS, Seattle, Wash. Union.
B. Oct. 22, 1846, Chillicothe, Ohio.
Co. K., 75th Ill. Inf. Paw Paw, Ill.
Aug. 12, 1862; Co. F, 1st Reg. U. S.
Vet. Vol. artificer. Dis. June 27, 1865.

I saved Old Glory from her grave in the battle of Chickamauga, September 20, 1863. Our flag bearer, a brave young lad, was shot in the head. The same shell that killed him tore our beloved flag from its staff. Before it touched the ground, I caught its shattered pole and rammed it into the butt of my gun, and kept its proud colors floating at the head of our command.

In this campaign, our movements were discovered by the Confederates and before we knew what was happening we were hemmed in between Missionary Ridge and Lookout Mountain. General Braxton Bragg had seized all the railroads and blockaded the Tennessee River. Our food supply had been cut off as well as reenforcements. It looked as though we were going to slowly starve to death. Two men of our forces were asked to volunteer to take a message through from Logan's headquarters to Sheridan. I was detailed to go, but the order was countermanded. The man who went in my place never came back.

It seemed days before any help came to us. General Smith engineered a plan that sent the blue coats on their way. Then General Grant arrived with more forces. It seemed that all of a sudden Union men began to pour in from all directions. General Braxton Bragg had his army of men fortified on the mountains surrounding us and they were in a safe position until reenforcements came to our aid. Men began climbing right up the steep mountainsides. They covered hill and dale like a nest of ants and soon overpowered the Confederates. There was a hot conflict for two days. I stuck to the fight as best I could, but was soon wounded. One of the balls that was taken out of my chest is a memoir of that battle that I keep.

I remember Abraham Lincoln well. One of the proudest times of my life was when he came to our house for dinner. He was a man of the people and everyone loved him.

As I near the age of a century, I am proud that I have many friends and no enemies. My advice to young people is to be honest, save money, buy a home, get married and rear a family.

I bear no enmity toward anyone and feel that we all fought for what we thought was right. The Gettysburg reunion was mutually enjoyed by the North and the South, I am sure.

RIDES A MULE IN DRESS PARADE

WILLIAM H. REEDY, Denver, Colo. Union.
B. July 7, 1844, Ralls Co., Mo. Co. C.
39th Mo. Vol. Inf., Louisiana, Mo.; Co. G,
14th Mo. Cav. Dis. Mar. 14, 1865, St. Louis, Mo.

Being of an even temperament, I don't know of anything exciting or romantic to relate.

I enlisted July 30, 1864, at Louisiana, Mo., and went from there to Hannibal, where I was mustered in about the 28th of June. From there I went by train to Florence and started south toward Jefferson City.

We camped in the fair grounds at Paris, Mo., with three other companies. While there, Quantrel's band of marauders, of which Jesse and Frank James were members, were camping at Centralia, about thirty miles distant. They took eleven of our soldiers, who were on furlough, off the train and lined them up. The people were outraged over this act. Company H and a company of the 39th Infantry, commanded by Colonel Johnston, mounted and went in pursuit of Quantrel's band. When they arrived, they counted off every fourth man to take care of the horses; and the others, armed with muskets and sabers, formed in line and marched toward the outlaw's camp. As soon as these companies fired a volley the enemy rushed on them, brandishing a revolver in each hand, and murdered all but five men. These five took flight as soon as they realized the situation and were saved.

The news of this disaster reached our camp about midnight. At this time, about twenty of our men were out scouting for other outlaws. The rest were asleep. Our Second Lieutenant awakened all the fellows in camp and ordered them to move to a school house. I was always a sound sleeper and the call did not arouse me. I slept on peacefully until a man went around making a final checkup and discovered me. I was quick to join my company. About this time, there were three rapid explosions of shells in the distance. Our Lieutenant was pacing around, as nervous as a June bride, asking what he should do. The rest of us were scared half to death, but no enemy came.

The first time I heard the roar of guns was when we neared a troop of men who were practicing. I began to realize then what it would feel like to face the fire in actual battle.

We camped for the winter in Glasco. Just before the holidays my company was ordered to Nashville, but I had the measles and had to go to the hospital, so was left behind.

I remained in the hospital until February, when my period of service terminated and I was mustered out at St. Louis.

About April 20th, I enlisted in Company G, 14th Missouri Cavalry in St. Louis. A horse and equipment were assigned to me and I left for Kansas.

I had a mighty good buddy about this time that I would do most anything for, and my regard for him sure got me into an embarrassing situation. He was detailed to go immediately on an important errand, and was assigned a mule to ride. Well, the most contrary thing on earth is a balking mule. My comrade's mount was in an uppety mood and put his big hoofs firmly on the ground and refused to budge; except when my comrade tried to get on his back, then up would go his hind heels and to the ground would go my buddy. Time was slipping by and Ed needed to be on his way. He came to me, with tears in his eyes and begged me to let him ride my horse. I couldn't refuse him, but, of course, I did not know then that I would soon be called to go on dress parade. When this order came, our troops came marching right alongside of me on horses, and there I was a-riding the mule. He was not stubborn then, nor did he try to balk. He stuck his proud nose in the air and pranced along as though he belonged there.

I was at Fort Riley for awhile and then went to a point on the Little Arkansas River, where I was mustered out.

My ninety-fourth birthday was spent on the train, returning home from the Blue and Gray Reunion at the Gettysburg battleground.

WITH "BUTCHER COMPANY" AT ANTIETAM

LOUIS F. RIEB, Pittsburgh, Pa. Union.
B. Feb. 4, 1840, Baden. Germany, Co. B,
123rd Reg. Penn. Vol. Alleghany, Pa.
Dis. May 13, 1863, Harrisburg, Pa.

My first attempt at enlistment was met with rejection by the examining physician. My second attempt was sponsored by Captain Hugh B. Murphy, so resulted in my acceptance. The physician said, "Let him go. If he dies, he will just die."

My physical condition at the time was not of the best, but nine months of outdoor life seemed to put new vigor into me. I was never sick or had occasion to be under a doctor's care during the entire term of service; except when I was wounded during the engagement at Fredericksburg, and sent to Point Lookout, Md., to recover.

Company B was made up largely of butchers from Alleghany, and was known as the "Butcher Company," though by trade I was a tinner. The day before our departure for Harrisburg, we were given a sumptuous dinner by the butchers of the old Alleghany Market.

Entraining for Harrisburg, we arrived in time for a good breakfast. Then on to Baltimore, where we were furnished dinner by the Union relief. Then on to Washington, expecting to get a good supper, but instead were served hardtack and coffee.

The next day we marched to Fairfax Seminary, Va., went into camp and had our first experience on picket duty. Shortly after we broke camp, we returned and crossed the Potomac River at Georgetown and went into Washington. Here we lay in the streets all night with no shelter of any kind. The next morning we exchanged our arms at the Navy Yard and encamped in an open tract of land near Washington, but still had no tents. On Monday morning we broke camp and entered on a forced march to Antietam, crossing South Mountain. On Sept. 17, 1862, we were ordered to load our guns and form in line of battle.

Our next march was toward Falmouth where we crossed over into Fredericksburg. I was in a battle there on December 13, 1862, where I was wounded. I was sent to the hospital at Point Lookout, Md., after a period of convalescence, I was at length ready to return to my regiment, which I reached in time to engage in the battle of Chancellorsville in May 1863. Shortly after, by reason of expiration of term of enlistment, I was mustered out of service and returned home to take up the duties of a private citizen.

In 1866, I started in business on East Ohio Street, Alleghany, Pa. (now Northside, Pittsburgh), and have been in the same location ever since. Now in my ninety-ninth year, I am able to be at my place of business every day.

I'm enjoying the reunion at Gettysburg as much as anyone could. I expect to attend the reunions so long as they last. So far as I know, I am the only survivor of both my company and regiment.

GAVE HIS LIFE TO SAVE HIS FLAG

By Lena Epperly MacDonald

My grandfather, Peyton G. Richardson, died the way he would have chosen to die-saving the flag for which he fought. That is the story brought back to his family by a companion in arms-a story since repeated to me by the daughter of that fellow comrade, wearer of the gray, a story I have every possible reason to believe unquestionably authentic.

Peyton G. Richardson answered the call of Jefferson Davis and the Confederacy and enlisted in Company I of the 54th Virginia Infantry, C. S. A., at Floyd, Va. In the same company there enlisted a neighbor, Jake Boyd by name, who had known my grandfather all his life. It was Mr. Boyd that brought back news of my grandfather's death to his family. It was Mr. Boyd's daughter, Mrs. Matilda Ann Earles, now and elderly woman, who told the story to me many times, stating that her father, Mr. Boyd, had repeated it frequently.

"It was at the siege of Atlanta which took place during May 13 to 16, 1864, that 'Pate' Richardson was killed. We were fighting with General Joseph E. Johnston's army and our company was them commanded by Captain Burrell Akers. The Yankees had been pushing us hard. We had lost a great many men. The Confederate loss, as it developed later, was 2,800 men for the three days.

"We were then at Resaca, Georgia, and fighting desperately. On May 16th the Yankees were again attacking in force and we were being slowly driven back. All at once our flag was shot down. Several of us moved to rescue it. I was within a few feet of 'Pate' Richardson and heard him say, 'I'll get it.' He did get that flag, too, and had it safe in our lines again when a Yankee bullet hit him. He died almost instantly but several of us noticed that he seemed to be kinda smiling as if he had done what he wanted to do before they got him. Looked to me like had died the way he wanted to die - doing something for the country he loved."

In commemoration of the heroism of Peyton G. Richardson and David Epperly, the Epperly-Richardson Banner will be presented to the Historical Division, United Daughters of the Confederacy, Montgomery, Alabama, in November, 1940, by their granddaughter, Lena Epperly MacDonald.

With highest esteem

Lena Epperly MacDonald
Sponsor for the Dist. of Col.
Staff of General Julius F.
Howell, Commander in.
Chief United Confederate
Veterans Washington
D.C. Oct 8th-11th 1940.

Peter Binkley

John S. Davisson

Charles Freeman Dunn

George Rummelhart

SURVIVORS OF THE BLUE

243

ON CHASE FOR BOOTH AFTER ASSASSINATION

GEORGE RUMMELHART, Omaha, Nebr. Union
B. May 25, 1848, Erie Co., Pa. Co. L
8th Ill. Cav. Jan. 26, 1864 St. Charles,
Ill. Dis. July 17, 1865, Benton Barracks, Mo.

One of the most thrilling events of my whole life was when I went on a chase for Booth after Abraham Lincoln was shot. On April 14, 1865, President Lincoln was enjoying the play, Our American Cousin, in the old Ford Theatre on Tenth Street in Washington. His box was several feet from the stage and was draped in a United States flag. About ten o'clock, Booth entered the theatre and presented credentials to the guard permitting him to enter Lincoln's box. It seems that none of the party were aware of his presence until he pressed a single-barreled derringer at Lincoln's head. Booth, in trying to escape, jumped onto the stage, but the spurs on his boots caught in the flag and he fell, breaking his leg. In spite of this, he made his exit and mounted a horse just outside the theatre and fled. We had a merry chase trying to find him. He was hid away in an old barn and we had to shoot him as he would not surrender.

Another exciting time was when my regiment was down on the Mississippi River and our boat sunk. All the men were transferred to another boat, but more than a hundred fine horses and other equipment were lost.

YOUNGEST COLONEL COMMANDING A REGIMENT OF THE ARMY OF THE POTOMAC

COLONEL H. C. RIZER, Washington, D. C. Union.
B. Feb. 1, 1844, Cumberland, Md. Co. C. 3rd
Reg. Potomac Home Brigade, Md. Vol. Inf. Sept.
16, 1861. Dis. May 29, 1865, Baltimore, Md.
Died July 21, 1938.

In the Army of the Potomac, I held every official rank in my regiment, except that of second lieutenant. I was corporal, sergeant, first lieutenant, captain, major, lieutenant-colonel, and colonel. I refused a brevet (honorary generalship) when I was mustered out-too many empty titles were being given out.

I served throughout the four years of the war, and the nearest I ever came to being wounded was when a sniper shot at me and it went through the sole of my boot. The shock of the near-casualty filled me with misgivings. Thinking that my leg was gone, I refused medical aid and grimly determined to keep fighting and help my regiment until my last ounce of strength should be spent—when all that happened was a bullet had pierced the sole of my shoe.

I regret that I could not join my two Confederate friends, General Emmett Waller and Major Bob Wilson, in attending the Gettysburg reunion. On Memorial Day, I represented the G. A. R. and they represented the Confederacy, when we flew in an airplane over Arlington Cemetery and strew rose petals on the graves of our deceased comrades. We spoke in a microphone while we were high in the clouds and the people in Washington heard us.

GETS ALL HIS WOUNDS FACING THE FIGHT

ROBERT P. SCOTT, Commander in Chief, Texas Div.,
U. C. V., Dallas, Texas. Confederate. B. May 7,
1846, Tallahatchie Co., Miss. Price's Brig.,
Co. C, White Co., Ark.

I hate to tell how I happened to join the army because I'm a peace loving citizen and don't believe in fighting, unless the safety of my home and loved ones is threatened, but when I fights I don't make no "piece meal" out of it. So, I will tell my story and the Lord can be my judge as to whether I was right.

I was near the barn, grinding corn on an old hand mill. It was just about dark, and our family were in the room where we usually gathered after supper. My mother was carding cotton, my two sisters were spinning, and father was sitting in a rocking chair scraping ax handles. A man with six-shooters on him entered the house, and I went up there to see what he was about. He was a man who ran the blockade for Devall Bluff. The old spy was a-bringing Yankees through the country. Well, when I got to the house, this man had my father by his long chin-whiskers, and was saying in no uncertain terms, "I'll cut your dam throat if you tell on me." I grabbed a pick and stabbed him twice in the back. For some reason or other he didn't try to shoot me, but ran out behind the house through the woods a-ways and got behind a tree. I slipped up on him, but he had keeled over-dead. I took his guns, went back to the house, and told my father what had happened. He said, "They will find this out and kill us." But I said, "No, I'll fix that." That night I hitched the mule to the single-tree, tied the man onto it, dragged him over to the river and dumped him in. I joined Captain McCoy's company the next day.

Two days after I joined we were down at Desert Bayou. We ran in on the Yankees and for the first time I had occasion to fight. I and McCoy were in front. We fired and then they fired. They killed McCoy. I ran behind a tree and reloaded my gun, but my company all retreated. A big Yankee came running up—I'll never forget how gentle I thought he looked-and charged on me. I put both barrels into him and he was dead. I ran and when I saw that all of my company were gone, I played rabbit and took to the woods as fast as I could.

Once, the enemy got me and twenty-four others penned up in a river bend in Louisiana, from which there apparently was no escape. Just as hope was abandoned, General Quantrell rode up and suggested that at daylight we try to break through the enemy lines. General Quantrell's theory was that the enemy guards would easily be overpowered and the Yankees, surprised at breakfast with their guns stacked, would be unable to resist. This proved all right and we escaped without a man being wounded.

In Eastern Louisiana, during the closing days of the war, my chin was nearly shot off by a bullet, it was barely hanging on, and my right eye was shot out. I fell, and about that time they hit me on the head with a saber, leaving an eight inch gash, then they stuck me through the left side. All my upper front teeth were shot out too. My legs were about the only part of my body that was left whole. I ran until I came to a house where the kind people tore up an old pillow slip and tied up my chin. Then I made my way on home. My mother administered the only other medical treatment I had. I'll tell you, there is no care that can beat that of a loving mother and the good old home remedies. Well, when I got well, I looked so ugly, I just knew the family was going to be ashamed of me, but mother said, "Bob, I'm mighty proud they got you in the face instead of the back."

I have attended forty reunions, traveling eight thousand miles to do so. I own a pistol 130 years old, which was handed down to me by my father. He lent it to a friend who used it in the Indian uprising.

I am one of the oldest United States Marshals now living, having served in Mississippi in 1872.

I buried the hatchet long ago with the North, and during this reunion I've shook hands with the boys in Blue and kissed their wives and daughters. David Pruitt is my attendant and we plan to go to Columbia, S. C., to the State Confederate reunion next month.

SOUTHERN CAUSE LOST, BUT SOUTHERN CHIVALRY WILL NEVER DIE

D. W. SEIGLER, Columbia, S. C.
Confederate. B. July 8, 1848, Orangeburg, Co. S. C.
Co. B, 20th S. C. Reg., Charleston, S. C.

Early one cold wintry morning, on December 5, 1864, a youth, just emerging into sixteen, felt that he could say, "Bravo, better battlefield than fire-side at home!" He bid adieu to an affectionate mother and father and devoted sisters, drove ten miles through an extremely cold western wind, and turned his face toward the battlefield.

Arriving at Windsor, a station on the Southern Railroad, we soon boarded the train for Charleston, S. C., arriving there at 7:30 p. m., having, as we thought, made a good run on regular schedule, a distance of one hundred and seven miles in twelve hours. We stopped at the Charleston Hotel, securing a room for the night for which we paid $15.00 in Confederate currency. It was impossible to get a meal there as Sherman's army was expected at any moment. We left Charleston with a view of reaching our army sometime during the day. It was encamped somewhere along the Salkehatchie River, not far from Pocataligo. We reached the camp about sunset and soon located the brigade, regiment, and company in which we were to enlist. Our names were enrolled by the Orderly Sergeant of Company B, 20th S. C. Regiment, Kershaws brigade. We were at once mustered into regular service and required to perform every duty incumbent upon a Confederate soldier.

About a week after enlisting, early one gloomy morning, we received orders to prepare to move. The great question with me for a time was how I should carry all my equipment. The problem was solved, by seeing how the other boys did, and I soon had my cartridge box belted around my waist, my canteen around my neck, my blanket over my shoulder, and rifle under my arm.

After a march of twenty-eight miles through mud and water, in which you could at no time see your feet, about dark we struck camp.

A guard was at once detailed. D. W. Siegler was the first name called. We were soon formed and marched out under a commissioned officer and carried into a dense swamp and stationed on the banks of the Salkehatchie River, with rigid instructions not to make a single step from under the shadow of the tree by which we were placed. We could plainly hear the Yanks talking. Our instruction was, if we saw anyone advancing from the opposite side of the river, to call halt one time and then fire. Soon after I was placed under a little pine. A large owl came and lit in the top of the tree. I could have touched him with my gun. Momentarily he yelled out, "Who, Who!" It seemed that he was saying to me, "Who are you?" I felt like answering, "I am the lad who felt now like saying, 'Bravo, better the fireside at home than the battlefield'."

My first night as a guard passed without any unusual occurrences. Our regiment remained at this encampment about ten days, bidding defiance to General Sherman's advance guard, but upon the approach of his main army, I had my first experience in a stampede. Before we were aware of it, they had us almost surrounded. We lost a few in killed, and quite a number in captured. My immediate company was so scattered that we did not get together again for a day. Upon roll-call the next morning, every man answered to his name, showing none of our immediate company killed or captured, evidencing that we were good and willing runners.

As soon as arrangements could be made, we were put aboard a freight train under heavy cannonading. The energy's guns were directed right down the railroad track and the shells whistled above our heads. How flat the boys would lie on the top of the car! We soon landed in Charleston, where we began preparing to evacuate the city by burning all warehouses containing provisions or cotton. Of course, cotton is valuable in warfare for use in making cushions for shells. Well, we spent the entire night destroying everything that could be of service to the enemy.

Last of all, we blew up our fine gunboat. A singular coincidence occurred immediately after it was blown up. As the smoke ascended from the explosion of hundreds of pounds of gunpowder, it formed a Palmetto tree, which for a time remained a perfect picture. Then it gradually vanished, the scene lasting probably five minutes. In a short time the enemy from the blockade off Charleston Bar began landing at the foot of Trad Street. A detachment of about one hundred men had been detailed to remain in the city long as possible to take out every man, cow and horse, but 'we were so pushed by the enemy that we had to leave everything and make our escape by going at double-quick speed for seven miles. I heard

a little girl say, "General Sherman was right when he said `War is Hell'."
That night we arrived at Monks Corner, some twenty miles from
Charleston, where General Joseph Johnston took command of our army,
and arranged for a general retreat with a view to reaching General Lee at
Richmond, if possible. We kept up a continuous march.

Since my war records were all burned, when my father had the
misfortune to lose his home by fire, I am unable to give any dates until the
surrender of General Johnston.

As previously stated, arrangements had been made for a general
retreat, which was now begun and continued until we arrived near Cheraw,
S. C., where Sherman's advance guard began pressing us too hard. A line
of battle was formed and the army was ordered to fortify itself. We soon
had substantial breastworks thrown up of logs and sand. We worked all
night on these fortifications and by daylight we felt perfectly safe behind
them, which we were. Just then the captain of my company received orders
to have five men detailed for sharpshooting. D. W. Siegler was the first
name called. My feelings just at that moment were hard to describe.

I never saw providential protection so visibly demonstrated as one
time when we were ordered to mount the breastworks and double-quick.
Times were so exciting that men had to be rushed as shots and shells were
falling like rain drops. When we were about a hundred yards from the
enemy line, we were ordered to fire, lie down and load, then rise and fire.
Our commanding officer soon saw that our little squad of a hundred men
would be sacrificed and no real good accomplished, so he gave orders to
fall back. Our comrades were falling on both sides of us, yet we were
untouched. The little lad never prayed more earnestly for God's kind
protection, and it was so visible that his faith was rewarded.

As we were retreating to our breastworks in full view of the enemy
who were advancing upon us with a full line of men at a double-quick, it
did not seem possible for a single man to escape. As we attempted to
mount our breastworks, a few of us succeeded in going over. It was there
that we witnessed the first slaughtering of men. The enemy charged our
works six times in a few hours and were repulsed every time. The killed
and wounded was high. Comparatively few of our men were killed as we
were so well protected by our breastworks. Sherman soon learned the only
way to rout us was by flanking. He stretched out his line and about
midnight had us on the run. We were soon on North Carolina soil. After a
time we arrived at Aversborro.

After another week of hard marching, we encamped near Bentonville, N. C. Sherman was pressing so close upon us that we again had to remind him that he could not run over us. After two days of hard fighting he saw the folly of his attempt. As before, he ordered a flank movement. We were soon in full retreat. This was the last battle I was in. We continued our retreat until near Greensboro, N. C.

General Sherman, under a flag of truce, notified General Johnston that he felt both armies had sacrificed enough men. They met in a farmhouse and an armistice was framed and the terms of Johnston's surrender was soon arranged. On April 26, 1865, we stacked our guns and were marched away under a Yankee band playing "Dixie." The Southern Cause was lost, but Southern Chivalry will never die!

Clarence Richards is my attendant at the Gettysburg reunion. We hope to attend many more. In fact, I hope to be the last one to go the last step of the way for the United Confederate Veterans.

RISKS DEATH, BUT NEVER FALLS TO DELIVER DISPATCHES

ROBERT B. SITTON, Horseshoe, N. C. Confederate.
B. Nov. 1, 1848, Buncombe Co., N. C. 14th N. C.
Cav., June 1, 1863, Asheville, N. C.

I served under the command of General Vance until he was captured in Tennessee about 1864. During this time we made a raid across the Smoky Mountains. There was only a dim road, ambulances, artillery, and a regular wagon train. The mountains were steep and slick with ice, so we had to tie ropes to the trees and let the wagon train down "block and tackle."

General Vance advanced to the rear of the Federal army and took them by surprise, capturing everything they had. He separated his forces and hemmed the Yankees in between. Then he went on into Tennessee and sent a message for us to come to him. We did not get the message in time, and ice was so thickly coated on the roads that we could not travel after night, so our command went down to Pigeon River and crossed French Broad River. The Yankees came in the rear of us, but we kept them back. General Vance thought he was out of danger, but the Yankees followed and captured him after night. He remained in prison until just before the surrender. He was one fine man, I tell you.

On December 25, 1864, General Palmer replaced General Vance. I was assigned to his staff as courier and served until the end of the war. A dispatch was never tendered to my care that was not delivered. Sometimes I had very close calls, but I always made my deliveries.

When I travelled in the night, the darkness helped conceal me from the enemy, but there was a time when it proved my undoing. My horse was swift and fearless, and when I mistook the stretch of a river for a clear road and drove into it, I had to get out the best way I could.

I arrived in Morgantown just before its invasion by the Yankees. People were fleeing for dear life. Women and children were making as fast time as they possibly could while dragging a few of their belongings. When a horse was available, as many as could clung on his back. There

255

were mothers with small children clinging to their skirts, and decrepit old folks wheedling themselves along. The countenances of all were tense with fright as they rushed along, to God knows where, but nevertheless fleeing. Every now and then someone would take time to warn me to turn back, but not I, I had a duty to perform-I would deliver my dispatch if it meant death in the attempt. To fail would jeopardize a whole army, I would not fail them. The receiver of the dispatch was waiting, brave and anxious, despite his dangerous position. He gave me an answer and then fled to safety-the last man to leave the picket post.

On my return the Yankees had my course blocked, so I tried to circle around them. They followed me in pretty close pursuit. When I reached a country house, I thought I would be safe in resting my horse, but it was not long before some Yanks came in sight. Another fellow, on a horse, came along about this time and the Yankees started chasing him, thinking that it was I.

Later that same evenings the Yanks almost got me. I was saved by my horse jumping a gulley that was too broad for their mounts. When it was too late to continue my journey, I stopped at the home of a very kind lady. Her husband did not want to go to war, so she kept him hid in the barn. She told me that I could sleep at her house if I would not bother anything. She fed me well and gave me a comfortable bed in one of the back rooms. I was so tired that I went sound to sleep-just dead to the world. In the wee, quite hours of morning, I felt a soft hand affectionately caressing and stroking my face. It startled me, but I was awakened so tenderly that I did not give any alarm. The lady was trying to warn me that the house was full of Yankees. I grabbed my clothes and got out of there in a hurry, escaping through the back way.

I don't know how on earth we ever lived on the little bit of food we got. Sometimes we only had parched corn. If providence was kind, we had cornmeal and bacon, but we never had salt or seasonings of any kind.

I attended the Gettysburg reunion with Sitton Allison as my attendant. I also attended the Columbia, S. C., reunion held in August. It is a great pleasure going to reunions and meeting all one's comrades. There is no bitterness now. We are proud that we had the courage to fight for the Cause that we believed in. We knew we were fighting against better organized and larger forces, that had the government behind them to furnish all their needs, but who can deny the courage of the Confederate Veterans.

A CONFEDERATE'S REASONS FOR THE WAR

PETER PIERRE SMITH, Washington, D. C. Confederate.
B. Apr. 19, 1844, St. Marys Co., Md. Co. B. 2nd
Md. Bat., Md. Line Troops.

The real issue out of which the War Between the States arose was that of Protective Tariff. The South was a cotton producing area, while the North was a manufacturing center. The South raised practically everything they required on their own soil. Cotton was the only commodity which they sold, and they produced the larger portion used throughout the world. They could buy more with their cotton in Europe than in the North and, naturally, the South wanted to buy in the cheapest market. The North felt that it needed protection from European competition, so set up a tariff wall around its industries. They wanted to force the South to buy their manufactured articles. The question became one of money capitalism in the North and feudal slave capitalism in the South. Anti-slavery and abolition were used merely as tools to keep their real objective obscured. Slavery was not an institution originally set up by the South, but the South was dependent upon slave labor.

When my mother and father were married, their parents gave them a number of slaves, among other things, with which to begin married life. Their original cost was very high. Naturally, good slaves were a valuable asset and an owner prized them as he would his home or any other property. Any man might justly be proud of being a large slaveholder. We were kind to them, gave them a decent home, and apportioned their work on the plantation so that everyone might do his part toward earning his keep. If a master had good slaves, his endeavors prospered and the slaves, as well as the master, were benefited.

As I said before anti-slavery and abolition were used as excuses by the North. They attempted to free our slaves without reimbursing us. Lincoln had got a bill through Congress to pay us a small amount for each slave that was set free, but I never knew the outcome of this movement.

The question of States Rights was predominant then, much more than it is today, and being a strong believer in States Rights led me to cast my lot with the Confederacy, for which Cause I believed in and fought for.

In 1862, my regiment went into winter quarters at Hanover Junction, Va. I was put on duty to guard a foreign deserter who was to be executed the following morning. The poor man could not stand the thought of death staring him in the face. It just set him wild. He dropped to his knees and in a loud, plaintive voice began praying, begging God to save him and declaring that it would break his dear old Christian mother's heart. This was too much for me. I put myself in his place and thought about how it would break my dear old mother's heart if anything happened to me. Well, I slipped a knife to him and turned my back. He was imprisoned in a canvas tent, which he slit in the back and climbed out. He was handcuffed and balls and chains bound his ankles, so he could not make much progress in getting away. Then he made the mistake of heading right toward the river. Of course, I could not speak to him, but I knew if he tried to swim the river with those weights on he would surely drown. I gave him plenty of time, to gain his bearings and reach safe ground before I fired my gun in the air. The corporal of the guard came rushing to my post to learn what had happened. I told him that my prisoner had got away, somehow. My buddy said to me, "Peter, be damned if I don't believe you let that prisoner get away." I gave him a pretty nasty look and said, "You'd better slow down on that kind of talk, unless you are aiming to get me in trouble around here." So he never mentioned the incident again so long as he lived, not even after the war.

I took part in the decisive battle of Gettysburg. It was there that a deep, long wound was inflicted on my leg and it has pained me all my life. Those things happen so quick that it is sometimes impossible to remember the surrounding circumstances. All I know is that a minnie ball struck me.

I was in all the engagements in the Valley of Virginia. Standing out in my memory as a veritable inferno was the battle of Cold Harbor. Then at Petersburg, I came near to being buried alive when the crater was blown up. My Company was right under it, but it did not reach our lines for about five hundred yards. Although two hundred Confederates were blown up in the air and many Federal soldiers were lost. My regiment had been sent out to locate where the mine was being dug. Grant had a bunch of niggers in his front line. They were loaded with whiskey and gun powder— whiskey to give them a feeling of boastful defiance and gun powder to fight us with. They came running toward us yelling, "No quarters, no quarters." Meaning that they were to take no prisoners but kill all of us. We started giving them the bayonet, and shot or captured nearly all who charged our lines. In later years, when I was employed at the Ebbitt Hotel, in Washington, we had a bell-boy, named Thomas Smallwood, who was the drummer boy for this outfit, and he verified this story.

In August 1864, one of my friends returned to camp from a furlough. He broke the sad news to me that my father had died in May, three months previous. Captain Crane, who was acting in the place of Colonel Hubbard (who had been wounded at Gettysburg and never returned to us), granted me a furlough, signed by him, Lt. Stone, and General Lee. I rode by train to Richmond and Hanover Junction and there I footed it home. When I arrived, our house was full of Yankees, who were using it as a headquarters. I had to slip in and keep hidden all the time I was there. When I started to leave, a guard on picket duty saw me jump the fence and took after me. He ran me into an open corn field. When he couldn't catch me, he got down on one knee to take aim and shoot, but his gun misfired. I saw that he was going to get me so I gave up. About sixty Yankees surrounded me about this time. They were going to try me as a spy, but my furlough signed by General Lee saved me. I was sent to Point Lookout Prison and kept in close confinement for sixty days, then put in a regular prison there. I was due to be sent to Richmond for exchange, but Lee surrendered, so I was a paroled prisoner of war.

An interesting experience was when Milroy's army eluded us and we captured it at Winchester. We had only one thousand men to their ten thousand, but we held them in check until Jackson's Corp, commanded by General Ewell, came to our support.

Then there was the time when orders came late one evening to double-quick it over to Gettysburg. In Harrisburg we came in contact with Mead's army and were ordered to charge. I've never seen men run so fast as the Yankees, as we went through the town we could have played marbles on their coat-tails.

Vivid in my memory are the courage and keen wit of a southern woman who was invaluable to the Confederacy as a spy. She was Belle Boyd, one of the finest horsewomen of her day and a beautiful creature to behold. She came into and went out of our camp at her pleasure. All the officers liked her and the men admired her. One day I was foraging on the outside of our lines when I heard the hoofs of horses at breakneck speed coming down the direction of Martinsburg to Winchester. I hid in the fence jamb to see what was happening. Here came Belle, just a-flying, with the

Yankees in right after her. She knew exactly where our picket line was. She lured her would-be-captors right into the trap and made them prisoners. These men were taken before the officer of the day and were shipped to Richmond. Even when Belle was captured and condemned for the third time, she turned the tables on the Federal officers-she married the last one who captured her. In later years she became an actress in England and then returned to America as a writer.

One thing about the Confederates, their horses being privately owned and trained were better saddle horses than the Federals' and the Confederates could usually outrun the Federals' mounted forces.

As the last survivor of my company and regiment, I want to say that we were opposed to fighting against the Stars and Stripes, but we were forced to fight for the protection of our rights. We stood the greatest test of courage to uphold the Cause we believed in. We endured the direness of a Lost Cause and its attending afflictions with faith, mercy and patience. We have lived to see the evolution of events prove that it is far better that we are united today, rather than a nation divided against itself and fighting as Europe is. I love my native country and its people, and I was happy to be privileged to attend a joint reunion with my brother soldiers-a wonderful symbol of the love and peace that we feel today as the United States.

YANKS AND JOHNNIE REBS HAVE THEIR GAMES TOGETHER BETWEEN BATTLES

ALFRED EDWIN STACEY, Eldbridge, N. Y. Union.
B. Jan. 20, 1846, Eldbridge, N. Y.
Co. L, 9th N. Y. Heavy Art., Sept. 5, 1864.

The spirit of patriotism was running high the day I joined the army. A gathering of townsmen had been called. Reverend Rogers, minister of the Baptist Church, who was usually a calm and meditative person, showed great excitement as he talked of our need for immediate action. His enthusiasm awakened the deep sense of loyalty and devotion of those present and a number of volunteers came forward.

I had some training as captain of a boy's military company, but that seemed mighty juvenile when I was thrown into the battle of Cedar Creek four days after enlistment. I was wounded twice during this battle. Once, while hustling to load my rifle, a bullet skinned across my nose. I still bear a vivid scar as a reminder of that escape.

We did not fight with our file of men far apart then as the army does today, and our Springfield rifles had a range of only about a half mile.

General Early had his Confederates camped about one quarter of a mile from ours. He came early one morning and drove the 8th and 19th. corps out of their beds, capturing and killing a lot of them. I belonged to the 6th Corp and they drove us back a considerable distance, taking our camp. Before nightfall we had beat them back and regained the ground they had taken. Sheridan came within nine feet of me and I heard him say, "We'll lick them out of their damned boots before night and sleep on their camp ground," and we did. There were one hundred Confederates on that camp ground that entered into their last long sleep that night.

Down on the line between Petersburg and Richmond, we were detached from our regiment and given a battery of thirty-pound parrot guns, the heaviest battery used in those days. We were also given six-inch co-horn mortars. I could have thrown a stone from our battery into the Confederate lines. Had they made a raid then, they could have captured all of us right off, but that was near the end of the war and they were indifferent about fighting and extra battle.

I was on guard at Battery Lee when Lincoln and his staff of officers were taking their last view of the situation.

The Confederates captured Fort Stedman one morning and we had it back by noon. Our battery kept two Confederate forts silenced all afternoon. I think it was General Meade in the next fort who sent a message to our captain asking if he had a man who could hit the Rebel headquarters, a little cottage about three miles away, under the command of General Hill. We didn't have a sighting gun, so it had to be done by eye. My brother Anthony was an expert gunner and his skill during that day had been observed by the officers. The captain had him take the sight with one shell to get the range, then fire a second shot. He planted a thirty-pound shell right against the side of the house and demolished it.

I did vidette duty on the Weldon railroad. The Johnnies used to come down this line about two or three times a week and capture from two to three hundred men from our pickets. After they made their capture, they put on the Union uniforms, disguising themselves, and went to [their lines?] We soon caught onto this trick and put an end to it.

You frequently hear of venom existing between Confederate and Union soldiers. As a veteran, I want to say that is more fiction than truth. We liked the Johnnies as fellows. Often when we were sent out for wood between the lines, we'd end up by visiting with the Johnnies. Of course, we didn't let the officers know about this. We were always swapping them sugar and coffee for tobacco. They had lots of tobacco, but didn't have much of anything else. We played many games together, but we had to hide from the officers to do it.

We used to invite the Johnnies into our camp and offer them jobs. We had teams to be driven where it was safe and for which they might receive $16 a month. That was more money than they had ever seen in the Confederate army and a few of them accepted the offer.

Now and then, when we'd go out looking for corn for our horses and mules, we'd run into a nest of slaves. I remember a plantation, back in the valley near Cedar Creek, where there were five women and three men. The clothes they wore were, well, you've probably never seen a dirty dish rag so filthy that you didn't want to handle it without a stick. They had a rag like that over each shoulder, with one down each leg, and one around the groin. We asked them if those were all the clothes they had. They said, "No we have Sunday-go-to-meeting clothes." We took a look at their so-called finery and they were awful rags. We told them to get in our wagon and we'd take them where they would be safe, get plenty to eat and wear, and be well treated. They were over-joyed to go with us.

When we were chasing Lee, we were resting in a little hollow near a prosperous looking plantation. The houses, barns and fences were painted white. Probably a hundred slaves were going about their daily tasks. They were dressed in clean cottons and were neat and orderly. They seemed happy and carefree and had every reason to be. Their security and surroundings were conducive to well-being. They had their own doctors and carpenters and everything they needed. So, I realized that there were many degrees of respectability among them, which depended largely upon their master's position.

Out of thirteen thousand men that enlisted from Onondaga County there are not over five living now. During the World War I was the only G. A. R. man from Onondaga on the draft board as the others were too old to serve.

In 1934-1935, I was elected Commander-in-Chief of the Grand Army of the Republic. In recommending me, a member of the Citizens Club said, "He earned all he got, he made a good soldier and that is all that counts."

My attendant at Gettysburg is George Cathers, whose grandfather was division general under Wellington in the battle of Waterloo.

WITH "THE FIGHTING SIXTH CORPS"

DEVALOIS W. STEVENS, Wasco, Ill. Union
B. Mar. 22, 1843, Elbridge, N. Y.
Co. G. 112th Reg. N. Y. Vol. Inf.
1st Brig. 3rd Div., Elbridge, N. Y.

Enlisting in August, we reached Washington on September 2nd. In two or three days we were in the battle of South Mountain, Md., not having a chance to drill. Two days later, we were in the battle of Williamsport in the foothills of South Mountain.

On September 17th, we were placed in the front ranks of the left wing of the battle of Antietam. McClellan defeated Lee after a hard battle. There were so many dead and wounded about us that the dead bodies were used like breastworks. Firing ceased at dark, but we were ordered to load our guns, fix bayonets, and stay in line of battle all night for a possible charge. The wounded were crying for help all around us, and it was soul-trying, I tell you, when we could not heed their cries.

Three battles, with all the horrors of war, occurred within two weeks after I left Syracuse-a terrible initiation into my war experience.

In the battle of Rappahannock Station, our brigade only, under General Schuyler, was engaged. Our pickets were on one side of the river and the Rebels on the other. The Rebels had built pontoon bridges across the river and thrown up breastworks a mile long to run a brigade of soldiers over. Our brigade was sent to drive them back. Our battle line formed at one o'clock and there was heavy fighting until dark. We thought the battle was over until the next day, at nine o'clock, we were ordered to load our guns and fix the bayonets. No one should speak, but forward march to within thirty feet of the enemy's breastworks. When the order came to fire and charge, we went over the breastworks and fought hand to hand. In fifteen minutes the Rebels surrendered. We took sixteen hundred prisoners and twelve cannons. We put a guard around the prisoners and marched them back to Sixth Corps Headquarters, amid the cheers of our division.

In December, 1862, our corps was in the front line of battle at Fredericksburg for forty-eight hours. Lee's men were fighting from behind a stone wall, which put us at a disadvantage.

Our next move was across the Rappahannock River into the foothills on the north side, reaching there at one o'clock at night, we were ordered to rest. We could build no fires to cook, so ate raw salt pork and hardtack-this after two days of heavy fighting. Two hours later, at three a.m., the order came to march until eleven o'clock at night. We did this for six consecutive days to reach Hooker and reinforce the Army of the Potomac. When they saw us come in they cheered and said, "Here comes the fighting Sixth Corps."

We reached Gettysburg at midnight on July 2nd. The next morning at daybreak, the third day of the battle of Gettysburg, one division was placed on the right wing, one in the center, and our division on the left to support Little Round Top. Two attempts were made by General Lee to take Little Round Top, but we drove his forces back. We followed Lee back into Virginia, the place we started from. Our men were near exhaustion after this strenuous experience.

When Grant went into the battle of the Wilderness there was a lot of musing among the soldiers as to why he wore white gloves and buttoned up his coat.

We suffered awful slaughters of men in the battles leading up to this one. The Confederates had the advantage here of an almost impenetrable forest and they gave hot contest. I was wounded by a musket ball that went through my left arm between the wrist and elbow, so I had to go to Mt. Pleasant Hospital.

At the Gettysburg reunion, on the seventy-fifth anniversary of this great battle, I sat on the monument dedicated to my division and had my picture taken.

D. W. Seigler

R. D. Hardester

M. A. Moore

Elbert Nunn

CONFEDERATE SURVIVORS

GUNS FIRE SEVEN SHOTS

DAVID L. STORY, Winchester, Mass. Union.
B. Feb. 18, 1843, Essex, Mass. Co. K. 40th
Reg. Mass. Beverly, Mass. Dis. June 16, 1865,
Richmond, Va.

I took part in one of the bloodiest small battles of the whole war. That was down at Olustee, Fla., where we lost over two-thirds of our men in three hours.

One morning the Johnnies charged us and we gave them one volley. They thought we would have to stop and reload our guns and they would come right on over and capture us, but we had guns that fired seven shots without stopping. We gave them another volley and they dropped just where they were-flat on the ground. We stopped firing and told them to come on in. They jumped up and came in and we took the whole lot of them. When they got inside our works, they looked both ways and said, "Where are all your men?" We told them, "This is all the men we have." They looked bewildered and said, "What! Have you got guns that wind up and fire all day?"

As I see the display of modern fireworks at this Gettysburg reunion, I fell mighty thankful that my warring days are over and I'll never have to face the volley of destruction they will spit out.

LIBBY AND ANDERSONVILLE PRISONS CURE HIM OF WAR SPIRIT

GILBERT D. STREETER, Orange, Mass. Union.
B. Aug. 4, 1846, Shelburn Falls, Mass.
Co. C. 27th Reg. Inf. Mass. Vol. Feb. 28, 1864.
Dis. June 9, 1865.

Joined a regiment that went to Norfolk and then to Fortress Monroe. My activities extended along the James River. Our first skirmish with the Rebels was on what was called Hickman Farm, and occurred the afternoon we landed at Bermuda Hundred. We engaged the enemy again at Oldfield Church.

On Sunday morning, May 16, 1864, we fought at Fort Darling, eight miles from Richmond. The Rebs captured about six hundred of my regiment there, including myself. They took us by boat to Richmond and put us in Libby Prison. The battlefield held no horrors greater than that place. It was lousy and filthy, filled with disease and suffering, and hunger and thirst. It is said that the men became so crazed by conditions there, they planned to make a break. The guards were afraid of the men and, in order to keep them in check, put out a grapevine rumor that the prison was encircled with dynamite that would be set off the moment the men got beyond bounds.

After a week in Libby, we were sent in cars to the Andersonville Stockade. At Andersonville, the wells went dry. For days there was no water and thousands died of thirst. It was here a legend originated that a group of Federal soldiers gathered in a circle at the foot of a hill and prayed to God to send them water to moisten their parched, swollen tongues. That prayer was answered when a little spring came trickling through the dry earth and provided water enough for all. That spring has been walled in and the story of its origin is carved in its stone wall.

The first of September, the leanest and weakest of the prisoners were picked out and sent to Charleston and later to Florence. So it was from Florence that I was paroled to our lines in March 1865.

The suffering in those "hell holes" the Rebs called prisons is substantiated by my own physical emaciation. Enlisting in the army a strong, robust lad, I came out a starved, raw-boned weakling of ninety pounds-a mere shadow of my former self. I'll tell you, ten and one-half months was enough war for me.

I reviewed the modern implements of warfare on parade here at the Gettysburg reunion with a prayer in my heart that they will never have to be used on human beings, and that President Roosevelt's attitude toward "Eternal Peace", expressed at the dedication of the monument, will live in the hearts of all future Presidents. Humans should be constructive, not destructive.

ON CHASE AFTER LEE

JOHN THOMPSON, Skaneateles, N. Y. Union.
B. Dec. 1, 1846, Victory, N. Y. Co, G, 40th
N. Y. Inf., Feb. 6, 1864, Auburn, N. Y.

I wasn't brave, but when the time came for me to fight for my country, well, it was like fighting for home and loved ones. Any man would go if he weren't a downright coward. My father and brother had been killed in the war and another brother was fighting, so I enlisted as soon as I got over a spell of fever.

I was in the battle of Hatcher Run and all the engagements around Petersburg. Then I went on a nine day chase after Lee. I didn't catch up with him until he surrendered at Appomattox.

The engagements around Petersburg lasted nine and a half months. We dug ditches and fought in them. We dug a mine under the Confederate main army and filled it with barrels of powder. This caused what was known as the Crater. When we fired the powder, the explosion underground blew up and killed a great number of the Confederates, then it formed a crater which sucked in our own men. They were struggling against all odds in the soft dirt when the Confederate's artillery opened up and mowed them down.

When General Lee surrendered at Appomattox, he went to the McLean home with Colonel Marshal and waited for General Grant, who arrived with General Sheridan, General Rawlins, Colonel Badeau and Colonel Parker. General Lee thought Colonel Parker, was a negro, but he was an Indian. They held a conference and came to terms. Six weeks later we were mustered out at Bailey's Cross Roads. During this time we were fed on beans, hardtack and coffee. Many times we got ahead of our wagon trains and ran entirely out of rations.

Soldiers in those days had to grab a bite to eat whenever they got a good chance. Sometimes we ate raw or half-done food, because we'd get an order to go into battle or on a march before we could finish cooking.

I remember Abraham Lincoln as a kind, tall gaunt man. He came with six of his staff to inspect the army at Petersburg. As he walked through our camp I just stood and looked at him.

"REBELS MOWED US DOWN LIKE GRASS"

A. F. TOLMAN, Manatee, Fla. Union.
B. Nov. 19, 1847, Warren, Maine.
Enlisted Camden, Maine, Aug. 15, 1864.
Dis. June 26, 1865.

In the year 1864, at the age of seventeen, I was enlisted in the Navy at Camden, Maine. I was examined in Portland and sent aboard a receiving ship at the Boston Navy Yard. It was then that we came to know gray backs (lice). They almost ate us up.

After a few weeks the Monandnock was ready, and her officers, crew and men were assigned. We had to throw away our lousy old clothing and buy new wearing apparel out of our monthly pay of $13.00. They were pretty navy suits of blue.

We left Boston for Fortress Monroe, our headquarters, and were all ready to take part at Fort Fisher, a strong rampart. The Monandnock had four fifteen-inch guns, two in each turret. Though we boys were green in war technique, we handled those guns like older hands. We were there two days, gave up the fight, and went back to Fortress Monroe. Then, on January 15, 1864, we went back to Fort Fisher. We rode out in a big storm on the powder boat that was to blow up the fort. The powder got wet and our plans could not be executed with the adeptness we had hoped for. One hundred and fifty men were detailed to go under the fort, lie flat on the ground, and wait until the land forces could get in back of the fort. A signal was to be given when the Navy boys should rise and make a charge. We were in a target position and the Rebels mowed our men down like grass. So, the order was changed to "No man from the ironclad can go ashore." We were lucky, because the land forces had a hand-to-hand fight that night. On the third day at ten o'clock the fort was surrendered. We blew it up, and blast was so terrific that the next morning arms and legs of men who were killed could be seen protruding from the ground, like so many posts.

One thing in particular, the fort had a six-inch rifle which did a lot of damage to our boat. The lieutenant went to the gunner and ordered, "Put that gun out of commission." The gunner tried three times to hit it, but missed by a large margin. The lieutenant grew impatient, and said, "Let me try it." He did, and the first shot hurled the gun down the mound.

I left my home to attend the Gettysburg reunion on June 16th. We stopped in Washington mid many other interesting places along the way. When the reunion was over, July 6th, we motored to Boston. We took in all the battlegrounds. Some sight.

THROUGH VIRGINIA WITH LEE AND JACKSON

FRANCIS MARION TRIMBLE, Stautnon, Va. Confederate
B. Aug. 3, 1844, Monterey, Va. Co. H, 31st Va. Inf.,
Monterey, Va.

All the boys in my community were joining the army. Naturally, I wanted to go to. I was not of army age though, so ran away from home without telling my father and mother.

Four of my uncles were already fighting: George W. Trimble, who was killed in the battle at Port Republic; Harvey Trimble, who died of fever while in the service; Jacob and Isaac Harper, who were both killed in battle.

Travelling by foot, I went with Jackson and Lee through the entire conquest of the Valley of Virginia. Grant's army crossed the Rapidan on May 5, 1864, and for six weeks we fought one of the most desperate attacks ever made. We were fighting to the south of Grant in what was known as the Wilderness. Grant had more than twice our number and was continually receiving reenforcements, while our army had to depend mainly on the forces at hand. They wedged in through pure might in numbers and drove us nearly to Richmond. Their losses during that six weeks were 55,000, which was more men than we had to start with. Bursting shells set fire to brush and many wounded men were burned to death on the battlefield.

Ragged and broken, our little army met a head-on attack from Grant at Spottsylvania, on May 8, 1864. We fought hand-to-hand with the enemy. A downpour of rain refreshed the atmosphere of a hot summer day, but made the mud stick faster than ever to our dirty rags and bodies. Bleeding and weary to the bone, I paused for a moment's breathing spell. All around me for a hundred-yard stretch the ground could hardly be seen for a mass of dead bodies. They were piled upon each other wherever they fell in battle. I was wounded in the side by a shell that gashed the flesh in three places and my clothes were literally riddled from my body. Oh, this was a bitter engagement. We fought until we were worn down and then fought some more. We were so greatly overpowered in number.

Then came the battle of Cold Harbor. We had to fight one day when the thermometer was about a hundred degrees. I was at Cedar Mountain and so many other places.

Sometimes with very little food to strengthen us, we went into battle. At best, we only had hardtack and bacon, but food and water were both scarce. The regiments wagon trains conveyed their food supplies.

We old Veterans were well provided for at the Gettysburg reunion, July 1938, and we had plenty of entertainment. S. D. Holsinger was my attendant and he treated me fit for a king.

THOSE WHO DIDN'T RUN AT BULL RUN
ARE STILL THERE

HENRY CLAY TURCK, New Orleans, La. Confederate.
B. Apr. 20, 1847, Lexington, Ky. Ky. Home Guards,
Lexington, Ky.

Sherman's Bummers were made up largely of conscripts and they were better destroyers than soldiers. When they came through my country there was a call for men to come out on the pike and defend the property from the raiders. They robbed us of all cattle and foodstuff in spite of all we could do.

Twenty-five Yanks were on the run after me at one time, but they never ketched me. I sneaked into a sewer and hid until they were gone.

We put the Yankees on the run at Bull Run. How they did run! Those who didn't run are still there.

A shot got me in the ankle and my leg had to be amputated three times. We had no high flalutin surgery in those days. Major Banks picked me up on the battlefield and got hold of a democrat, sort of spring wagon, and took me to Cincinnati to the hospital. I am one out of sixty thousand to survive a third amputation of the leg. This is according to the Royal British Medical Society. My ole wooden leg his served me for seventy-five years. One thing in my state, they can't hang a man with a wooden leg. No, sir, they hang him with a rope.

I'm having the time of my life at Gettysburg and I'll be down in Columbia next month to the state Confederate Convention. I never miss a reunion as it is the most fun I have in life.

IMPRESSIONS OF A 95-YEAR-OLD VETERAN

JOHN WESLEY TURNBOUGH, Eldorado, Okla. Confederate.
B. June 6, 1844, Union Co., Ark. Falcon Guards Co,
E, 11th Reg. East Ark. Vol., Falcon, Ark.

My greatest experience was when General Pope engaged our little army at Fort Thompson and New Madrid, on the Mississippi River, in Mo. That being my first experience under heavy cannonading, I realized that we were in war.

In April 1862, my company surrendered and we had a good time with the Union soldiers for a few days, until we were sent to prison at Camp Douglas, Illinois.

I experienced many keen emotions, seeing many actions, and the conduct of men under fire in battle. I remember when General Sherman landed his army at Grand Gulf, Miss., and started on his march across the state. General Stephen D. Lee had ten thousand calvarymen that kept up excitement for all of us. I served as a scout on outpost duty, more or less, as I liked active service. As a scout I had many adventures, good and bad.

The rations of my company consisted of beef, cornmeal and potatoes, with some flour now and then.

I got along all right with my comrades, and I also liked the northern soldiers who had charge of me while I was a prisoner. If we had been asked what we were joining and fighting for, our answers would have been as vague as our reasons or minds were on any great national question. Most of us just volunteered because the others were, and during the four years we learned a serious and lasting lesson.

I will say, the War Between the States was a very historical war. The cause of it was that there were two great aristocratic monopolies competing for the control of America. In the North and East it was financial, in the South it was chattel slavery, and their antagonism toward each other forced the division of the states and the civil war between the states. At Gettysburg the great decisive battle was fought. The Southern Cause was lost and the great financial power was permanently established. Chattel slavery was forever abolished in the United States of America.

That gave place for the rise of economic slavery as we see it today, which I must say is much worse than chattel slavery.

The Southern States were held down for many years under a horde of appointed officers called carpetbaggers. But in the Seventies we got shet of the "carpetbaggers", and our own bunch of politicians have proved to be very little better. The Thirteen States of the South were recognized only as a conquered province, only good for taxation and speculation. Still we were a living people, forced into extreme poverty, such as would shame a civilized people.

I must say that this sick and confused world has my deepest sympathy, knowing that they do not know who nor where they are. For the great Divine Light seems to have been withdrawn from us and left the world wandering in darkness.

Want to give an expression of my convictions of the Gettysburg reunion and the veterans of the North and the South. To me, we look like a pitiful fifteen hundred very old men, most of us quite feeble, needing the good will of the nation and all kind-hearted people. I think the people of Pennsylvania and Gettysburg are a noble, kind, and great people, worthy of a page in present day history. The old veterans are worthy of any honor or kindness the nation or states may show them, for we all responded in 1861, full of patriotism, for what we then thought was right.

I am now ninety-four years old and still do all of my own writing. In closing, I will say to the living veterans and the sons and daughters of those who have passed on. We did our duty as good citizens, patriotic to our country then involved in war and I close with kind regards for all people far and near.

UNDER THE STARS AND BARS WITH ROBERT E. LEE

W. F. VAN SWEARINGEN, Charlotte, N. C. Confederate.

I was born near Pioneer Mills, Cabarrus County, N. C., Oct. 2, 1842. My father was born in the seventeenth century, 1799, and owned much land and quite a bunch of slaves. Mother was born in 1805. I had a fairly good education as offered by the schools of my days.

A squad of seven Cabarrus County boys joined a Stanly County company on the 4th day of February, 1862, at Wilmington, N. C. I was a little over nineteen years of age. When sworn in before the proper officers the boys got off a good laugh on me. I was told first to kiss the Bible. I never saw anyone kiss the Bible before and I did it with quite a loud smack as I would have kissed a pretty girl at a dance-it was all on me. We were quartered in a suburb of Wilmington in good, new houses, with plenty to eat and drilling twice a day. After about six weeks we had orders to cook two days' rations and leave for New Bern. Arriving there we got out of the freight cars, got forty rounds of cartridges, loaded our guns and got back into the cars. There was great confusion on the streets-horses hitched to vehicles running wild. The enemy's big shells were dropped about the city from gunboats.

After crossing the long bridge a short distance, our train ran slowly, finally stopping. We could see numbers of soldiers, crippled, falling back to the rear. Our men got out of the cars and a gun accidentally fired and shot my brother in the arm. He was sent home, and a week afterwards nine buckshot were taken from his arm. Our troops got there barely in time to retreat to Kingston; stayed there quite a while and from there we went Richmond, near the Chickahominy River swamps, where I contracted a long spell of fever.

I was a private in Company K, Twenty-eighth North Carolina Volunteers-Captain Moody's company. The principal battles in which I engaged were: Hanover Court House, Gettysburg, Wilderness, Spottsylvania Court House, Chancellorsville, Petersburg, and was present at Appomattox at the end of the conflict.

Brother Warriors

I was wounded the third day's fight at Gettysburg. I was in the second line of battle crossing a plank fence. My rifle fell on one side and I fell on the other, about seventy-five or eighty yards from the enemy, behind a stone wall on Cemetery Ridge. Our troops went only a short distance, after I was wounded, when they fell back, many killed or disabled. The battle slackened up somewhat and I felt the blood trickling down my breast and I saw plainly that it meant death to retreat across the open field a half mile or more. The dead and wounded were many on both sides. Just under the crest of the hill scores of fine artillery horses lay crippled, writhing in death-from Lee's battery of nearly one hundred guns for one hour just previous.

I will never forget a young Mississippi man of the Fifty-fifth Regiment crying and looking for a doctor, holding his bowels in his hand, torn by a piece of shell. I directed him to a Federal surgeon not far away.

I close this Gettysburg chapter saying that after the armies fell back I was placed in a building formerly used as a female seminary a three-story brick building. Many Federal troops were there also. In the third story or attic was a shell lodged in the roof, shot from Lee's cannon the first day's fight.

After several days the provost guard let the wounded walk on the battlefield, with strict instructions not to carry anything away. There I saw my dead brother's cartridge box with his initials on it, also his hat. The old-fashioned belt went around the shoulder, the front was saturated with blood, and a hole from a Minnie ball in his strap told the tale. Here and there were many mounds of earth thrown up over the dead. Such is cruel war.

I here carry the reader back to the first day's conflict in West Gettysburg. Our regiment was not brought into the real battle but swept the field in battle array with some casualties, mostly from the sharp shooters. Let me here tell a tale of sympathy that went out to a woman and two little children. Between two converging lines of battle, with a baby in her arms and another holding to her dress. She was dragging a small trunk, passing through our lines, and was evidently from the wrecked house which had been perforated with bullets. Our Colonel had two guards take her back one and a half miles to safety.

I was taken to Fort Delaware a prison of war, stayed there in that horrible place about five weeks, and was exchanged and paroled home. When my wound was well I was notified to report back to our regiment, which I did.

My wound was a flesh one, a bullet entering my body where the shoulder and neck unite. I also received a light wound in the leg at the Battle of the Wilderness, which disabled me for three days. Our regiment got orders to go and catch a bunch of Federals in a thick woods, which we did, they having got lost or cut off from their main army. A few men got killed; they at once surrendered 137 men.

General Longstreet, coming just in the nick of time, in the very early morning of May 5 (I believe), saved Lee from defeat. Longstreet was from the western army. Here Grant began his flanking movement and kept it up until Lee got before him long before he got to Richmond.

Right near and in sight of Spottsylvania Court House a desperate battle was fought, beginning early in the morning and lasting much of the day. This was the 8th day of May, 1864. The Twenty-eighth Regiment was on the lower end of the so-called "horseshoe". Grant had broken Lee's line at the point of the horseshoe.

Talking about bravery! In this battle General Lane and First Lieutenant Crowell of our company were more than conspicuous—what I call reckless exposure, almost inviting death. The enemy all of a sudden sprung up like jack rabbits, front and flank, bullets were spattering the mud over me, when they came on me at once, floating a large United States flag. It was as beautiful as the one that was raised in my father's yard just previous to secession when the hot presidential election was on; when the "Star of the West" was fired upon in Charleston harbor; when the devils of civil war were unchained for four years; when billions of treasury were spent; when hundreds of thousands of soldiers were killed and maimed for life.

Grant's men wore caps and were dressed in dark blue uniforms with plenty of brass buttons and buckles, which made good targets. I could scarcely tell a word they spoke to me, hollering out loudly "Johnny; Johnny, down." When they saw I had no gun, one old foreigner opened his knife and attempted to cut the strap that held my cartridge box. These men were glad to get me and other prisoners to Grant's headquarters about a mile away to get out of temporary fighting. Here the telegraph instrument constantly clattered under an awning, flashing the news to President Lincoln at Washington. These wires were on small poles not as large as a man's arm. Here, too, I saw thousands upon thousands of Federal soldiers held in readiness to be hurried to any point needed. Here also I saw thousands of large fat beef cattle following the army. Here I saw many hundreds of large covered army wagons, with six mules or horses to the wagon, loaded with all kinds of provisions for the different army corps, numbering up to the Seventh Army Corps. Can the reader of this letter tell how many Lee had. No? I will answer this for you. He had three. What a vast difference. Wonderful how Lee kept Grant out of Richmond so long.

When captured the second time, I was taken to Point Lookout, Maryland, with hundreds of other prisoners. The drinking water here was fearfully bad. After two and a half month's confinement I was but a living skeleton walking about. Orders came for an exchange of prisoners man for man; only those that looked like death could pass, and that after being examined by two different doctors in two different buildings. I here state that Major Brady, in command of this post, was very kind and considerate of our men. This man once did me a good favor, just two or three days previous to our exchange.

I came near losing my life in this prison. In the early morning, a few minutes before daylight, someone in our big bell tent asked who was whistling so loudly just on the outside. I said it was a negro soldier. He heard the remark, came into the tent cursing, cocked his gun and wanted to shoot or stab with his bayonet the man who made the remark. No one knew or would tell on me. The bottom rail here was sure on top. This was the day we left Point Lookout for Dixie. On the trip down our vessel stopped a short while at Fortress Monroe, where Jefferson Davis was imprisoned for many months. Arriving at City Point, on the James River, a band saluted us and played "Dixie" and "Home, Sweet Home," and otherwise cheered us up. After quite a while I got to be myself again and joined our company near Petersburg. I found several of our boys had been slain in battle while others were in hospitals and some in Northern prisons. I bought a box of nice, substantial food for the boys. Provisions in Petersburg were at an awful price.

While on picket duty one day the latter part of March, 1865, we observed some buzzards flying in the woods near the ground between the two contending armies which were a half mile apart. Lieutenant Stone, Private Shotel, and I went to investigate and when about fifty yards from our objective point we observed the enemy's pickets on duty about sixty yards away; we easily slipped back to our rifle pits undiscovered.

Lieutenant Crowell was killed near the hour of midnight while fortifying a well so that our men could get water. After completing the job, he struck a match to see how it looked on the outside, and no sooner done than a bullet passed through his head.

A lake of fire and brimstone could hardly have stopped Grant's men at Fort Gregg just a few days previous to the surrender. This was on Sunday morning when A. P. Hill was killed. The attack on Lee's lines was made just at the dawn of day, when the big morning star in the East was nearly an hour high. This was about the first of April. Oh, how their officers begged, pleaded with, and cursed their men for not moving more swiftly, all obstructions being overthrown, and here Lee's army was cut in two; an easy job for the enemy's cavalry to capture many hundreds of our men.

Let me state here a secret that was kept from me and all others until the war was over, and I was glad I didn't know it, for I had enough of prison life already. It is this:

Three of the last seven original men in our mess or tent vowed in secret that they would be taken prisoners the first honorable opportunity that offered. Those men were the very best of soldiers, but they saw the "handwriting on the wall," as I did at Spottsylvania Court House. These men, as well as many thousands of others, were liberated some time in the summer of 1865 after peace was declared.

Here I am about to close my epistle and have not said a word about the Battle of Chancellorsville. I was in most of General Jackson's famous marches and battles. In the first days of May, General Hooker crossed the Rappahannock River at three different points, miles apart, with his vast army, throwing pontoon bridges over the river in the night. Here Jackson marched his men twenty-six miles, I believe, in one day, attacking the enemy on his extreme right flank late in the evening. They were taken by complete surprise and ran pell-mell, leaving several half-skinned beef, cattle, batteries of artillery and camp equipment. We pressed them probably two miles in a dense woods when night came on. If the men could have stood still one hour longer we could have captured a whole army corps. About dark they fired a terrible volley on us, using shrapnel and canister from their cannon; this occurred mostly on the plank road just at dark and there was some sharp shooting in the night. This was the night Jackson was mortally wounded and died later at Guinea Station. He, with his staff of officers, rode out in front about nine o'clock to reconnoiter the enemy front, being probably a hundred yards away; on returning they made a rattling noise and our men, mistaking them for the enemy's cavalry, fired into them. It is said, and I have never heard it contradicted, that the Eighteenth North Carolina did the firing.

Here we lay on our guns. About eleven o'clock at night the enemy assaulted us with a heavy loss as we heard from prisoners next day. Nearly all night we could hear the Yankee felling timber, hollering and talking, and this timber obstructed our quick assault next morning.

Sleep! At times we couldn't stay awake. Once we slept all night, knowing what was before us the following Sunday morning. You old soldiers, many a time you've heard the sharp notes of the whippoorwill; this night was an exception; they seemed to be quite tame and did hardly quit their lonesome music when volleys of shooting took place. They seemed to say "Witter-witter-whippoor-will"; this was repeated quickly for hours. Sunday morning the work of death began early; our men went forward and with a determined effort were victorious after a very stubborn battle. The Seventh North Carolina Volunteers suffered the worst. Here we lost many fine men. It was victory for the South if it was dearly bought. We almost drove the enemy into the river but they were stubborn to the very late hours of Sunday evening, and we were glad too when we heard the Union Army had crossed the river. Here we captured large quantities of ammunition in boxes of one thousand rounds each, looked like a freight car full.

Heavy fighting was going on at the same time down the river not far from Fredericksburg, where the enemy was repulsed and had to recross the river and give up the job of "On to Richmond."

What a hard time Lee's shattered army had in the retreat from Petersburg and Richmond on that Sunday night. Nearly all Sunday evening desultory firing at each other was going on. I had seen the end of the war was close by but the enemy did not slacken up much. Lieutenant Stone came to me and told me if I didn't quit shooting he would put me under arrest. I knew he would not, for he had no spare men.

When Lee and Jackson invaded Pennsylvania, in 1863, a soldier of our company became infatuated with a young lady at Berryville, Virginia, a small town. Our army was in motion and the acquaintance was brief. If my memory serves me right he was wounded and taken prisoner. After a few months he was exchanged at the Battle of Sharpsburg. Twelve months later, on the second invasion of Pennsylvania, our regiment was camped near this little town again, and this soldier, William Biles, got permission from our captain to go forward and claim his bride, which he did. Early next morning he fell in line as we marched through the village and such a Rebel yell went up amid the smiles and waving of handkerchief from the few ladies present. After the war he brought his wife to his home in Stanley County, North Carolina, a happy man.

Our regiment was the last in crossing the Appomattox River about ten or eleven o'clock at night. Barrels of tar and turpentine were placed at each end of the bridge and set afire, making a quick and spectacular sight to look on. We had some fighting on the way to Farmville, Grant's men almost running over us. Lee burned his wagon trains and the spokes were chopped from the wheels of those that couldn't be burned.

I was present at the surrender and felt mighty bad to stack arms over to the enemy. It looked silly to see those blue-coated men cutting down the old apple tree and digging up the stump, making use of every part of it as souvenirs of the war. This was the 9th of April, 1865.

Oh, God, this was a bitter cup that no one exactly knows, only those present. Sherman was very near right when he said, "War is hell." Of our company of one hundred and twenty-four men at Wilmington, only thirteen stacked arms at Appomattox. Where were the one hundred and eleven men? Echo answers, where?

I had to walk all the way back to my North Carolina home and was all but famished for want of subsistence. Meeting mother at home at last-oh, how sweet it was! Some of the servants not far away ran to the house and told mother I was nearly home. She hurried out from the house and met me in the lane near the barn, taking me by one hand, kissing and hugging me, and patting me on the back, saying, "Wilbur, Wilbur, Wilbur, where is your brother?" I told her he got killed at Gettysburg. This was a sad meeting mingled with joy, and I am not ashamed to tell my readers this brings tears to my eyes as I write these lines.

At the close of the War Between the States, Mr. W. F. Van Swearingen, Sr., moved from his home in Cabarrus County, North Carolina, to Lancaster, South Carolina, where he was engaged in the mercantile business for many years. He was appointed Postmaster by President Harrison and later on elected Auditor of Lancaster County. He moved to Charlotte, where he lived to be 87 years old. He died in 1930.

EXCHANGED TATTERED RAGS FOR SPLENDID ARRAY

JAMES W. VINES, Giatto, W. Va. Confederate.
B. Nov. 28, 1844, Monroe Co., Va. Co. A,
King's Battalion, 1862.

The boys of my home town assembled in the center of an open field on Wolfe Creek to organize for the war. Our company was stationed at King's Salt Works for awhile before going into battle.

My initiation into service was in testing implements of warfare before they were sent to the battlefields. I examined eight-inch shells which contained highly explosive powder, held intact by a cushion. I accidentally dropped one and the cap struck a rock. It exploded at my feet and inflicted a foot wound that put me in the hospital from June to September 19th. That is the only time I was in a hospital during the war. Emery and Henry College served as a hospital.

Sheridan wrought destruction in the Valley of Virginia. His trail was left destitute of dwellings of any kind. He burned all the foodstuff that he could not take with him. We encountered him at Winchester and fought against the right wing of his army. That was one of the hardest fights I was in. As I remember, we started at sun up and continued until ten o'clock. The Federal Officers ordered a reenforcement of soldiers to the front about two o'clock in the afternoon. General Crook responded and brought an army consisting of a great many negroes. We turned loose on them with our artillery and a smoke went out over the field that left ten thousand negroes killed or wounded. The Union won this battle, but they paid dearly for it. They took our guns and killed a great many of our men. History does not account for as large number of men as were really killed. Papers containing accounts of the casualties were kept from us as much as possible. Our army was so scattered that it would be hard to say just how many of our men were missing. This battle consisted of four sieges at different points before it ended and covered an area of forty miles. The Union's army consisted of 40,000 men against our 32,000.

The battle of Cedar Creek was fought on October 19, 1864. Our division, with Colonel King commanding, was located on the left wing of

General Sheridan's army. At five o'clock a cannon was fired. This meant that fighting would commence on the following day. We started early in the morning and continued most of the day. The Yankees charged us several times, firing all around us, trying to drive us from our position. Some of the boys in our ranks were so frightened that they tried to drive their cannons into the ground for shelter. Both sides lost heavily in this battle. Our army became terribly shattered due to heavy losses.

Once when I straggled a little out of bounds, a cavalryman rode up from behind and struck me over the head with a saber, cutting a long gash in my temple and almost knocking me off my feet. He ordered me to unhitch some horses from a wrecked wagon. I pretended that I was going to carry out his orders, but instead I slipped between the horses and ducked under the wagon. He aimed a gun at me, but I jumped behind the wagon just in time to miss the shot. The bullet hit the wagon at an angle that caused it to glance and strike my foot below the ankle. I have carried a painful scar through life from that wound. It made a very large hole almost through my foot.

With my foot nearly off, I could not attempt a getaway. A Confederate trooper saw what was happening and contrived to save me. It looked like the next minute I would get a load of lead that would spell my finish. The trooper shot the Yankee off his horse. I staggered to the breastworks and on through the field where I met the Colonel. He saw that I had been wounded and sent me on leave.

I travelled all night, struggling along with my wounded foot. When I stopped the Yankees almost caught me. I escaped and went to New Market, Va. At last, I found a wagon in a shed where I thought I might find a few moments of peace. I climbed in and went to sleep, but it was not long before Sergeant Shankin discovered me. He ordered me on guard duty at daylight. I looked a mess, I had lost my knapsack and supplies and my clothing was torn and covered with blood from head to foot. I went to Colonel King's office and told him of my wound, but he ordered me to obey the command given me by my superior. Later, when they examined me and realized my condition, I was granted a thirty day furlough. I remained at the camp to recuperate.

I needed a general cleaning up, so I went to the quartermaster's office to ask for supplies. He was not in, so I reached in the tent and pulled out the first article of clothing I could get my hands on. It turned out to be an officer's dress coat. Oh, it was a beautiful garment, all trimmed with gold braid and a long cape! I can't say that I would have specially chosen that style for myself, but since I had it I wasn't going to the risk of trying to make an exchange. Thus, elegantly arrayed, I proceeded to the creek where I bathed, and washed my own tattered garments.

War is horrible, but there are always incidents that stand out. I remember a twelve pound shell striking a man's body and blowing it up in mutilated fragments.

Out of the 1,883 old vets here at Gettysburg, there hasn't been a fight that I've heard of. Those Yankees still like our camps and they've been slipping over here and eating with us. We "jake" them a little over old times and they seem to like it.

WOUNDED SOLDIER HELPS PERFORM OPERATIONS

R. H. WALL, Gerton, N. C. Confederate.
B. Dec. 15, 1840, Rutherford Co., N. C.
Co. I, 56th Reg. N. C. S. T., Rutherford, N. C.

A wound in the left side of my chest felled me in the siege of Petersburg. For hours I lay on the battlefield with an open, bulging wound. My strength was rapidly failing and I knew that any exertion would prove fatal to me. Just when my plight seemed utterly hopeless, someone came along and carried me to the hospital. After the doctor dressed my wound I felt much better, though very weak. I guess that I sort of forget my own pains when I took a look about me at the maimed bodies—loads of them. Anyway, the surgeon needed all the help he could get and I sat beside him all night long, holding a lantern while he amputated arms and legs. There were so many wounded and dying that it seemed an endless job trying to take care of them.

The next morning, I was granted a thirty-day fur-lough to go home and get well. It was extended for a longer period, but, before I could return to my regiment, typhoid fever struck me and I had to stay at home sixty-five days longer.

FIGHTS BUSHWHACKERS

W. H. WALL, Elkton, N. C. Confederate.
B. Jan. 8, 1848, Wilkes Co., N. C.
Co. C, 21st Reg., Elkton, N. C.

You see, the way I was enlisted was like this. Back in 1864, there was a heap of people who ran away from the army and hid in the woods to keep from fighting. Of course, they were a cowardly gang, bad about stealing, and in general a terror to the neighborhoods. We called them bushwhackers. Well, I enlisted to protect citizens and property against these freebooters.

Our home guard in Wilkes County made a raid on the bushwhackers, but they were too strong for us. They fired on us from ambush. Doke Sparks was killed, and Buck Colkerhan and Jack Baugus were wounded. The next day the captain of the bushwhackers, with eighty men, went over to Tennessee and joined the Yankee army because they thought they would be safer on that side. That is one reason for a lot of the atrocities committed in the name of the Union Army, so many of their forces were carrying these skunks.

When word came of the surrender, 1 was at Old Fort, N. C., on my way to join in the fight at Knoxville.

I'm having a big time at Gettysburg. Florence Wall is my attendant. One of the finest things about this reunion is having someone to see that our every wish is granted.

SERVICE UNDER TWO FLAGS

EMMETT M. WALLER, Commander-in-Chief, D. C. and Md.
Div., U, C. V., Washington.
B. near Memphis, Tenn., 1847. 13th Tenn.
Cav. June 6, 1861.

The plantation of my parents was quite typical of the well-to-do southern planter. Our household was well regulated according to the tranquility of life so wholeheartedly enjoyed at that time, and we owned a great number of slaves who were content and happy with their family life in their negro quarters. We bought and paid for our slaves just as we had purchased other property which we owned legally. We did not regard them as being in bondage, but valued them as chattels for which we had paid a worthy price. As servants and farm hands, they were indispensable on any large plantation. They gladly gave their labor and in return received full value in a good home and security from all worldly problems. They loved their master, were proud of him, and often reveled in the prestige that his relative wealth and social position afforded them.

Our home was within the sweep of Sherman's army. It took his men three days to pass through our plantation. I shall never forget the helplessness we felt when his men entered our home and took possession. While the family looked on they destroyed its beautiful and expensive furnishings. They used an old ax in splintering our exquisite piano. Then they drove the family out and burned the home to the ground, as well as all the other buildings, with the exception of the negro quarters. They utilized all our supplies for their army, even using the fence rails for campfires.

Our old negro foreman, apprehensive of the welfare of my young mother, put her astride a mule and fled twenty-five miles with her into Memphis, vowing he would kill the first person who dared to try and harm a hair on her head.

Thus deprived of a home, I, at the age of fourteen, on the 6th day of June, 1861, enlisted as a drummer boy in the Thirteenth Tennessee Infantry, to serve for a one-year period.

In the battle of Murfreesboro, I was badly wounded just above the ankle. The main artery was ruptured and I nearly bled to death. Completely exhausted from the loss of blood, I was left on the field to die, but a Union officer saved my life. He picked me up and carried me to the Federal hospital. After I recovered from my wound, I was allowed to walk freely about the town. I used to go out and play marbles with the Yankee boys. I got pretty lonesome though and one day, while in the railroad station, I started crying. A Union major came along and asked me what the trouble was. When I told him, he got a railroad pass and sent me back to Memphis, where my mother was staying.

I was discharged immediately after the battle of Pittsburg Landing, Tenn., in which I participated. Then I was sent to the Kentucky State College. The next summer all the northern boys went home, but we southern boys had no homes to go to, so we started out to join General Forrest at Jackson, Miss. There were sixteen of us to begin with, but as we travelled along our number increased to three hundred. It was dangerous travelling, as the Yankee cavalry was always on the lookout for us, but southern sympathizers helped to direct us along. We travelled all night and hid out during the day.

When we arrived at the Cumberland River, we captured a cabin boat. We promised the captain that we would do no harm if he would carry us across the river. When he had conveyed all but sixty of us, a gunboat came along and halted the captain in the middle of the river. In making our get-away, the gunboat fired cannon balls after us, which fell as far as three miles from where we had disembarked.

Then we came to the Tennessee River, which was wide and swift. The current swept downstream with such force that it took strength and courage for our men or horses to attempt swimming it. We managed to get some of the best horses across the current to a little island. That made it easier to get the rest to follow. My horse turned around three times in midstream and returned to the shore despite my earnest coaxing. It took all night for our group to complete this crossing. In the meantime the sixty boys who had been left on the banks of the Cumberland River, and whom we thought the Yankees might have caught, arrived. They had overcome many hazards and our delay gave them time to catch up with us. We made our way on to Jackson, Miss., where we joined General Nathan Bedford Forrest.

I was assigned as escort to General Bell and was in all the engagements in which Brigadier General Forrest's Cavalry forces participated, including

Paducah, Ky.; Fort Pillow, Price's Cross Roads, Miss., and Johnsonville, on the Tennessee River. I participated in all the engagements which were fought in this advance and acted as the rear guard in the retreat of General Hoods' troops, which meant that I was under fire virtually every day from the time General Hood's lines were broken at Nashville until we crossed the Tennessee River in our retreat. I was awarded a medal of honor by the Confederacy for outstanding valor on the field of battle.

Before the battle of Franklin, when General Pat Cleburne called for two escorts, I was assigned to him. Well, sir, I don't know how many horses were shot from under him, but there were plenty. Once, when his horse was killed, I offered him mine. Just as he started to mount, the horse fell mortally wounded. General Cleburne wasn't to be outdone, putting his hat on the end of his sword and raising it high, he marched forward still leading his men into the fray. In that day general officers fought at the head of their troops-not five or six miles in the rear. General Cleburne was killed right on the Union breastworks. I was beside him when he fell. I and another fellow dragged him away. We got him into a ditch and later took him to a farm house. Well, sir, on the porch of that farm house there were six other Confederate general officers-dead.

Once in the midst of a skirmish, I passed under a persimmon tree that was loaded with ripe, mellow fruit, just touched by the frost. You never heard of a Confederate soldier who wasn't hungry—well, my mouth just watered at the sight of them and I couldn't forego the temptation to risk getting a few. Before I could quite reach them a sniper got me. I didn't go to the hospital with that wound, but I missed the luscious tidbits and it was mighty uncomfortable riding my horse for a while after that.

When the war was over and I returned to the site of our old home it looked pretty forlorn. There was nothing left but the negro quarters. Some of the slaves who hoped for our return had remained and were carrying on as best they could with broken-down cavalry horses.

The horse I rode home was so worn out that his head was drooping to the ground and he could hardly drag one foot ahead of the other. The old foreman, who rescued my mother, saw me coming down the road and ran to meet me. Torn between joy and sadness, the tears were rolling down his black cheeks. "Oh, Boss, dare ain't nuthing lef'," I was sympathetically informed. Then catching in a glance the condition of my horse, his hands began digging around in the pockets of his ragged over-alls. Withdrawing $2.60, all the money he had been able to accumulate in the many, many days, he pressed it into my hand, saying, "Boss, I guess yo' hav ter go ter Memphis, dis'll take yo' on de train."

After the War Between the States, I enlisted in the Eleventh Infantry of the United States Army. I was with the first group to reach the scene of the massacre of General Custer's command by the Sioux. I was discharged in 1878 and reenlisted in the Fifth Cavalry, serving that regiment until I was placed on the retired list in June 1902.

At ninety-two, life is still full of interests for me. I attended the Gettysburg reunion in July 1938. Major W. F. Van Swearingen arranged the trip for me and comrade Robert Wilson. Since 1903, I have gone regularly, every day, to my business as custodian clerk of All Souls' Unitarian Church.

Introduced to Congress as one of the "Oldest Living Defenders of the Flag," Colonel Waller was recited for distinguished military service. (See Congressional Record, June 14, 1935.)

Cyrus Stamet, a "Yank", John Wesley Turnbough and M. D. Vance, both "Johnny Rebs" typify the spirit of Brother Warriors

Robert W. Wilson, Emmett Waller and Peter Pierre Smith proudly hold the Flag for which they fought.

SOLDIERS TAKE OATH OF ALLEGIANCE

P. EDWIN WEST, Brewerton, N. Y. Union.
B. May 22, 1847, Constantia, N. Y. Co. F,
189th N. Y. Inf., Sept. 1, 1864, Constantia, N. Y.

The way I happened to enlist, my brother was home on furlough and I wanted to go back with him. My parents wouldn't hear to it. A few days later, I got my back up and told them that unless they consented I would go where I was not known and enlist. I wanted to go down there to see how the thing worked. Finally, they came to their minds and let me go. I told the recruiting officer that I was seventeen, but he put me down as eighteen.

The first battle I was in was on March 29, 1864, at a place called-dammit, 'can't think of the name- oh yes, Gravel Run. On April 2, I was in a battle on Lewis' Farm. Now then, on Lewis' Farm there were four out of my company killed. We were lying down, supporting the battery when the Brigadier General says, "Send them over a few mosquitoes." We opened up and let 'em have a. few. It quieted the enemy and we didn't hear anything more from them for awhile. I later went down to Five Forks, where we had a battle.

General Meade took over General Hooker's forces and was supporting Grant when Lee surrendered at Appomattox. I was right there when it all took place. Lee's army were a ragged looking bunch. Two-thirds of them didn't even have guns and they had been without rations for three days. General Grant issued twenty-five thousand of our rations to them. You see, they had to go home on foot and some of them had a good ways to go. Well, the fourth day, our supply train came and we got something to eat, but by that time I didn't care much whether I ate or not.

After the surrender, we were busy for three or four days while the Confederates took the Oath of Allegiance. We formed two lines through which the Confederates marched into the hall where they gave up their arms. They kissed the Bible and took the Oath, then marched on.

We were sent to guard the Richmond and Danville railroad for a few days and were then sent to Washington. We camped on Arlington Heights, just across the Potomac River from Washington. Governor Fenton, of New

York, came there to examine the New York State Troops. In a few days we were sent to Elmira, N. Y., paid off, and discharged.

Well, I guess the bravest thing I did was to shoot a razor-back hog. That was up in the Blue Ridge Mountains. I was out quail hunting and heard something behind me. Looking around, I saw a razor-back hog coming for me with her mouth wide open. My gun was loaded with acorns and I let her have a full dose, right in the mouth. She went down and I supposed she was dead. The next day, I got a couple of fellows to go with me to find her. She was gone, so I commenced making a search about the place. I kinda got close to a clump of bushes and it commenced rustling. Then something behind it started at a double-quick pace through the shrubs. I ran to keep up with it and every once in a while an acorn would crack down in front of us and a pig would jump out of it and run.

CONFEDERATE SOLDIER WRITES HOME

CONFEDERATE STATES OF AMERICA
Virginia, Manassas, June 4, 1861
Stand firmly by your cannon,
Let ball and grape-shot fly,
And trust in God and Davis,
And keep your powder dry.

Mrs. Fannie C. Hoffman,
Coosa, Ala.

Dear Duchey:

I received yours of August 2nd of Mr. Collins of Auburn, and I was glad to hear that you were all well. I would have written to you sooner, but it was and is almost a matter of utter impossibility to get paper as it is worth ten cents per sheet.

You may well say that we won a great and glorious victory! We employed on our part about fifteen thousand troops against forty thousand at least of the enemy. Our loss in killed and wounded was about eight to ten hundred, theirs at the lowest estimate exceeded twelve thousand and they admit the loss of twenty-two thousand missing.

Oh, Duchey, it was a horrid sight! Our soldiers were engaged in burying the dead about nine days. We are expecting every day a more formidable conflict as the parties on both sides are daily receiving reinforcements. The engagements will be no doubt not far distant from this point. Perhaps we will march on Washington or Alexandria in a few days.

Prince George Bonaparte left here a day or two ago, paid General Beauregard a visit and surveyed the battlefield and is strongly attracted to the interests of the Southern Confederacy, and it is his opinion that England and France will both interfere in removing Lincoln's blockade or proclaim war against the northern government and, if so, the war will be a short one and we will soon be with loved ones at home, then peace and prosperity will again smile upon our down-trodden and depressed Sunny South.

Let foreseen considerations result as they may, by the all-wise and omnipotent hands of providence pervading us, we can whip them anyway.

We have a great deal of sickness in the camps. Little Charley has been quite sick with the measles, but I feel now he is convalescing. His brother James is nearby; he came last week and stayed two or three days with him.

Your brother Mark is about two or three miles from here. He left here about an hour ago. You wanted to know what kind of clothes would be suitable. Two pairs of woolen pants for me, one or two for Charley and a couple of pairs of socks.

Kiss all my dear little grandchildren for me and tell Annie that we will soon drive the Yankees away and then grandpa will come home and drive McRamery to the buggy.

Duchey, you will please forward this letter to Cousey, with instructions to Cousey to send it to Becky, and on to Leonora and the children, they must all write to me. Direct all letters to Manassas junction in care of Capt. J. A. Strother, Border Rangers.

I know not, dear children, whether we are destined to meet in this life anymore or not. Before another span of day, you will hear of another great battle which has been fought, and I may be among the slain, and if so, my children farewell and let us cherish bright hopes that we will meet in a happier clime where strife will cease to be.

Nothing more-your friend and father and friend,
From : Private M. J. Westmoreland
Mark J. Westmoreland
Cons. Co. Lomax Reg.
Col. Gordon, commanding

Submitted by Vera Mae Westmoreland, granddaughter of Mark J. Westmoreland.

RESTS COMFORTABLY INDOORS WHILE HIS GUARD STANDS IN THE RAIN

MOSES R. WETZEL, Carlisle, Pa. Union
B. Apr. 10, 1843, Carlisle, Pa. Co. C,
158th Reg. Pa. Inf. Oct. 16, 1862,
Chambersburg, Pa. Dis. Aug. 10, 1863.

I served as a fifer, seeing service under Generals Burnside, Hooker, and Meade. This took me through the campaigns in Virginia, North Carolina, Maryland and Pennsylvania.

General George Brinton McClellan was a man greatly loved by his soldiers, but Lincoln considered his march to Richmond a failure and relieved him in November 1862. General Ambrose Everett Burnside took his command and marched on Fredericksburg. The Union's loss of 12,300 against the Confederate's loss of 4,500, caused great criticism. Burnside's command was given over to General Joseph Hooker. Hooker was an egotist and a vain boaster. He led his 97,000 into the battle of Chancellorsville against the Confederates 67,600, only to be beaten and suffer a loss of 16,000 men in three days. General Hooker's command was then given over to General George Meade, just before the battle of Gettysburg, in which they were conspicuous.

The colonel of our regiment used to imbibe a little too freely and on such occasions he was easy to anger. It was difficult for the drummers or fifers to play in the rain as the instruments were damaged by moisture. When this happened the old colonel use to storm and rave. I was ordered in the guardhouse for a brief period for failing to play my fife. I was called before the colonel to answer the charge. He sought to punish me by assigning an area near his tent to be clear of small shrubs. I pleaded that I had no implement with which to do the work. He withdrew a small knife from his pocket which he gave to me and I was forced to use it as best I could. Not satisfied that he had subdued what he considered a cantankerous spirit, he sent me back to the guardhouse. This amused me greatly for I was privileged to remain indoors and enjoy leisure and comfort while my guard had to stand for a long time holding his heavy gun with the rain pouring in his face and soaking his body.

The Steamship Thomas Collier ran aground near Pamlico Sound and we were forty miles from help of any kind. We lightened the vessel by throwing coal overboard, but were in a quandary as how to prize the boat out of the mud. Two men volunteered to row forty miles to obtain help. They made it in one night and the next day they sent help by a sternwheeler. We were transferred to another vessel and proceeded on our way.

If there was anything that tickled a private, it was to see and officer in an embarrassing predicament. They pretend such excellence and probed at the privates on the least provocatin. Well, one day the general took our regiment of new recruits to a nearby timber to drill in the manual of arms. He gave me an order that was mistaken by the men as "Fire!" "Pop, pop, pop," went the rifles. The general became enraged and his horse went wild with excitement. He commanded, "Cease that firing!" After everyone had been properly subdued he lined us up and had us send a volley through the woods that echoed equal to a battle.

The customs of living have had many a change in my lifetime. Most things show a definite improvement, but I believe the most significant step forward during the last seventy years in Christian County is the advancement in agricultural science, with the mechanical aids for farming which have been developed. I used to cut grain with a hand sickle. Now it is no job at all.

They've been showing us a lot of modern implements of warfare at this reunion (Gettysburg). When another war is fought it will be with machinery. During the Civil War we were dependent on manual strength, endurance and strategy.

I am the last survivor of the F. M. Long G. A. R. Post in Taylorville.

GETS WOUNDS SWIPING POTATOES

I. M. WICKERSHAM, Omaha, Neb. Union.
B. Aug. 2, 1846, Cynthiana, Ohio, Co. F, 2nd Reg. Ohio
Heavy Art. Feb. 22, 1864, Hillsboro, Ohio.
Dis. Aug. 1, 1865, Nashville, Tenn.

I had been detailed on guard duty at Nashville, but a sudden change in orders kept me at camp. That is how I happened to escape when the Johnnies captured the waterworks and took some of our soldiers. We defeated them on December 16, 1864, at Nashville.

I only got shot once. That was the night when our rations got cut off. With some other boys, I started out foraging. We came to a nice field of potatoes and were making a scoop when a shot hit me, but it wasn't serious. We got back to camp with quite a few of our swipings.

When I was seventy-eight, I got badly hurt and have had to walk on crutches ever since. I was stepping off a train and was thrown under a truck. Don't think that I don't get plenty of fun out of living though, for I do.

CUTS SEVENTY-FIVE SHOCKS OF CORN FOR PRIVILEGE TO ENLIST

ALLEN CAPERTON WIKLE, Sinks Grove, W. Va. Confederate.
B. Sept. 7, 1845, Union W. Va. Phil Thurmond's
Rangers, Packs Ferry, Summers Co., W. Va.

One evening, in October, while cutting corn, I made up my mind that I wanted to help my comrades win their battle. I was so thrilled at the thought of going that I cut seventy-five large shocks of corn that day, for my dear old Dad said I couldn't go to war until I got my corn cut. The next morning, my cousin, One Wikle, and I started out for Packs Ferry to enlist. The President of the United States never felt prouder than we did on our way down there. It was miles and miles and we had to walk every step of the way, but we made it in one day. Nowadays folks are too puny to walk one mile to church.

Our captain, Phil Thurmond, drilled us for about one week before we started on a scoot across Kennys Mountain, a march of four days and nights. The only food they had to start us off with was a handful of crackers. We were supposed to forage along the way, but pickings were as scarce as hen's teeth and we only found water once. We went in search of Yankees, but couldn't find any on that trip, so returned and rested.

Then we went to Big Sewell Mountain. We weren't very long in rounding up a few on that trip. Somewhere from the loft of a house they began shooting at us. We fortified ourselves behind trees and shrubs and gave them back as good as they sent until twenty-five surrendered.

At Meadow Bridge we had a battle with some more pickets. We didn't lose a man and happy were we, but we killed several pickets. Don't know the number.

In 1865, we raided Nicholas Company and took Fort Ramsey. One Yankee undertook to get away. Our man was running after him, trying his best to shoot him, but the gun wouldn't go off. Finally, he caught up with the Yankee and knocked him down with the gun. The Yank pleaded not to be killed. He told the Yank, "I wouldn't harm a hair on your head, but you should of stopped after you were captured." He tried out his gun, to see what was wrong that it hadn't fired, and it went off every time. Though it had failed lots of times when he tried to shoot the Yank. We never lost a man in that raid. Captain Payne's horse was shot from under him, but he escaped unharmed.

After we took Fort Ramsey we went back to camp and that was the last fight I was in. Just a short time after that "Peace!" was shouted throughout the camp, so I went home and married Nancy Ballard and we settled down to raising a family.

Next to getting married the greatest thrill I ever had was attending the Gettysburg reunion. I stood the travel and camp life fine and I am thankful for the perfect health I am blessed with.

SLEEPS WITH HEAD ON BODY OF DEAD SOLDIER

JOHN M. WILDMAN, Cortland, N. Y. Union.
B. Sept. 26, 1838.

I am 101 years old and though I enjoy good health and a fine appetite, my age is against me in remembering very much about the war.

I went with the boys in Blue through the battles of Bull Run, Antietam, and Little Round Top. At Gettysburg, one of my comrades, Jay Hull, caught a shot right in the forehead and it came out at the back of his head. Can you believe it, he actually lived to get strong and healthy! His home was down here at Babcocks Mill.

Many times the soldiers were so worn out that the moment an opportunity came to rest they did not question where or how, but slumped down in their tracks. I was horrified one morning to find that what seemed a comfortable head-rest, as I snoozed peacefully through the night, was the body of a dead soldier. I had lain in mud all night with the dead body supporting my head and shoulders above the slush.

They say 100,000 folks have been to our Gettysburg encampment to see us. I'm mighty glad you came and I hope you won't retreat from us Union soldiers.

The author found this delightful old warrior seated in a camp chair on the lawn in front of his tent. As she approached him smiling, he observed her in a quizzical manner for a moment and then inquired, "And who might you be, young lady?" She replied, "Just a little Rebel from Florida, getting the thrill of invading a Yankee camp." He extended his hand in welcome and answered in a kind voice, "My child, there are no Rebels in this country."

RAN YANKS TWO MILES'
BUT WAS LEADING THEM

BENJAMIN FRANKLIN WILLIAMS, Atlanta, Ga. Confederate.
B. Mar, 1853, Stewart Co., Ga.

At the age of nine I was engaged in the war. My older brothers and father carried gun powder and shots. I carried supplies. I was too young to enlist as a soldier and carry a gun, but I did duty at the Quartermaster Supply Department throughout the four years of the war.

My father served as an enrolling officer at the beginning of the war. He got up a company of young boys and drilled them. When the last call came for volunteers, father went to the war. The company of young boys he had prepared gave their services by hauling supplies to the camp depots. These provisions were gathered around the country from the farmers, who gave a certain portion of their foodstuff to the quartermaster at the camp commissary. I carried lots of supplies to Wheeler's cavalry.

One exciting come off was when I ran a bunch of Yankees about two miles by myself. You bet, I was leading them-they tried to catch me, but I outrun 'em. They shot once in a while, just to see how fast I could run, but if they meant to hit me, I outrun the bullets.

You've heard us folks down here in Georgia referred to as Georgia Crackers. Well, that label dates back to the ox-cart days. A long time ago travelling was mighty slow. People drove oxen hitched to little covered wagons. In order to get to town to do a little trading a fellow had to start out in the middle of the night. Now, oxen are slow animals and sometimes they like to just stop and stand still in the road. The drivers carried rawhide whips which they twirled in the air and snapped with a loud crack. The noise drove the oxen on. Lots of times the crack of the whip awakened people living along the roads to town and they would remark, "There goes a cracker."

I am commander of Camp Evan P. Howell, U. C. V., No. 1825, which is the largest camp in Georgia. Mrs. W. D. Langley is my adjutant, and was my attendant at Gettysburg.

SNEAKS THROUGH UNION LINES
TO JOIN THE CONFEDERACY

ROBERT E. WILSON, Washington, D. C. Confederate.
B. Mar. 17, 1846, Prince Georges Co., Md. Co. D.
1st Md. Cav. Frederick Co., Va.

I and another fellow sneaked through the Union lines to join the Confederacy. We left Prince Georges County, Md., early in 1864, pushing our way up through Union territory, around the Potomac River and down to Winchester. Before our tracks had time to grow cold we were back in Maryland participating in raids as Confederate soldiers, under the command of General Early.

I and a squad were detailed to carry stock down to Albermarle County, Va., during which time General Early made a raid on Chambersburg, Pa. He burned the town and returned to Virginia. We again joined General Early in Virginia and participated almost daily in the valley engagements. I was in battles at Martinsburg, Horseshoe Bottom, Falling Waters, Shepardstown, Burkeville, and Buckland Mills.

On September 19th, about three o'clock in the morning, we were ordered from Buckland Mills to Winchester. We made the march over there and fought the whole day through, supporting our artillery. The enemy charged and we drove them back. Later they made a charge on the extreme left of General Linborden's line, breaking his forces and compelling us to fall back to Fisher's Hill.

On September 20th, we lay in line of battle all night and until about noon of the following day. We lost a good many men and much artillery before we were forced to fall back. After this, we were sent to Port Republic, where we stayed for about ten days, until General Rosser was sent up from Richmond to reinforce General Early.

On October 19th, General Early surprised General Sheridan at Cedar Creek. We routed them until Sheridan made that famous dash from Winchester and rallied his men. With a substantial reinforcement Sheridan returned and followed General Early up the valley and took about twenty-five hundred prisoners. General Sheridan sent troops to hold the fort at

Mount Jackson and we followed them. We held them in check there until our ammunition gave out.

The latter part of November, we were sent to Prince William County, obviously to spend the winter, but on account of the movements of other forces we were sent to Liberty Mills. We had quite a fight there and were forced back to Gordonsville. The Union soldiers followed us and we fought all the next day, our activities extending up through the Cattail Mountains.

At this time, I got a furlough for thirty-five days and went to Charlottesville. After my furlough, I was ordered to Richmond. On my way there I met up with and joined General Rosser's brigade. After a day or so, I met my command and went with it to Petersburg.

About the first of April we were ordered to Dunlap Station, right across from the enemy's big guns. We had orders not to talk loud nor make any campfires at night. General Lee ordered the destruction of war material laying on the tracks, but countermanded the order. Later, the enemy started firing and we were ordered to destroy everything to prevent its capture. We then travelled nine days and nights, marching and counter-marching, skirmishing and fighting, back to Petersburg.

Upon leaving Petersburg, we fought our way along through Forty-five Forks, Denwood Court House, Farmville, High Bridge, and across the river to Appomattox Court House. General Sheridan got there ahead of us and opened fire early that morning. On our extreme left, General Gordon was doing most of the fighting and I think he did the last fighting in Virginia.

People call me Major Wilson, but that title was thrust upon me. The older men, who were officers during the war, died sooner and their titles were passed on down to a lot of bucks who never rated them. You get doty when you get as old as I am, but I ain't a major, never was. I was a private in the ranks.

I'm enjoying the Gettysburg reunion and expect to go to Columbia next month. I flew up to Gettysburg in an airplane with Col. H. C. Rizer, a Union soldier and close friend of mine. On Memorial Day, we flew, with General Emmett N. Waller, and strew rose petals on the old veterans' graves. I participate in all Confederate activities. I attend all state and national reunions, and for a quarter of a century I have attended every meeting held in the Confederate Memorial Home on Vermont Avenue. I haven't missed a single Jackson and Lee Memorial Evening. I am ninety-three years old and feel "fit as a fiddle." I'm never sick and never suffer a pain. Old soldiers never die, they just fade away.

On February 24, 1939, I was called to the death bed of Robert E. Wilson. I shall never forget the inspiration of this visit. As I came into the dining room where he lay, his cot and sleeping apparel were snowy white, like his beautiful hair. His countenance was sweet and calm. His feeble, wrinkled hands held mine in a fairly firm clasp as I sat with him. Once, I bowed my head for a long while when he asked me to pray with him. His voice was weak, but clear. He said, "Thank you for coming. You know, I feel all right, haven't a pain in the world, but I'm 'just fading away'." He believed in man's rebirth from the material to the spiritual world and told me that he was going Tuesday. On the day he named, at twenty-five minutes past three o'clock, February 27, 1939, he "faded away." He faced death a hero, just as he faced the cannon's roar in the dangerous charges made with General Early in the Shenandoah Valley as a Confederate soldier. He raised his hand to signify his obedience to his Savior's command, smiled, and said, "I am ready, everything is all right." His courage never faltered for he knew, "The last enemy that shall be destroyed is death."-Martha Norris McLeod

LEE'S SURRENDER

C. WINGROVE, Clay Center, Kans. Union.
B. Jan. 6, 1846, French Creek, W. Va.
Co. M, 3rd Reg. W. Va. Cav., Mar. 10, 1864,
Buckhannon, W. Va. Dis. June 30, 1865.

I went with the 3rd West Virginia Cavalry through the entire engagement. The happiest day of my whole life was when I heard that the war was going to end. I saw General Lee when he dismounted and I saw General Grant and his officers arrive. General Lee made a neat, portly appearance and Grant seemed to regret his shaggy appearance. But they had known each other before, when they fought together down in Mexico. General Lee asked General Grant to put his terms in writing, which he did with a pencil. He told General Lee that his men would not be molested as long as they obeyed the law. I saw General Grant when he said to General Lee, "Keep your sword," and when he said that the Confederates could keep their horses, to "go home and farm."

There were a lot of things we had to fight besides the Rebels. For instance, the gray backs and green backs gave us plenty to think about. Now, the gray backs are a self-satisfied group and have to be picked off, one by one; while the green backs are more tempermental and have to be handled differently. They stuck to us by the hundreds until we learned to steal a march on them. We'd go out in the cold, take off our clothes, and rush back to the camp fire and they'd jump into it to get warm.

BOMBARDMENTS OF FORT FISHER

WILLIS H. WINN, Hohokus, N. J., Union.
B. June 22, 1847, Salem, Mass. Navy
Battleship Colorado, Sept. 27, 1864.
Dis. Sept. 7, 1867, Brooklyn Navy Yard.

Wilmington was an important city of the Confederacy. Despite the vigilance of the Union fleet, many blockade runners managed to slip in and out bringing valuable supplies to the southern army. The mouth of Cape Fear River was guarded by Fort Fisher, a very powerful defense. On December 25, 1864, fifty Federal war ships and ironclads under Admiral Porter and a land force under General Butler bombarded the fort without success. The next day a two hundred and a fifty ton torpedo was exploded and, when this did not make the Johnnies surrender, we had to go after more ammunition. My ship was pierced with sixty-four guns and there were 650 men aboard. We returned on January 15th and captured the fort. This bombardment lasted from two until nine o'clock in the evening. A gruesome incident on our ship was when a colored sailor, whom we all liked and called "White Nigger," got a shot right in the neck. His head snapped right from his body and rolled across the deck.

I was stationed most of the time at a riffle gun on the forecastle. At one time we were ordered ashore. We had to dig in as close as possible until orders were given to charge. We were told not to touch anything lying on the ground as there was danger of contacting explosive materials.

We shot down the Confederate flag, but it kept popping right back up, like a defiant target. Their soldiers tried desperately to keep its colors floating. As soon as we'd kill a flag bearer, another one would step up and take his place. As fast as they went up, they were shot down, until about sixty or seventy men lost their lives.

After the war, our battleship became a flagship. For two years we visited many foreign ports; England, France, Spain, Italy, Portugal, and other countries of consequence.

I had a great thrill when Dr. McClennan, the ship's surgeon, told me that I could have the honor of firing the last shot before we should leave the ship. I was stationed at the gun, ready to fire, but, when the time came, Dr. McClennan stepped up and fired the last shot. I felt disappointed, but soon got my satisfaction when a shell fell alongside of our ship. It was feared for a moment that it might explode and cause a great deal of damage. Dr. McClennan was the worse frightened of all. He ran about in such an excited fury that the rest of us forgot the danger of the situation and gave way to an uproar of laughter.

The Gettysburg reunion is a happy occasion with former enemies united in a common bond of interest. A spirit of good will and joviality permeates the camps. We are all happy today to be a part of this great union. I've met a lot of men who were in the famous battles here seventy-five years ago.

RAISES OBJECTIONS TO OWN FUNERAL

HOMER S. WOODWORTH, Omaha, Neb. Union.
B. Dec. 28, 1842, Angola, Ind. Co. B,
100th Ind. Inf. Vol., York, Ind.
August 15, 1862.

When the call came for volunteers in August 1862, I walked forty-five miles from my country home to Fort Wayne where a company was being organized. I was the last boy to enlist in Company B. Its quota had been filled and the captain told me that I had better go to another county as I could only be a private if I joined his company. I replied, "That is all I want."

We received orders right away to go to Indianapolis and join three other companies which comprised the 100th. Regiment. We went to Madison for a few days and then up the river to Camp Gray, then to Covington, Ky., where we did a little soldiering.

One of the most interesting parts of my routine was drilling, especially since my close friend, Gill Rhoades, was a drill-master and frequently let me help him instruct the men. While this privilege seemed important, the proudest time of all was when we dressed up in fancy regalia and paraded on horseback in grand review.

Down in Tennessee we marched after General Braxton Bragg, but could not catch him. He's the general who perched his army up on Lookout Mountain and Missionary Ridge and kept General Rosecrans' army hemmed in the horseshoe until they were nearly starved to death. They actually had to kill their mules and eat them. Grant finally came with an overwhelming force and drove Bragg away.

We started on a march into Mississippi, but, by the time we arrived at Holly Springs, I took malaria fever and had to go to the hospital, known at that time as the Magnolia House. We were not comfortable there very long as General Earl Van Dorn, a Texas cavalryman, came in at Grant's rear and captured the place on December 20, 1862.

General Grant had ammunition stored in a large barn at Holly Springs. He ordered that a part of the supplies be carried out into the streets and a fire set to the barn. It caused an awful explosion which could be heard for miles. The vibrations caused the windows and doors of my hospital room to crash in and hit me on the head. I was badly cut. Being unable to defend ourselves, a number of us were taken prisoners and later the whole camp was clipped off. I tell you, it was a trying time. Those rebels kept us there long enough to relieve us of our cash and other valuables. Yes, sir, they took $140 from me, alone.

When the smallpox epidemic broke out I was doing guard duty on a railroad, my comrade, Jerome Dillingham, was stricken and died three days later. I was pretty sick with it and was recuperating when we were called to take part in the siege of Vicksburg. This was one of the chief objectives, second only to the Confederate capitol, as the Confederates had it so strongly fortified as to make it impossible for us to navigate the river. After a great many attempts were made, Grant settled down to a six weeks siege. Incessant firing from land and water poured shot and shell into the city like a rainfall until the residents were forced to abandon it and take to the hillsides, where they lived in caves. On July 4, 1863, the Confederates surrendered thirty thousand prisoners and four hundred guns.

My regiment was ordered to Jackson, but a number of us were not well enough to go, so our major remained behind with us. When we finally got on our way and were caught in a severe storm. Major Parrot was killed by a falling tree and many of our men were injured. We got as far as Black River, but were nearly all sick.

I was put in a small tent, twelve by twenty feet in size, which they called a hospital. There was no bedding of any kind and we had to use brush and moss for coverings. The sick and dying were all crowded in together. Men died at the rate of two or three a day. There were no coffins available and there was not time enough to give the sick needed attention, much less go through burial ceremonies after they were dead. The corpses were taken out of the tent and placed in a shady spot until the opportunity came to bury them. I was unconscious most of the burial. I lay there unaware of what was going on most of the time and it was hard to tell whether I was dead or alive. Henry Hand reported me as "dead," and I was placed out in the shade with other bodies for until a man came along and tried to throw me across his shoulder. My grave was ready. All they needed now was to dump me in and fill it over with dirt. The uncomfortable position on the man's shoulder caused me to let out a loud groan. He jumped as though a ghost had shouted at him and dropped me to the ground. I protested being buried alive. Comrade Hand called a doctor, a colonel, who examined me and said, "You can't live more than a few days." General Sherman ordered my discharge and transportation home. Harvey Hurt went along as my escort. We traveled by boat, train and stage coach from Black River, Miss., to Angola. I was carried the entire distance on a canvas stretcher. My parents had heard a report that I was dead. They could hardly believe their eyes when they saw me. It took me a year and a half to recover enough to drive my fine horse and buggy.

We had a large chorus at the Gettysburg Reunion, made up of Union and Confederate veterans and had a big time singing together and seeing who could tell the biggest yarn. Of course, I beat them all.

It took a year's correspondence to secure this 98 year old veteran's story. He was so busy travelling all over the southwest that he hardly had time to write in detail. The author had letters from him in numerous states. The picture of him in this book is his own photography.

JUST A DRUMMER BOY

JOHN YOUNG, Pine Bluff, Ark. Confederate.
B. Drew Co., Ark. Co. G. 5th Ark. Reg.
Little Rock, Ark.

I was just a drummer boy in the service. I was not in the ranks, only a drummer. How long I was in the service I can't tell. I only know we nearly starved.

I had a great deal of trouble when I was vaccinated for smallpox. For three months and twelve days people were dying.

The Last Meeting of the Blue and Gray at Gettysburg was fine. Everyone seemed to enjoy being there and I didn't hear of a single fight during our stay. We've got a mighty good government and should all try to make good citizens.

REMINISCENCES OF SLAVES

GENERAL LEE'S BODY SERVANT

WILLIAM MACK LEE. Slave.
B. Westmoreland Co., Va.,
July 28, 1838.

I 'tends all de Confederate Reunions ter meet de surviving followers of my ole marster, de General Robert E. Lee. I luv ter talk about him en ter answer de questions about his life.

'En missus, I allus has ter do whut de young white ladies wants, but 'sense me if I don' smile. Marse Robert warn't much of a smilin' man, but he's de bes' man I ever know'd.

I'm goin' on eighty-nine en I'm kinda stove up. Ol' niggah been shot, you know. But you's lookin' fine and I hopes you lives ter be a hundred.

I'm pretty hearty niggah. I 'beys de law of Gawd, de law of man, de law of nature, en votes de Democratic ticket.

What de medals covering my coat! Dey stan's fer de reunions I've 'tended. I got one fer ebery yeah. De people, dey all knows me en dey all luvs Marse Robert, en likes to heah me tell about him in de days o' de war.

Marse Robert asked me one time, "Willie Mack, who teached yo' to steal?" An' I tol' Marse Robert, "Nobody neber tol' no niggah ter steal, it's just born in him, dass all." But my marster, he teached Willie Mack stealin' is wrong, an' a whole lot of other things is wrong. Marse Robert was a prayin' man, an' I reckon thass why I turned out ter be er preacher.

I spent four yeahs, four months, en four days with Marse Robert during de war, and after de war, although a free diggah, I stayed wid him fer nearly fifteen yeahs.

Marse Robert sont me ter school in Washington, en I be er minister. I'se proud ob de fact that I'se got many compliments of distinguished white ministers, in whose churches I'se filled de pulpit.

Brother Warriors

Interviewed in April, 1927, at the Confederate Reunion, Tampa, Florida.

A SLAVE FIGHTS FOR HIS FREEDOM

JOSEPH CLOVESE, Slidell, La. Union.
B. Jan. 30, 1844, St. Bernard Parish, La.
Co. C., 63 U. S. C. Inf., Blake Correll, Miss.
Dis. Jan. 9, 1866, Devall Bluff, Ark.

I was born a slave on the plantation of Emile Longeais, who was a native of France. My father's mother was a French speaking negro. I lived and worked on the farm until I enlisted in the war. I wanted my freedom and was glad to fight for it. When I heard that a regiment was being made up at the court house at Vicksburg, I set out for there. We were drilled for awhile and then sent to Davis Bend, where Mr. Jeff Davis lived. Later we were in a scrimmage at Waterproof, La., but no one was killed.

I spent two years, three months, and nine days in the army and was mustered out at DeValls Bluff, Ark. I can only say that I served as best I could. We were in much danger sometimes. At Vicksburg there was much killing and hard fighting, but we marched forward and advanced upon the enemy.

The greatest thing I saw was the changing of the river by General Grant. Grant changed the current of the river by taking it up in a spade and the water flowed the other way. But when Captain West said, "Boys, we have won the battle, ain't you glad," we all rejoiced and were ready for going home.

DIDN'T WANT TO BE A FREE MAN

R. A. GWYNN, Birmingham, Ala.
Confederate Slave. B. Jan. 6, 1849, Pontotoc
Co., Miss. Fitzgerald Henry Guard of Tenn., Fitzgerald, Tenn.

I was born in slavery down on my dear ole massa's plantation. I'se jes a nigger frum the verry bottom uv my heart, en proud uv it. En I respects en loves my white folkses. I nebber hab no trouble wid them in my whole life.

I useter belong to Marse Phil Holcomb, but I was sold from one marse to an-other en finally I belonged to Marse Bob Kyle. Ole marse luved me jes like I was a jewel and he tuk jes as much care uv me. I never went back on him, no sir, I was jes as loyal to the verry last.

Ole marse lived in the biggest en finest house in the country. Setting back about fifty yards from group of small cabins. My ma use to take care of the "Big House" was the "Niggar Quarters," or a the chillun en they all called her "Mammy." My marse had a fine team of horses en I use to drive the carriage for him. Them wuz the good ole days when we had plenty to eat en a good place to live.

Ole marse uster allus teach us to live right en when I grew up I studied my Bible and started preaching. That wuz sixty years ago.

About all I kin remember about de war wuz that there wuz a lot of troops marching en a lot of hullabaloo en talk about the Yankees coming down to free the niggers en a lot of talk about "Brotherhood." But I didn't want ter be free, en I didn't want ter be a white man. I wanted my marse jes to be "ole marse" and I jes wanted to be one of his "niggers."

I was down in Columbus, Ga., when the fighting started. Lordy, how dem cannons did roar. I was scared as if a ghost had 'peared.

When de war wuz over, ole marse en missus kum out and told us, "Yo' all is free now, there is my houses that is always been your'n, go en lib dere jes as long as yo' wants to en do what yo' please." So us all stayed right there, jes' like before, only ole massa divided de crop wid us one half for the other.

Brother Warriors

Mos' de niggers didn't hab no place to go and nuthing to do. Freedom warn't whut it wuz primped up to be.

R. W. Gwynn and Simon Phillips

Jackson F. Fischer

S. J. Miles

SLAVES WHO DIFFERED IN OPINIONS OF FREEDOM

YANKEES PROMISE HIM FORTY ACRES OF LAND AND A MULE

SIMON PHILLIPS, Birmingham, Ala. Confederate Slave.
B. 1848, Hale Co., Ala. 51st Cav.

I wuz de property of Massa Bryant Watkins. I wuz whut day called a slave, but it wuz mighty fine goings, I'll tell yer. Massa Watkins gib me young Marsters John en Robert, his two sons, who wuz about my age, en I tuk care ob dem clean up to de time dey went ter de war. Ebbery whar dey went, dere wuz I.

Missus, ebberyone luvs 'is property, it's only natural, en yo' grandpaps luved us caze us belonged ter 'em, en so fer as being a slave goes, us wuz treated one hundred percent better by de white folks den than us is ter day. I tell yo', my ole massa wuz sho one good man, en dere wuz plenty more jes like 'im.

Didn't nebber heah of no stealin' en no killin' in dat day. Why? Caze nigger warn't hongery, he hab good place ter lib en plenty ter eat. Dere were som rambunkious young bucks in dose days dat run away, den dey hab ter hab patterollers ter guard de slaves en keep 'em frum running away. If us wanted ter leave ole massa's farm, dey gib us a pass for so many hours, en if us stay more'n dat time, de patteroller he ketched us en mor'n wore us out wid a raw hide whip. Sumtimes, day hab ter get out de hounds ter ketch runaway slaves, but us nebber hab much trouble in dat way till de Yankees started stealin' us niggers jes 'fo de war.

In dat day, warn't no sech thing as marriage among the black folks. If I see a gal dat luks good ter me, I tol' ole massa, and he make er trade with her massa that I could hab her. If he give her to me, den I didn't need no pass ter go ter see her. I could go over dere ebery night without being bothered. If my ole massa liked de gal, den he'd make trade ter buy her en bring her over ter our nigger quarters, en gib us er house to lib in. But all de chillun born ter us belonged ter her former massa. My ole massa gib Mr. Brown two big bucks (negro men) fer my gal. She wuz wuth more'n dat.

Bed time on de plantation wuz nine o'clock ebery night, 'cept Satiday. De patteroller went through de quarters ter see dat all lights wuz out en eberything quiet.

So fer as religion goes, yo' krow de nigger luv his religion more'n ennybody. Whatever a massa believed in, all his niggers believed de same. If he be Baptist, they be Baptist. If he be sum other faith, dey be sum other faith. De minister who preached to de white folks at eleven o'clock on Sunday morning preached to de niggers on Sunday night. That wuz always a big time fer us. The minister's text mos' ob de time was "Obey Your Massa." De cullered folks didn't hab no church dey held dere meetings under de big oak tree. If de preacher preached good, us shouted loud; if he prayed good, us danced.

Saturday night wuz "frolic night," en de slaves could stay up jes as late as dey wanted ter.

Ole massa gib us de bes' food in de world. Us raised mos' ob it on de farm en had er smoke house fer de meats, en er bin fer de potatoes, en er crib fer de corn. Nuthin' had er lock on it, craze warn't no need fer stealin'.

De nigger quarters wuz set often frum the "Big House," en each cullered family had er log cabin. Dey wern't fine mansions, but er heap better'n mos' de niggers hab now.

When young Marsters John en Robert jined de army, I, naturally, went wid 'em. Lots of de niggers run across de line en jined de Yankees, but dey wuz mostly good fer nuthing scoundrels. Ole massa nebber desert me in time ob peace en I don't desert him in time ob danger.

When us knew de Yankees wuz coming, us went out en hid ebberything out on er hill on de other side of de swamp. Us buried de silver en other things en den swept out de tracks wid pine tops so dey couldn't find 'em. Us'd taken all de stock en hosses way off, en de only thing lef' wuz er little two-year-old colt in de pasture. De Yankees kum en tried ter ketch him, but he'd jump en dodge en rear till finally dey got er rope on him en held him down. Den dey put er saddle en bridle on 'im, en one ob dem got on, dey opened de gate en off dey went. Man, dat colt did run. Dere wuz er straight road off frum de house, en jes as far as yo' could see dat colt wuz running, wid dat Yankee sittin' right on 'im.

Ole massa had er mare he sho luved. She wuz named Anne, after ole missus, en when de Yankees brought her up to de house, after finding her in de woods, he jes broke down en cried. All de nigger chillun cried too, but dey didn't know why. Dey wuz jes crying caze de massa wuz crying.

During de war, once, we went two or three days wid out food. It wuz den de nigger got into de chicken stealin' habit. We'd jes rake 'em off de 'em up wid dirt. Us didn't hab no salt, en when de fence en throw 'em in er trench ob coals en cover chicken got dun, us jes pull off de skin en feathers en eat 'em. Dat's de bes' checken in the world.

After de war wuz over en ole massa didn't show up right away, all de niggers went out ter look fer him. We wuz scared he might be wounded er killed. One nigger sit down en jes hollered en groaned, "Ole massa is gone." Us wuz all mighty glad ter see him come home.

I don' go ter no reunions of the North en South tergether, don' ker if dey do wants ter pay my way fer goin'. I don' want ter hab nuthing ter do wid dem Yankees, caze dey promised me forty acres ob land and a mule if dey won de war. When all dey dun wuz gib me er piece ob paper en take all my money. De Yankee would say, "Here yo' deed, Simon, as sho Moses lift up de serpent in the Wilderness, also I lift Simon out ob $10."

RECIEVES EMANCIPATION

S. J. Miles, Omaha, Nebr. Union Slave.
B. Dec. 3, 1842, Mobile, Ala. Co. E,
96 Reg. U. S. Colored Inf. Vol. April 19,
1865. Dis. Jan. 29, 1866, New Orleans, La.

Dis ole cullored man dun seen all de fighting he goin' ter see. I wuz right down thar whar de niggers fust dun dere fightin'. I wuz in de war two and a half yeahs. I wuz in all dem places in Mississippi. I enlisted cause I wuz born in slavery en I didn' wan' be no slave. I believed in brotherhood, wid de luv uv God in yo' hearts fer all men, black and white.

I kum off de field in Mobile. I wuz glad ter git my emancipation.

EMANCIPATION PROCLAMATION (1863)

Whereas, on the twenty-second day of September, in the year of our Lord one thousand eight hundred and sixty-two, a proclamation was issued by the President of the United States, containing, among other things, the following, to wit:

"That on the first day of January, in the year of our Lord one thousand eight hundred and sixty-three, all persons held as slaves within the United States, or designated part of a State, the people whereof shall then be in rebellion against the United States, shall be then, thenceforward, and forever free; and the Executive Government of the United States, including the military and naval authority thereof, will recognize and maintain the freedom of such persons, and will do no act or acts to repress such persons, or any of them, in any efforts they may make for their actual freedom.

"That the Executive will, on the first day of January aforesaid, by proclamation, designate the States and parts of States, if any, in which the people thereof respectively, shall then be in rebellion against the United States; and the fact that any State, or the people thereof, shall on that day be in good faith represented in the Congress of the United States by members chosen thereto at elections wherein a majority of the qualified voters of such State shall have participated, shall in the absence of strong countervailing testimony, be deemed conclusive evidence that such State, and the people thereof, are not then in rebellion against the United States."

Now, therefore, I, Abraham Lincoln, President of the United States, by virtue of the power in me vested as commander-in-chief of the Army and Navy of the United States, in time of actual armed rebellion against authority and government of the United States, and as a fit and necessary war measure for suppressing said rebellion, do, on this first day of January, in the year of our Lord one thousand eight hundred and sixty-three, and in accordance with my purpose so to do, publicly proclaimed for the full period of one hundred days from the day first above mentioned, order and designate as the States and parts of States wherein the people thereof, respectively, are this day in rebellion against the United States, the following to wit:

Arkansas, Texas, Louisiana (except the parishes of St. Bernard, Plaquemines, Jefferson, St. John, St. Charles, St. James, Ascension, Assumption, Terre-bonne, Lafourche, St. Mary, St. Martin, and Orleans, including the city of New Orleans), Mississippi, Alabama, Florida, Georgia, South Carolina, North Carolina, and Virginia (except the forty-eight counties designated as West Virginia, and also the counties of Berkley, Accomac, Northampton, Elizabeth City, York, Princess Ann, and Norfolk, including the cities of Norfolk and Portsmouth), and which excepted parts are, for the present, left precisely as if this proclamation were not issued.

And by virtue of the power and for the purpose aforesaid, I do order and declare that all persons held as slaves within said designated States and parts of States are, and henceforward shall be, free: and that the Executive Government of the United States, including the military and naval authorities thereof, will recognize and maintain the freedom of said persons.

And I hereby enjoin upon the people so declared to be free to abstain from all violence, unless in necessary self-defense; and I recommend to them that, in all cases when allowed, they labor faithfully for reasonable wages.

And I further declare and make known, that such persons of suitable condition, will be received into the armed service of the United States to garrison forts, positions, stations, and other places, and to man vessels of all sorts in said service.

And upon this act, sincerely believed to be an act of justice, warranted by the constitution, upon military necessity, I invoke the considerate judgment of mankind and the gracious favor of Almighty God.

In witness whereof, I have hereunto set my hand, and caused the seal of the United States to be affixed.

Done at the city of Washington, this first day of January, in the year of our Lord one thousand eight hundred and sixty-three, and of the Independence of the United States of America the eighty-seventh.

ABRAHAM LINCOLN
L.S.
By the President:
William H. Seward,
Secretary of State.

(The war for the maintenance of the Union had been going on for a year and a half before Lincoln issued the preliminary proclamation quoted in the beginning of the present document. The emancipation proclamation of January 1, 1863, enlarged the basis of the conflict, and from the point of view of foreign nations gave the North the advantage of a moral as well as a political issue.)

RECOLLECTIONS OF MY SLAVERY DAYS

WILLIAM HENRY SINGLETON, New Haven, Conn. Union,
B. Aug. 10, 1835, New Bern, N. C. Org. 35th U. S.
Colored Inf., New Bern, N. C.

I have lived through the greatest epoch of history, N. C. That was not so many years, you see, after having been born August 10, 1835, at New Bern, the adoption of the Declaration of Independence and the winning of the Revolutionary War. But in the country of the Declaration of Independence, I was born a slave, for I was a black man; and, because I was black, it was believed I had no soul. I had no rights that anybody was bound to respect, for in the eyes of the law I was but a thing. I was bought, sold, and whipped. Once, I was whipped simply because it was thought I had opened a book.

But I lived to see the institution of slavery, into which I was born and of which I was for many years a victim, pass away. I wore the uniform of those boys in blue, who, through four years of suffering, wiped away with their blood the stain of slavery and purged the Republic of its sin. I met, too, that great man, who led those men as their Commander in Chief; he shook hands with me, yes, talked to me. I can still see his sad, tired, worn face as he spoke to me that day. And in those days, since I was whipped simply because it was thought I had opened a book, I have seen the books of the world opened to my race. And with the help and sympathy of God's good people, I have seen them make a beginning in education. And, in my old age, when a nation across the seas sought to enslave the world, as once my race was enslaved, I saw the boys of my race take their place in the armies of the Republic and help save freedom for the world.

My master belonged to a high, proud family, and his estate was one of the largest in Craven County, N. C. He had more slaves than any other planter thereabouts.

The first thing I remember is playing on the plantation with my little brothers and with the other slave children, while the men and women slaves were in the cotton, corn, and potato fields, working during the day. We children were taken care of by an old slave lady at a central house. She had grown too old to work and so acted as a kind of nurse for the slave children during the day. I was about four years old at that time. I had two brothers younger than I, and one two years older. Nights we went home with our mother.

The slaves lived in a row of houses a ways from the main house where our mother lived. Of course, my mother was supplied with all the food we wanted and we did not need much clothing because the weather was warm. I had nobody that I called father. I only knew my mother. Her name was Lettis. All the slaves on a plantation had the same name as their master. When a plantation changed owners the slaves changed their names. The slaves on our plantation, for instance, were known as Singleton's men and women. John Winthrop had a plantation adjoining ours and all the slaves on that plantation were called Winthrop staves. Our plantation had formerly been owned by the widow Williams. The slaves were then known as her slaves, but when she married my master, he succeeded to her plantation and all the slaves, including my mother, were called from that time on by his name.

In the war, I took part in an attack as a guide and had a horse shot from under me. A few days later, I told Colonel Leggett, my officer, that I would not fight any more unless I was prepared to defend myself. He said, "We never will take niggers in the army to fight. The war will be over before your people ever get in." I replied, "The war will not be over until I have had a chance to spill my blood; if that is your feeling toward me, pay me what you owe me and I will take it and go." He owed me five dollars and he paid me. I took that five dollars and hired the A.M.E. Zion Church, at New Bern, and commenced to recruit a regiment of colored men. I secured a thousand men and they appointed me as their colonel. I drilled them with corn stalks for guns. We had no way, of course, of getting guns and equipment. We drilled once a week. I supported myself by whatever I could get to do and my men did likewise.

I spoke to General Burnside about getting my regiment into the Federal service, but he said he could do nothing about it. It was to General Burnside, however, and my later association with him as his servant, that I owe what I now regard as one of the greatest experiences of my life. One day at the General's headquarters, his adjutant pointed to a man who was talking to the General in an inner room and said, "Do you know that man in there?" I said, "No." He said, "That is our President, Mr. Lincoln." In a few minutes the conference in the inner room apparently ended and Mr. Lincoln and General Burnside came out. I do not know whether he had told President Lincoln about me before or not, but the General pointed to me and said, "This is the little fellow who got up a colored regiment." President Lincoln shook hands with me and said, "It is a good thing; what do you want?" I said, "I have a thousand men, we want to help fight to free our race. We want to know if you will take us in the service?" He said, "You have good pluck, but I cannot take you now, because you are contraband of war and not American citizens yet, but hold on to your society and there may be a chance for you." So saying, he passed on. The only recollection I have of him is that of a tall, dark complexioned, raw-boned man, with a pleasant face. I looked at him as he passed on in company with General Burnside and I never saw him again.

On January 1, 1863, President Lincoln's emancipation proclamation became effective, which made me and all the rest of my race free. Never again could we be bought and sold, or whipped, or made to work without pay. We were not treated as things without souls, but as human beings. Of course, I do not remember that I thought it all out in this way when I learned what President Lincoln had done. I am sure I did not and the men in my regiment did not. I had gone back to New Bern then. The thing we expected was that we would be taken into the Federal service at once. It was not until May 28, 1863, however, that the thing we had hoped for so long came to pass; when Colonel James C. Beecher, a brother of Henry Ward Beecher, that great champion of our race, came and took command of the regiment.

I was appointed sergeant of Company G, being the first colored man that furnished the government a thousand men in the Civil War. The regiment was at first called the Ist North Carolina Colored Regiment. It later became known as the 35th Regiment, United States Colored Troops. Soon afterwards, we were armed and equipped, and shipped to South Carolina and stationed at Charleston Harbor. From that time until June 1866, when we were mustered out at Charleston, South Carolina, I was in active service, ranking as First Sergeant, Company G, 35th United States Colored Infantry. J. C. White was the captain of that company, and Colonel James C. Beecher was the commander of the regiment. We saw active service in South Carolina, Florida and Georgia.

I was wounded in the right leg at the Battle of Olustee, Florida. After the war ended, we were stationed for a time in South Carolina, doing guard duty, and were finally mustered out of the service on June 1, 1866. My honorable discharge from the service, dated on that day, although worn and not very legible now, is one of my most prized possessions.

Shortly after the war ended, I was converted in a Methodist Church of the A.M.E. Zion connection, in North Carolina. So, when I came to New Haven, Connecticut, I joined the A.M.E. Zion Church of this city. It was in that church that I learned to read, although I had learned the alphabet and how to spell simple words while I was in the army. I became ambitious to learn all I could, so read as many books as I could, and availed myself of all the opportunities that were presented to educate myself. I saved money from my salary too.

After the war, my mother and brothers remained near New Bern and hired a little place known as the Salter Place. When I had money enough I bought this place, but there was such a strong feeling against me at New Bern for the part I had taken in the war that I could not go back there. The Klu Klux Klan said they would shoot me. My mother lived on the place until her death some years later, but I could not go back even to see her buried. My brothers remained on the place, but they did not live very long after my mother. I then sold the property through a Mr. Wheeler of New Bern.

My wife is making a good attendant for me at this Gettysburg reunion. Many of my old friends are here and we are having an enjoyable trip.

"Des Moines, Ia. Sept. 8, 1938. The Grand Army of the Republic mourned today the loss of one of its most courageous members, Col. William Henry Singleton, 103, believed to have been the only commissioned negro officer in the Civil War. He died of a heart attack last night after he had participated with his comrades in the annual parade of the national G. A. R. His wife said the strain of the long journey from their New Haven, Connecticut, home and the excitement of the parade apparently had induced his death. His 118 comrades defied a 90-degree heat and tried bravely to parade for fifteen blocks through downtown streets.—
The Washington Herald"

SLAVES VALUABLE PROPEITY

DAVID FIELDS, Hendersonville, N. C. Slave.

I'se jes en ole slavery darkey. I wuz born on my massa's plantation near Hendersonville, about de yar 1851, en I wuz ten years oh when de war broke out.

My massa wuz Massa Sebring Feiston. After de war us niggers wuz jes turned out into de cold world wid out nuthing at all ter lib on. Us wuz honest cullered folkses, cauz us had er good massa who teached us ter lib right, en if we hadn't been good, he'd er jes bandoned us.

In de war, po' ole massa lost ebbery thing he had. Dem Yankee scouts, dey go through de house en hepped demselves. Missus tried to hide her gold band ring in a jar, but dey tuk dat too.

When dey burned his house en he hab nuthing ter eat, en no place ter go, jes a few clothes, he gib me sum of 'is clothes. He say to his niggers: "Yo' all is free now, yo' ken go whar yo' wants." My ma, she tuk in washing en hired me out ter Mr. Byers ter plow a yoke of steers. Mr. Byers, he paid me a whole bushel of corn a week ter work fer 'em. De corn kep' ma en us younguns in hominy en corn meal, en we didn't hab much other vittuls ter go wid it, mos' black coffee en molasses.

My ole massa wuz as good as de Lawd hisself. He nebber tanned our hides lak sum massas did. He luved us. He say, "I nebber sell none of my niggers." Dat meant a lot too, fer I wuz a big buck, en wuth from $1,000 to $1,500, mor'n all de niggers in de whole country wuth ter day.

Ole missus wuz an Allen befo' her marriage. She wuz even better'n ole massa. Menny's de cold, dark night she kum trapsing down ter de cabins ter 'tend de sick. Nuthing wuz too good fer her niggers. Ole missus' daughter libs in dis verry town now en takes care ob me. She say, "I don' nebber fergit my papa's niggers." If she wuz a rich woman, I'd be a faring like a King ter day, but I guess it bes' as 'tis, fer if I wuz rich I'd be a rip snorter; as 'tis I can't do dat en get along, so I'se a God fearing nigger.

In slavery days us black folkses wuth plenty money. Dey put us on de block en say: "Here a nigger, how much am I offered fer. He's a fine, healthy buck, en will make yo' a fine nigger." Then a man would look him over en say: "I'll give yo' so much." Den anuther one would bid higher, 'pending on how he looked. Dey brought frum $500 to $1,500. Whoever got 'im put 'im in a waggin en hauled 'im off jes like he wuz cattle.

De Yankees kum onto de farms during de war en git a lot ob de niggers ter sneak out. Dis caused our ole massa ter put de patterollers out to watch us. De patteroller ketched 'im if he try to run away and punished 'im.

MAGAZINE EXPLOSION MISTAKEN FOR GABRIEL'S TRUMPET

JACKSON F. FISCHER, Shreveport, La., Union Slave.
B. Feb. 16, 1847, Mobile, Ala. Co. F, 97th
La. Reg. Mobile, Ala. May 2, 1865. Dis.
Sept. 1867, New Orleans, La. Attended Gettysburg Reunion.

Before the war, I was owned by Colonel F. L. Owens, Greens Mill, New Orleans, La. I joined the army at my home in Mobile, Alabama. I joined the Yank Army. I joined the 97th Regiment and the Company was F. Captain Lew was the Captain, Colonel Robinson was the Colonel. I was about fifteen years old.

I volunteered to go to Coveby as the war was not ended. Finally, we got orders to march out for Coveby. We tore down our tents and packed up, but before we got very far from the camp we received orders to go back to camp and stay there until the war ended, so we did. We did garrison duty. We guarded the bank for awhile night and day, also the hospital and jail, the cotton compress and sometimes the public square; also the magazine, a place for caring for the cannon balls and bomb shells. We were drilled to march, fight sham battles, and also for dress parade and military drills. I did steady service for three years.

A scary time was when the magazine blew up about two miles from our camp and killed several people. Houses were wrecked, and windows knocked out of houses at a distance. One old lady thought that Judgment Day had come and cried, "Thank God, Israel is blowing his trumpet." Bodies of men were sailing up about a mile in the air.

The war ended and we were mustered out of service. We took a steamboat by the name of "Red Chief" for New Orleans. The first thing that happened was the pilot ran onto a big barge. Then that night when we got out in the big water, we met a storm which lasted for seven hours, and were blown back fifteen miles by the wind. The captain and mate gave us up, but we came out safe. We arrived in port twenty-four hours late, taking a day and half to get to New Orleans. We landed near Calenton Greeven, on the Mississippi River, and stayed there until we were discharged from service.

_____

Government war record indicates that this soldier was wounded.

A SLAVE FIGHTS FOR THE UNION

JOSEPH WADDLE, Omaha, Nebr. Union.
B. Aug. 7, 1849, Springfield, Mo.
Co. H, 79th Reg. Kan. U. S. C. T. Dis.
Nov 9, 1865.

De ole marster where I wuz born in slavery was named Waddle, but I don' remember his given name. My mother's name was Hanna. Joseph Waddle is the name ole marster giv me, but all my friends call me "Professor."

I don' remember whether we thought of freedom or anything else much as I wuz only fourteen. I jes know that for two years and seven months I served as an orderly and drummer. When I was discharged I went to Fort Scott.

You know, I've been living around Omaha since 1880 and I've lived in the state of Nebraska since 1872.

De medals on my uniform are given to me at the reunions. I never miss a state G.A.R. reunion and I've been to several national conventions.

DEY SOLD US CULLERED FOLKS LIKE HOSSES

GEORGIANA JONES, Columbia, S. C. Slave.

I jes ken member de days fo' de war I wuz a pickaninny den aroun' nine year old. Sherman, he kum ter our plantation en tuk ebbery solitary thing he wanted. I ken member he dug up all ole massa's whiskey en sot it on de groun'. Us cullered younguns seen it, en de Yankees tol' us to drink all us wanted. We nebber tasted nuthing lak dat befo' in all us lives, en us lit in. De whiskey didn't taste good, so us jes drunk de wine, en all got tight.

My massa en missus wuz rich folkses. Dey had a country place, but lived mos' de time in de big city. Us cullered younguns sho luv her, she wuz so good ter us. She brung us candy frum de city, so us allus looked forward ter her kuming ter see us. She uster throw pennies onter de groun' en hab one big time laughing at us scrambling for dem.

Dere wuz all kinds of massas and missuses, jes like dere is all kinds of bosses ter day. Some is good, sum is bad. Well, mine wuz the good ones. Sum folkses jes naturally mean, while others can't be ennything but good.

Our missus allus see dat us wuz took care of. She kum ter see us if we wuz sick, en if us wuz bad sick, she sont for de doctor.

Lawsy, missus, dey use to sell us cullered folkses jes like dey do de hosses en cattle nowadays. Dey put us onter de block en de fellow who has the mostes money gits us. De mothers frum dey chillum sumtimes.

De Yankees kum mighty nigh gifting ole massa during de war. Us had ter hide him ter keep dem frum killing 'em. Dere wuz er passel uv Yankees in our cabin, when here kum ole massa on 'is hoss. My ole mammy didn't wan' nobody ter harm ole massa, so she slipped out, grabbed de hoss' reins en turned his head de other way. Us hid him in the swamp till de Yankees done gone.

De Yankees tuk all our cows, en chickens, en other grub, but dey didn't burn our big house. I'm a telling yer, times wuz mighty hard fer grub ter eat. We uster pick up de corn, where de hosses had et, en beat it up fine en make bread outen it.

Yer oughter seen the depot where de food wuz kep', dey blowed it into thunderation, en, Lordy mercy, yer should er seen de cullered folkses dey killed.

Missus, one thing us pickaninnies wuz ascared of wuz de patteroller. He wuz allus a big man wid er gun, who watched de darkies en kep' em frum running er way to sum other plantation. Dey figured dey had paid big money fur us, I guess, but dey couldn't keep us from running away. When my mammy wanted ter scare me ter make me go ter sleep, she say, "De patteroller sho gwinter git yo' if yo' don' watch out."

Following is an addition of an update on General Julius Franklin Howell, Commander in Chief of the United Confederate Veterans, upon his 100th birthday.

The handwritten note is General Howell's own handwriting.

To -
Our Beloved President
Franklin Delano Roosevelt
Commander-in-Chief
of the
Armed Forces of the
United States of America

From -
Genl Julius Franklin Howell
Commander-in-Chief
United Confederate Veterans
Washington City, D.C.
October 8-11, 1940

Brother Warriors

At the age of 100, Gen. Julius Franklin Howell, past national commander of the United Confederate Veterans, is going strong, with thriving insurance business, a wife less than half his age, a pungent sense of humor and a memory sometimes too keen for pleasure.

Before catching the train for Washington to attend Confederate Memorial exercises tomorrow, he worked at his office in Bristol, Va., til 6 p.m., typing business letters. Although he can still hear a stage whisper, Gen. Howell did put his foot down two years ago and refused to serve another term as president of the Board of Trustees of Intermont College on the ground he couldn't hear all the arguments at board meetings.

When he celebrated a century of good living last January 17, a lot of organizations, including the Baptist Church, passed resolutions honoring him.

They said a good many things I don't deserve," he remarked. "I don't mean to say they intentionally lied."

Gen. Howell doesn't let all the attention he receives go to his head. Resplendent in the uniform of the United Confederate Veterans, he points out he was "only a corporal." He won't even tell you about the impromptu speech he made before Congress two years ago.

Poignantly, he recalls the day the Confederates evacuated Richmond. He had been wounded. His horse had died, and unable to find another, Gen. Howell was a foot soldier: As the Confederates marched out of the town, liquor from barrels they had broken ran in the gutters. Many of the town's inhabitants walked alongside the troops rolling barrels flour, carrying clothing and meat. From across the river, they could see the town burning as the Union troops went through.

At the age of 19, he returned from the wars, convinced that a world had ended. His father insisted that he continue his education. Gen. Howell believes that is one reason he has lived so long. He learned to take the broad view of life. He regained his zest for living.

Gen. Howell went to normal school in Illinois, then to the University of Pennsylvania and to Harvard. He became a professor of the history of English at the University of Arkansas, was appointed president of Mountain Home College in Arkansas and then of Intermont College in Virginia.

Gem Howell's first wife died after they had been married for 63 years. Six of their nine children still are living. He has 16 grandchildren and about nine great-grand-children, I've stopped counting them."

Yet at the age of 88 he began looking around for a wife.

"I lived with my daughter for a while. But a daughter can't take the place of a wife. If I was going to go on living, I would have to marry again. I considered quite a, few. I courted several of them but kept on looking until I met the right one."

The Howells have been married for 12 years now. They are in Washington as the guests of the Confederate Memorial Committee and of Mrs. Lena Epperly MacDonald of the New Colonial Hotel. Today the general is attending ceremonies marking the birthday of Confederate President Jefferson Davis at the Capitol. Tomorrow Gen. Howell will take part in ceremonies for the Confederate dead at Arlington National Cemetery.

Gen. Howell, 100, Works All Day
Before Catching Train to D. C.

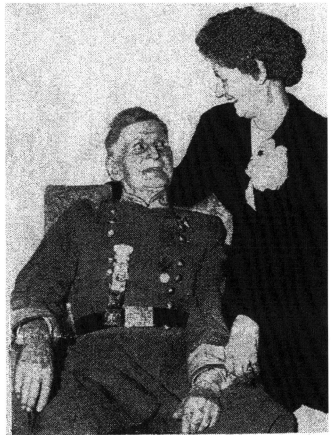

100 AND GOING STRONG-Gen. Julius F. Howell, pictured here with his wife, brought a century's experiences with him to take part in the Confederate memorial exercise here.

Star Staff Photo

Brother Warriors

About the Author

Martha Norris McLeod was born June 4, 1900 at the McLeod home in Crawfordville (Wakulla County), Florida. She was the fifth child of Judge R. Don McLeod and Mattie Judson Norris.

Martha received her early education in the public schools of Wakulla County. In her business life, she worked for the United States government for twenty years. She was assistant liquidator at the Customs House in Tampa, Florida, prior to moving to Washington, DC in 1933. In Washington she became editor of the News Digest published by the Department of Agriculture. She also served as publicity chairman of Young Democrats of America and rendered services to National Democratic Headquarters and the Absentee Voters Bureau.

As a young woman, Martha attended reunions of the United Confederate Veterans with her father throughout Florida and Georgia. She also served as Maid of Honor representing Florida at many of the conventions. During these events, she spent a great deal of time interviewing both Union and Confederate Veterans, and in 1940, she published these true stories in a book titled Brother Warriors.

In a ceremony held in Washington, DC, at Confederate Memorial Hall on June 30, 1941, Martha's book was formally presented to President Franklin D. Roosevelt by General Julius F. Howell, Commander-in-Chief of the United Confederate Veterans, and General William W. Nixon, Commander-in-Chief of the Grand Army of the Republic.

Martha was subsequently invited to join the National League of Pen Women. During World War II, she wrote and broadcast visionary radio programs teaching the nation how and what to recycle. She also served as a Red Cross worker at Walter Reed Hospital and the National Naval Medical Center at Bethesda. After the war, she studied physiotherapy and graduated with honors in that field in Chicago. In 1948 she returned to the south, moving to Thomasville, Georgia, where she established her own Physiotherapy Clinic and treated many patients from southern Georgia and north Florida.

In 1955, Martha organized the Southeastern Region for the Clan MacLeod Society of America, consisting at the time of Georgia, Alabama and Florida. In August 1956 the first world-wide Clan Parliament was called by Chief Flora MacLeod at Dunvegan Castle, Isle of Skye, Scotland, and Martha attended representing the Southeastern Region. Queen Elizabeth, the Duke of Edinburgh, and Princess Margaret attended Dunvegan Castle for a luncheon with the MacLeods during the event. In February 1957, Chief Flora MacLeod visited Thomasville as Martha's house guest for a fortnight. She was entertained at social events in Tallahassee, Thomasville and Jacksonville.

Martha's father, Roderick Donald McLeod, known as R. Don, was Wakulla County Judge from 1901-1929, and was also a Confederate Veteran of the War Between the States, having served as a 16-year old soldier in the Battle of Atlanta. Because of this relationship, Martha was one of the last surviving "Real Daughters" of the Anna Jackson 224 Chapter, United Daughters of the Confederacy (UDC), Tallahassee, Florida. She always took part in activities remembering the dead of the War Between the States, and in Confederate Memorial Day ceremonies. In honor of her father, the R. Don McLeod 2469 Chapter, UDC, was established in Wakulla County Florida on 12 September 1982.

In 1978 Martha moved from Thomasville to Tallahassee, where she resided for 21 years, and remained active with her many social and historical interests. Martha also did extensive genealogical research on the MacLeod Clan and her own McLeod Family. She documented the research in two books: MacLeod Ancestry Ancient and Present, published in 1974, and MacLeod Heritage and Ancestry, published in 1988 when she was 88 years old. In 1995 she was nominated to the Florida Women's Hall of Fame.

Martha Norris McLeod died June 15, 1999, eleven days after her 99th birthday. Her enthusiastic devotion to her community, family, and her heritage was admired by all.

R. Don McLeod, Captain, U.S. Navy (Retired)
Grand-nephew of Martha Norris McLeod
Great-grandson of R. Don McLeod, Confederate and Judge

Brother Warriors

Brother Warriors

Made in the USA
Columbia, SC
11 August 2019